LATENT VARIABLE MODELS
An Introduction to Factor, Path, and Structural Analysis
SECOND EDITION

John C. Loehlin
University of Texas at Austin

LATENT VARIABLE MODELS
An Introduction to Factor, Path, and Structural Analysis
SECOND EDITION

LEA   LAWRENCE ERLBAUM ASSOCIATES, PUBLISHERS
1992   Hillsdale, New Jersey   London

Lawrence Erlbaum Associates, Inc., Publishers
365 Broadway
Hillsdale, New Jersey 07642

Library of Congress Cataloging-in-Publication Data

Loehlin, John C.
    Latent variable models : an introduction to factor, path, and structural analysis / by John C. Loehlin. — 2nd ed.
        p.   cm.
    Includes bibliographical references and index.
    ISBN 0-8058-1083-8. — ISBN 0-8058-1084-6
    1. Latent variables.   2. Latent structure analysis.   3. Factor analysis.   4. Path analysis.   I. Title.
    QA278.6.L64   1992
    51925'35—dc20   91-39173
                                                        CIP

Printed in the United States of America
10   9   8   7   6   5   4   3   2   1

Contents

Preface

This book is intended as an introduction to an exciting growth area in social science methodology--the use of multiple-latent-variable models. Psychologists and other social scientists have long been familiar with one subvariety of such modeling: factor analysis--or, more properly, exploratory factor analysis. In recent decades, confirmatory factor analysis, path analysis, and structural equation modeling have come out of specialized niches and are making their bid to become basic tools in the research repertoire of the social scientist, particularly the one who is forced to deal with complex real-life phenomena in the round: the sociologist, the political scientist, the social, educational, clinical, industrial, personality, or developmental psychologist, the marketing researcher, and the like.

All these methods are at heart one, as I have tried to emphasize in the chapters to follow. I have used preliminary versions of this book in teaching graduate students from psychology and related disciplines, and have found the particular approach used--via path diagrams--to be effective in helping not-too-mathematical students grasp underlying relationships, as opposed to merely going through the motions of running computer programs. In some sections of the book a certain amount of elementary matrix algebra is employed; an appendix on the topic is provided for those who may need help here.

In the interests of accessibility, I have tried to maintain a relatively informal style, and to keep the main text fairly uncluttered with references. The notes at the end of each chapter are intended to provide the serious student with a path into the technical literature, as well as to draw his or her attention to some issues beyond the scope of the basic treatment.

The book is not closely tied to a particular computer program or package, although there is some special attention paid to LISREL and EQS. I assume that most users will have access to a latent-variable model-fitting program on the order of LISREL, EQS, CALIS, COSAN, AMOS, or EzPATH, and an exploratory factor analysis package, such as those in SPSS, BMDP, or SAS. In some places, a matrix manipulation facility such as that in MINITAB, SAS, or

SPSS would be helpful. I have provided some introductory material but have not tried to tell students all they need to know to run actual programs--such information is often local, ephemeral, or both. The instructor should expect to provide some handouts and perhaps a bit of hands-on assistance in getting students started. The reader going it on his or her own will require access to current manuals for the computer programs to be used.

Finally, it gives me great pleasure to acknowledge the help and encouragement that others have provided. Perhaps first credit should go to the students who endured earlier versions of the manuscript and cheerfully pointed out various errors and obscurities. These brave pioneers included Mike Bailey, Cheryl Beauvais, Alan Bergman, Beth Geer, Steve Gregorich, Priscilla Griffith, Jean Hart, Pam Henderson, Wes Hoover, Vivian Jenkins, Tock Lim, Scott Liu, Jacqueline Lovette, Frank Mulhern, Steve Predmore, Naftali Raz, and Lori Roggman. Among other colleagues who have been kind enough to read and comment on various parts of the manuscript are Carole Holahan, Phil Gough, Maria Pennock-Roman, Peter Bentler, and several anonymous reviewers. I am especially grateful to Jack McArdle for extensive comments on the manuscript as a whole, and to Jack Cohen for his persuasive voice with the publishers. Of course, these persons should not be blamed for any defects that may remain. For one thing, I didn't always take everybody's advice.

I am grateful to the University of Chicago Press, to *Multivariate Behavioral Research,* and to the Hafner Publishing Co. for permission to reprint or adapt published materials, and to the many previous researchers and writers cited in the book--or, for that matter, not cited--whose contributions have defined this rapidly developing and exciting field.

Finally, I owe a special debt to the members of my family: Jennifer and James, who worked their term papers in around my sessions at the MacIntosh, and Marj, who provided unfailing support throughout.

J. C. L.

Note to the second edition: Much of the first edition is still here, but a certain amount of new material has been added, some exercises changed, and one topic (multidimensional scaling) dropped to make room. Also, I've tried to make the book more helpful to those who are using programs other than LISREL. I still appreciate the contributions of the people I thanked before. In addition, I am grateful to Peter Bentler, Robert Cudeck, and Jeff Tanaka for their helpful comments on draft material for the present edition, and to the American Mathematical Society for permission to adapt Table H.

Chapter One:
Path Models in Factor, Path, and Structural Analysis

Scientists dealing with behavior, especially those who observe it occurring in its natural settings, rarely have the luxury of the simple bivariate experiment, in which a single independent variable is manipulated and the consequences are observed for a single dependent variable. Even those scientists who think they do are often mistaken: The variables they directly manipulate and observe typically are not the ones of real theoretical interest but are merely some convenient variables acting as proxies or indexes for them. A full experimental analysis would again turn out to be multivariate, with a number of alternative experimental manipulations on the one side, and a number of alternative response measures on the other.

Over many years numerous statistical techniques have been developed for dealing with situations in which multiple variables, some unobserved, are involved. Such techniques often involve heroic amounts of computation. Until the advent of powerful digital computers and associated software, the use of these methods tended to be restricted to the dedicated few, but in the last couple of decades it has been feasible for any interested behavioral scientist to take a multivariate approach to his or her data. Many have done so. The explosive growth in the use of computer software packages such as SPSS, BMDP, SAS, and LISREL is one evidence of this. All these packages contain programs capable of doing one form or another of multivariate analysis involving unobserved variables.

The common features of the methods discussed in this book are that (a) multiple variables--three or more--are involved, and that (b) one or more of these variables is unobserved, or *latent*. Neither of these criteria provides a decisive boundary. Bivariate methods may often be regarded as special cases of multivariate methods. Some of the methods we discuss can be--and often are--applied in situations where all the variables are, in fact, observed. Nevertheless, the main focus of our interest is on what we call, following Bentler (1980), *latent variable analysis*, a term encompassing such specific methods as factor analysis, path analysis, and structural equation analysis, all of which share these defining features.

Path Diagrams

An easy and convenient representation of the relationships among a number of variables is the *path diagram.* In such a diagram we use capital letters, A, B, X, Y, and so on, to represent variables. The connections among variables are represented in path diagrams by two kinds of arrows: A straight, one-headed arrow represents a causal relationship between two variables, and a curved, two-headed arrow represents a simple correlation between them.

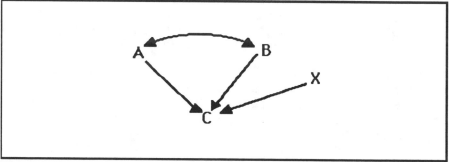

Fig. 1.1 Example of a simple path diagram.

Figure 1.1 shows an example of a path diagram. Variables A, B, and X each is assumed to have a causal effect on variable C. Variables A and B are assumed to be correlated with each other. Variable X is assumed to affect C but to be uncorrelated with either A or B. Variable C might (for example) represent young children's intelligence. Variables A and B could represent father's and mother's intelligence, assumed to have a causal influence on their child's intelligence. (The diagram is silent as to whether this influence is environmental, genetic, or both.) The curved arrow between A and B allows for the likely possibility that father's and mother's intelligence will be correlated. Arrow X represents the fact that there are other variables, independent of mother's and father's intelligence, that can affect a child's intelligence.

Figure 1.2 shows another example of a path diagram. T is assumed to affect both A and B, and each of the latter variables is also affected by an additional variable; these are labeled U and V, respectively. This path diagram could represent the reliability of a test, as described in classical psychometric test theory. A and B would stand (say) for scores on two alternate forms of a test. T would represent the unobserved true score on the trait being measured, which is assumed to affect the observed scores on both forms of the test. U and V would represent factors specific to each form of the test or to the occasions on

2

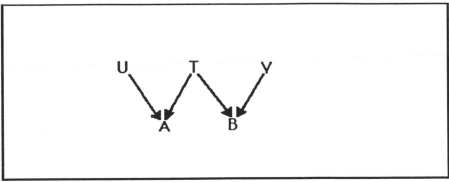

Fig. 1.2 Another path diagram: test reliability.

which it was administered, which would affect any given performance but be unrelated to the true trait. (In classical psychometric test theory, the variance in A and B resulting from the influence of T would be called *true score variance* and that caused by U or V would be called *error variance*. The proportion of the variance of A or B due to T would be called the *reliability* of the test.)

Figure 1.3 shows a path representation of events over time. In this case, the capital letters A and B are used to designate two variables, with subscripts to identify the occasions on which they are measured: Both A and B are measured at time 1, A is measured again at time 2, and B at time 3. In this case, the diagram indicates that both A_1 and B_1 are assumed to affect A_2, but that the effect of A_1 on B at time 3 is wholly via A_2: There is no direct arrow drawn leading from A_1 to B_3. It is assumed that A_1 and B_1 are correlated, and that A_2 and B_3 are subject to additional influences independent of A and B, here

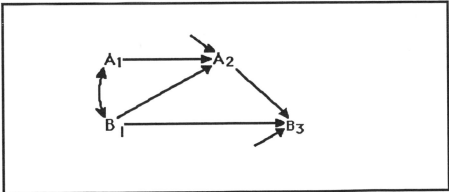

Fig. 1.3 A path diagram involving events over time.

3

represented by short, unlabeled arrows. These additional influences could have been labeled, say, X and Y, but are often left unlabeled in path diagrams, as here, to indicate that they refer to other, unspecified influences on the variable to which they point. Such arrows are called *residual arrows* to indicate that they represent causes residual to those explicitly identified in the diagram.

The meaning of *cause* in a path diagram

Straight arrows in path diagrams are said to represent *causal relationships*--but in what sense of the sometimes slippery word *cause* ? In fact, we do not need to adopt any strict or narrow definition of *cause* in this book, because path diagrams can be--and are--used to represent causes of various different kinds, as the examples we have considered suggest. The essential feature for the use of a causal arrow in a path diagram is the assumption that a change in the variable at the tail of the arrow will result in a change in the variable at the head of the arrow, all else being equal (i.e., with all other variables in the diagram held constant). Note the one-way nature of this process: Imposing a change on the variable at the head of the arrow does *not* bring about a change in the tail variable. A variety of common uses of the word *cause* can be expressed in these terms, and hence can legitimately be represented by a causal arrow in a path diagram.

Completeness of a path diagram

Variables in a path diagram may be grouped in two classes: those that do not receive causal inputs from any other variable in the path diagram, and those that receive one or more such causal inputs. Variables in the first of these two classes are referred to as *exogenous, independent,* or *source variables.* Variables in the second class are called *endogenous, dependent,* or *downstream variables.* *Exogenous variables* (Greek: "of external origin") are so called because their causal sources lie external to the path diagram; they are causally *independent* with respect to other variables in the diagram: Straight arrows may lead away from them but never toward them. These variables represent causal *sources* in the diagram. Examples of such source variables in Fig. 1.3 are A_1, B_1, and the two unlabeled residual variables.

Endogenous variables ("of internal origin") have causal sources that lie within the path diagram; they are causally *dependent* on other variables--one or more straight arrows lead into them. These variables lie causally *downstream* from source variables. Examples of downstream variables in Fig. 1.3 are A_2 and B_3.

In Fig. 1.2, U, T, and V are source variables, and A and B are downstream variables. Look back at Fig. 1.1. Which are the source and downstream variables in this path diagram? (I hope you identified A, B, and X as source variables, and C as downstream.)

4

In a proper and complete path diagram, all the source variables are interconnected by curved arrows, to indicate that they may be intercorrelated--unless it is explicitly assumed that a correlation is zero, in which case the curved arrow is omitted. Thus the absence of a curved arrow between two source variables in a path diagram, as between X and A in Fig. 1.1, or T and U in Fig. 1.2, is not an expression of ignorance but an explicit statement about assumptions underlying the diagram.

Downstream variables, on the other hand, are never connected by curved arrows in path diagrams. (Actually, some authors use downstream curved arrows as a shorthand to indicate correlations among downstream variables caused by other variables than those included in the diagram. We use correlations between residual arrows for this purpose, which is consistent with our convention, because the latter are source variables.) Residual arrows point to downstream variables, never at source variables. Completeness of a path diagram requires that a residual arrow be attached to every downstream variable unless it is explicitly assumed that all the causes of variation of that variable are included among the variables upstream from it in the diagram. (This convention is also not universally adhered to: Occasionally, path diagrams are published with the notation "residual arrows omitted." This is an unfortunate practice because it leads to ambiguity in interpreting the diagram: Does the author intend that all the variation in a downstream variable is accounted for within the diagram, or not?)

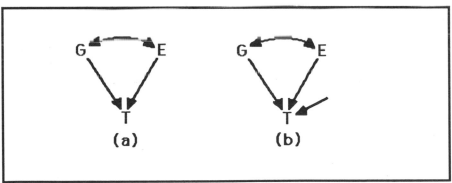

Fig. 1.4 Path diagrams illustrating the implication of an omitted residual arrow.

Figure 1.4 shows an example in which the presence or absence of a residual arrow makes a difference. The source variables G and E refer to the genetic and environmental influences on a trait T. The downstream variable T in Fig. 1.4 (a) has no residual arrow. That represents the assumption that the variation of T is completely explained by the genetic and environmental influences upon it. This is a theoretical assumption that one might sometimes wish to make. Fig. 1.4 (b), however, represents the assumption that genetic and environmental influences are not sufficient to explain the variation of T, that some additional factor or factors--perhaps measurement error or gene-environment interaction--may need to be taken into account in explaining T. Obviously, the assumptions in Figures 1.4 (a) and (b) are quite different, and one would not want it assumed that (a) was the case when in fact (b) was intended.

Finally, all significant direct causal connections between source and downstream variables, or between one downstream variable and another, should be included as straight arrows in the diagram. Omission of an arrow between A_1 and B_3 in Fig. 1.3 is a positive statement: that A_1 is assumed to affect B_3 only by way of A_2.

The notion of completeness in path diagrams should not be taken to mean that the ideal path diagram is one containing as many variables as possible connected by as many arrows as possible. Exactly the opposite is true. The smallest number of variables connected by the smallest number of arrows that can do the job is the path diagram to be sought for, because it represents the most parsimonious explanation of the phenomenon under consideration. Big, messy path diagrams are likely to give trouble in many ways. Nevertheless, often the simplest explanation of an interesting behavioral or biological phenomenon does involve causal relationships among a number of variables, not all observable. A path diagram provides a way of representing in a clear and straightforward fashion what is assumed to be going on in such a case.

Notice that most path diagrams could in principle be extended indefinitely back past their source variables: These could be taken as downstream variables in an extended path diagram, and the correlations among them explained by the linkages among their own causes. Thus, the parents in Fig. 1.1 could be taken as children in their own families, and the correlation between them explained by a model of the psychological and sociological mechanisms that result in mates having similar IQs. Or in Fig. 1.3, one could have measured A and B at a preceding time 0, resulting in a diagram in which the correlation between A_1 and B_1 is replaced by a superstructure of causal arrows from A_0 and B_0, themselves probably correlated. There is no hard and fast rule in such cases, other than the general maxim that simpler is better, which usually means that if going back entails multiplying variables, do not do it unless you have to. Sometimes, of course, you have to, when some key variable lies further upstream.

Other assumptions in path diagrams

It is assumed in path diagrams that causes are unitary, that is, in a case such as Fig. 1.2, that it is meaningful to think of a single variable T that is the cause of A and B, and not (say) two separate and distinct aspects of a phenomenon T, one of which causes A and one B. In the latter case, a better representation would be to replace T by two different (possibly correlated) variables.

An exception to the rule of unitary causes is residual variables, which typically represent multiple causes of a variable that are external to the path diagram. Perhaps for this reason, path analysts do not always solve for the path coefficients associated with the residual arrows in their diagrams. It is, however, good practice to solve at least for the proportion of variance associated with such residual causes (more on this later). It is nearly always useful to know what proportion of the variation of each downstream variable is accounted for by the causes explicitly included within the path diagram, and what proportion is not.

Another assumption made in path diagrams is that the causal relationships represented by straight arrows are linear. This is usually not terribly restricting: Mild departures from linearity are often reasonably approximated by linear relationships, and if not, it may be possible to transform variables so as to linearize their relationships with other variables. The use of log income, rather than income, or reciprocals of latency measures, or arcsine transformations of proportions, would be examples of transformations often used by behavioral scientists for this purpose. In drawing a path diagram, one ordinarily does not have to worry about such details. One can always make the blanket assumption that one's variables are measured on scales for which relationships are reasonably linear. But in evaluating the strength of causal effects with real data, the issue of nonlinearity may arise. If variable A has a positive effect on variable B in part of its range and a negative effect in another, it would be hard to assign a single number to represent the effect of A on B. However, if A is suitably redefined, perhaps as an absolute deviation from some optimum value, this may be possible. In Chapter 7 we consider some direct approaches to dealing with nonlinear relationships of latent variables.

A note on the orientation of path diagrams

Path diagrams are ordinarily arranged on the page with the flow of causation going more or less from left to right or from top to bottom, although occasionally one sees other arrangements, such as a path diagram radiating out from the center. Figures 1.1, 1.2, and 1.4 are examples of top-to-bottom orientation, Fig. 1.3 of left-to-right. Any of these is perfectly acceptable, although sociologists seem to have some preference for the left-to-right arrangement and geneticists for top-to-bottom. Both are used in this book, with the choice often determined by such trivial considerations as how well the diagram fits on the page.

Feedbacks and mutual influences

In our examples so far we have restricted ourselves to path diagrams in which, after the source variables, there was a simple downstream flow of causation: no paths that loop back on themselves or the like. Most of the cases we consider in this book have this one-way causal flow, but path representations can be used to deal with more complex situations involving causal loops, as we see later in Chapter 4. Examples of two such non-one-way cases are shown in Fig. 1.5. In Fig. 1.5 (a) there is a mutual causal influence between variables C and D: Each affects the other. A causal sequence could go from A to C to D to C to D again and so on. In Fig. 1.5 (b) there is an extended feedback loop: A affects B, which affects C, which in turn affects A.

(a)   **(b)**

Fig. 1.5 Path diagrams with (a) mutual influences and (b) a feedback loop.

Direct and indirect causal paths

Sometimes it is useful to distinguish between *direct* and *indirect* causal effects in path diagrams. A direct effect is represented by a single causal arrow between the two variables concerned. In Fig. 1.5 (b) variable B has a direct effect on variable C. There is a causal arrow leading from B to C. If B is changed we expect to observe a change in C. Variable A, however, has only an indirect effect on C because there is no direct arrow from A to C. There is, however, an indirect causal effect transmitted via variable B. If A changes, B will change, and B's change will affect C, other things being equal. Thus, A can be said to have a causal effect on C, although an indirect one. In Fig. 1.5 (a) variable B has a direct effect on variable D, an indirect effect on variable C, and no causal effect at all on variable A.

8

Path Analysis

Path diagrams are useful enough as simple descriptive devices, but they can be much more than that. Starting from empirical data, one can solve for a numerical value of each curved and straight arrow in a diagram to indicate the relative strength of that correlation or causal influence. Numerical values, of course, imply scales on which they are measured. For most of this chapter we assume that all variables in the path diagram are expressed in standard score form, that is, with a mean of 0 and a standard deviation of 1. Covariances and correlations are thus identical. This simplifies matters of presentation, and is a useful way of proceeding in many practical situations. Later, we see how the procedures can be applied to data in original raw score units, and consider some of the situations in which this approach is to be preferred. We also assume for the present that we are dealing with unlooped path diagrams.

The steps of constructing and solving path diagrams are referred to collectively as *path analysis,* a method originally developed by the American geneticist Sewall Wright as early as 1920, but only extensively applied in the social and behavioral sciences during the last couple of decades.

Wright's rules

Briefly, Wright showed that if a situation can be presented as a proper path diagram, then the correlation between any two variables in the diagram can be expressed as the *sum of the compound paths connecting these two points,* where a compound path is a path along arrows that follows three rules:

        (a) no loops;
        (b) no going forward then backward;
        (c) a maximum of one curved arrow per path.

The first rule means that a compound path must not go twice through the same variable. In Fig. 1.6 (a) the compound path ACF would be a legitimate path between A and F, but the path ACDECF would not be because it involves going twice through variable C.

The second rule means that on a particular path, after one has once gone forward along one or more arrows, it is not legitimate to proceed backward along others. (Going backward first and then forward is, however, quite proper.) In Fig. 1.6 (b) the compound path BAC is a legitimate way to go from B to C; the path BDC is not. In the former, one goes backward along an arrow (B to A) and then forward (A to C), which is allowable, but path BDC would require going forward then backward, which is not. This asymmetry may seem a bit less arbitrary if one realizes that it serves to permit events in the diagram to be connected by common causes (A), but not by common consequences (D).

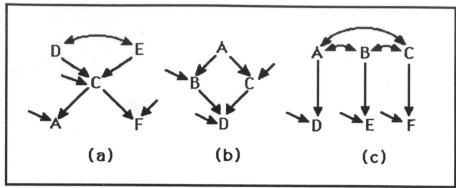

Fig. 1.6 Illustrations of Wright's rules.

The third rule is illustrated in Fig. 1.6 (c). DACF is a legitimate compound path between D and F; DABCF is not, because it would require traversing two curved arrows. Likewise, DABE is a legitimate path between D and E, but DACBE is not.

   Figure 1.7 serves to provide examples of tracing paths in a path diagram according to Wright's rules. This figure incorporates three source variables, A, B, and C, and three downstream variables, D, E, and F. I have designated each arrow by a lower case letter for convenience in representing compound paths. Each lower case letter stands for the *value* or magnitude of the particular causal effect or correlation. A simple rule indicates how these values are combined: *The numerical value of a compound path is equal to the product of the values of its constituent arrows.* Thus, simply writing the lower case letters of a path in sequence is at the same time writing an expression for the numerical value of that path.

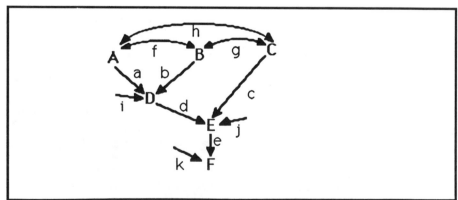

Fig. 1.7 Examples of tracing paths in a path diagram.

For example, what is the correlation between variables A and D in Fig. 1.7? Two paths are legal: *a* and *fb*. A path like *hgb* would be excluded by the rule about only one curved arrow, and paths going further down the diagram like *adcgb* would violate both the rules about no forward then backward and no loops. So the numerical value of r_{AD} can be expressed as *a +fb*. I hope that you can see that $r_{BD} = b +fa$, and that $r_{CD} = gb +ha$.

What about r_{AB}? Just *f*. Path *hg* would violate the third rule, and paths like *ab* or *adcg* would violate the second. It is, of course, quite reasonable that r_{AB} should equal *f*, because that is just what the curved arrow between A and B means. Likewise $r_{BC} = g$ and $r_{AC} = h$.

Let us consider a slightly more complicated case: r_{AE}. There are three paths: *ad, fbd,* and *hc*. Note that although variable D is passed through twice, this is perfectly legal, because it is only passed through once on any given path. You might wish to pause at this point to work out r_{BE} and r_{CE} for yourself. (I hope you got *bd +fad +gc* and *c +gbd +had*.)

Finally, consider the correlation between A and F. This works out to *ade +fbde +hce*. Notice that this can be rewritten as (*ad +fbd +hc*)*e*, or simply (r_{AE})*e* ; that is, once we have solved for the correlation r_{AE}, we can think of

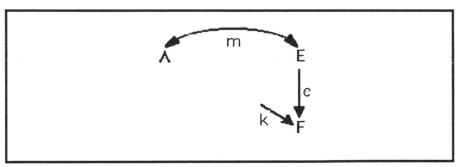

Fig. 1.8 A simplified version of Fig. 1.7.

the path diagram as having the simple form shown in Fig. 1.8, of two variables A and E whose correlation (call it now *m*) is known, plus a causal path *e* from variable E to F. In working with complex path diagrams, this technique of substituting a single value for a discrete subunit of the diagram is often helpful. Note that this simplification can be made because the causation of F is separable in the diagram from the network of paths connecting A and E. If there had also been a direct path from, say, B to F, this could not properly be represented in Fig. 1.8, and this particular simplification would not be possible.

You should now try your hand at the five remaining correlations in Fig.1.7:

r_{DE}, r_{EF}, r_{BF}, r_{CF}, and r_{DF}. The answers are not given until later in the chapter, to minimize the temptation of peeking at them first.

Numerical solution of a path diagram

Given that we can express each of the correlations among a set of observed variables in a path diagram as a sum of compound paths, can we reverse this process and solve for the values of the causal paths given the correlations? The answer is that often we can.

Consider the example of Fig. 1.1, redrawn as Fig. 1.9. Recall that variables A and B were fathers' and mothers' intelligence, and C was children's intelligence. X is a residual variable, representing other unmeasured influences on child's intelligence that are independent of the parents'

Fig. 1.9 The example of Fig. 1.1, with observed inter-correlations of A, B, and C.

intelligence. Suppose that in some suitable population of families we were to observe the correlations shown on the right in Fig. 1.9. We can now, using our newfound knowledge of path analysis (and ignoring X for the moment), write the following three equations:

$$r_{AB} = c$$
$$r_{AC} = a + cb$$
$$r_{BC} = b + ca.$$

Because we know the observed values r_{AB}, r_{AC}, and r_{BC}, we have three simultaneous equations in three unknowns:

$$c = .50$$
$$a + cb = .65$$
$$b + ca = .70.$$

Substitution for c in the second and third equations yields two equations in two unknowns:

$$a + .50b = .65$$
$$.50a + b = .70.$$

These equations are readily solved to yield $a = .40$ and $b = .50$. Thus, if we were to observe the set of intercorrelations given in Fig. 1.9, *and if our causal model is correct,* we could conclude that the causal influences of fathers' and mothers' intelligence on child's intelligence could be represented by values of .40 and .50, respectively, for the causal paths a and b.

What do these numbers mean? They are, in fact, standardized partial regression coefficients. We call them *path coefficients,* for short. Because they are *regression coefficients,* they tell us to what extent a change on the variable at the tail of the arrow is transmitted to the variable at the head of the arrow. Because they are *partial* regression coefficients, this is the change that occurs with all other variables in the diagram held constant. Because they are *standardized* partial regression coefficients, we are talking about changes measured in standard deviation units. Specifically, the value of .40 for a means that if we were to select fathers who were one standard deviation above the mean for intelligence--but keeping mothers at the mean--their offspring would average four-tenths of a standard deviation above the population mean. (Unless otherwise specified, we are assuming in this chapter that the numbers we deal with are population values, so that issues of statistical inference do not complicate the picture.)

Because paths a and b are standardized partial regression coefficients, also known in multiple regression problems as *beta weights,* one might wonder if we can solve for them as such, by treating the path analysis as a sort of multiple regression problem. The answer is, yes we can, at least in cases where all variables are measured. In the present example, A, B, and C are assumed known, so we can solve for a and b by considering this as a multiple regression problem in predicting C from A and B.

Using standard formulas (e.g., McNemar, 1969, p. 192):

$$\beta_1 = (.65 - .70 \times .50)/(1 - .50^2) = .40$$
$$\beta_2 = (.70 - .65 \times .50)/(1 - .50^2) = .50,$$

or exactly the same results as before.

Viewing the problem in this way, we can also interpret the squared multiple correlation between C and A and B as the proportion of the variance of C which is accounted for by A and B jointly. In this case $R^2_{C \cdot AB} = \beta_1 r_{AC} + \beta_2 r_{BC} = .40 \times .65 + .50 \times .70 = .61$. Another way in which we can arrive at the same figure from the path diagram is by following a path-tracing procedure:

The predicted variance of C is *the sum of the compound paths from* C *to itself via* A *or* B *or both*. In this case there is the path to A and back, with value a^2, the path to B and back, with value b^2, and the two paths *acb* and *bca* : $.40^2 + .50^2 + 2 \times .40 \times .50 \times .50 = .16 + .25 + .20 = .61$.

Either of these approaches will also allow us to solve for the value of the path *d,* which leads from the unmeasured residual X. The variance that A and B jointly account for is R^2, or .61. The variance that X accounts for is thus $1 - R^2$, that is, $1 - .61$, or .39. This, therefore, must be the square of the correlation between X and C. So the value of *d* is $\sqrt{.39}$, or .62.

As long as all variables are measured, one can proceed to solve for the causal paths in a path diagram as beta weights in a series of multiple regression analyses. Thus, in Fig. 1.7 one could solve for *a* and *b* from the correlations among A, B, and D; for *d* and *c* from the correlations among D, C, and E; and for *e* as the simple correlation between E and F. The residuals *i, j,* and *k* can then be obtained as $\sqrt{(1 - R^2)}$ in the various multiple regressions.

In general, however, we must deal with path diagrams involving unmeasured, latent variables. We cannot directly calculate the correlations of these with observed variables, so a simple multiple regression approach does not work. We need, instead, to carry out some variant of the first approach--that is, to solve a set of simultaneous equations with at least as many equations as there are unknown values to be obtained.

Fig. 1.10 The example of Fig. 1.2, with observed correlation of .80 between alternate forms A and B of a test.

Consider the example of Fig. 1.2, test reliability, repeated for convenience as Fig. 1.10. We wish to solve for the values of the causal paths between the true score T and the observed scores A and B. But T is an unobserved, latent variable; all we have is the observed correlation .80 between forms A and B of the test. How can we proceed? If we are willing to assume that A and B have the same relation to T, which they should have if they are really parallel alternate forms of a test, we can write from the path diagram the equation

$$r_{AB} = t^2 = .80,$$

14

from which it follows that $t = \sqrt{.80} = .89$. It further follows that t^2 or 80% of the variance of each of the alternate test forms is attributable to the true score on the trait, that 20% is therefore due to error, and that the values of the residual paths from U and V are $\sqrt{.20}$ or .45.

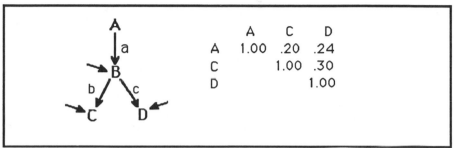

	A	C	D
A	1.00	.20	.24
C		1.00	.30
D			1.00

Fig. 1.11 Another simple path diagram with a latent variable.

Figure 1.11 presents another case of a path diagram containing a latent variable. It is assumed that A, C, and D are measured. Their intercorrelations are given to the right of the figure. B is not measured, so we do not know its correlations with A, C, and D. We can, however, write three equations for the three known correlations in terms of the three paths *a, b,* and *c,* and (as it turns out) these three equations can be solved for the values of the three causal paths.

The equations are:

$$r_{AC} = ab$$
$$r_{AD} = ac$$
$$r_{CD} = bc.$$

A solution is:

$$r_{AC}\, r_{CD}/r_{AD} = ab \times bc\,/ac\ = b^2 = .20 \times .30/.24 = .25;\ \ b = .50$$
$$a = r_{AC}/b\ = .20/.50 = .40$$
$$c = r_{AD}/a\ = .24/.40 = .60.$$

Note that another possible solution would be numerically the same, but with all paths negative, because b^2 also has a negative square root.

(By the way, to end the suspense about the problem regarding Fig. 1.7: $r_{DE} = d + ahc + bgc$, $r_{EF} = e$, $r_{BF} = bde + fade + gce$, $r_{CF} = ce + gbde + hade$, $r_{DF} = de + ahce + bgce$.)

Under-, over-, and just-determined path diagrams

Figure 1.12 (a) shows another simple path diagram. It is somewhat like Fig. 1.11 upside down: Instead of one cause of the latent variable and two effects, there are now two causes and one effect.

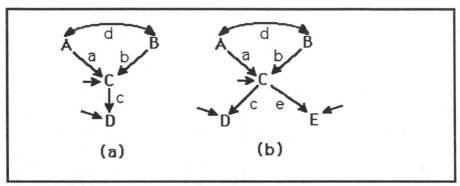

Fig. 1.12 Examples of under- and overdetermined path diagrams.

However, this change has made a critical difference. There are still just three intercorrelations among the three observed variables A, B, and D, yielding three equations. But now there are four unknown values to be estimated: a, b, c, and d. One observed correlation, r_{AB}, estimates d directly. That leaves only two equations, $r_{AD} = ac$ and $r_{BD} = bc$, to estimate the three unknowns a, b, and c. Therefore, no unique solution is possible, and the path diagram is said to be *underdetermined*.

In the preceding problem of Fig. 1.11, there were three equations in three unknowns, and an exact solution was possible. Such a case is described as *just determined*. Fig. 1.12 (b) shows a third case, of an *overdetermined* path diagram. As in the left-hand figure, C is a latent variable and A and B are source variables, but an additional measured downstream variable E has been added. Now there are six observed intercorrelations among the observed variables A, B, D, and E, yielding six equations, whereas we have only added one unknown, giving five unknowns to be solved for. More equations than unknowns does not guarantee overdetermination, but in this case, for most observed sets of correlations, there will be no single solution for the unknowns that will satisfy all six equations simultaneously. What is ordinarily done in such cases is to seek values for the unknowns that come as close as possible to accounting for the observed intercorrelations (we defer until the next chapter a consideration of what "as close as possible" means).

It might be thought that just-determined path diagrams, because they permit exact solutions, would be the ideal to be sought for, but in fact, for the behavioral scientist, overdetermined path diagrams are usually to be preferred. The reason is that the data of the behavioral scientist typically contain both sampling and measurement error, and an exact fit to these data is an exact fit to the error as well as to the truth they contain. If we assume that errors are more or less random, a best overall fit to the redundant data of an overdetermined path diagram will usually provide a better approximation to the underlying true population values. In addition, as we see later, overdetermined path diagrams may permit statistical tests of goodness of fit, which just-determined diagrams do not.

A computer-oriented symbolism for path diagrams--RAM

A way of drawing path diagrams that has advantages for translating them into computer representations has been developed by J. J. McArdle. He calls his general approach to path modeling Reticular Action Modeling, or RAM.

Fig. 1.13 The path model of Fig. 1.11 (left) shown in RAM symbolism (right).

Figure 1.13 shows on the left a path model presented earlier in this chapter, and on the right the same model in a RAM representation. The following points may be noted: (1) Latent variables are designated by placing them in circles, observed variables by placing them in squares. (This is a widespread convention among latent variable modelers, not just specific to RAM.) In addition to squares and circles for variables, RAM uses triangles to designate constants, which are important in models involving means, discussed later in the book. (2) Residual variables are represented explicitly as latent variables (X, Y, Z). (3) Two-headed curved arrows leaving and re-entering the same variable are used to represent the variance of source variables. When they are unlabeled, as here, they are assumed to have a value of 1.0--thus, these are standardized variables. Curved arrows connecting two different source variables represent their covariance or correlation, in the usual manner of path diagrams.

Although a little cumbersome in some respects, which is why we will not be using it routinely in this book, RAM symbolism, by rendering explicitly a number of things often left implicit in path diagrams, facilitates a direct translation into computer representations. We will see examples in Chapter 2.

Factor Models

An important subdivision of latent variable analysis is traditionally known as *factor analysis*. In recent discussions of factor analysis, a distinction is often drawn between *exploratory* and *confirmatory* varieties. In exploratory factor analysis, which is what is usually thought of as factor analysis if no qualification is attached, one seeks, under rather general assumptions, for a latent variable structure that could account for the intercorrelations of an observed set of variables. In confirmatory factor analysis, on the other hand, one takes a specific hypothesized structure and sees how well it accounts for the observed relationships in the data.

Traditionally, textbooks on factor analysis discuss the topic of exploratory factor analysis at length and in detail, and then they put in something about confirmatory factor analysis in the later chapters. In this book, however, we will find it instructive to proceed in the opposite direction: to consider first confirmatory factor analysis, and defer an extended examination of exploratory factor analysis until later (Chapters 5 and 6). The reason for this is that path models provide a natural and convenient way of representing the hypothesized causal structures involving latent variables that the confirmatory factor analyst wishes to compare to real-world data.

The origins of factor analysis: Charles Spearman and the two-factor theory of intelligence

As it happens, the original form of factor analysis, invented by the British psychologist Charles Spearman shortly after 1900, was more confirmatory than exploratory, in the sense that Spearman had an explicit theory of intellectual performance that he wished to test against data. Spearman did not use a path representation, Wright not yet having invented it, but Fig. 1.14 represents the essentials of Spearman's theory in the form of a path diagram.

Spearman hypothesized that performance on each of a number of intellectual tasks shared something in common with performance on all other intellectual tasks, a factor of general intellectual ability that Spearman called "g." Performance on each task also involved a factor of skills specific to that task, hence the designation *two-factor theory*. In Spearman's (1904) words: "All branches of intellectual activity have in common one fundamental function (or group of functions), whereas the remaining or specific elements of the activity seem in every case to be wholly different from that in all the others" (p. 284).

18

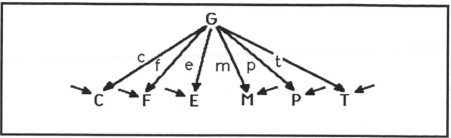

Fig. 1.14 Path representation of Spearman's two-factor theory.

Spearman obtained several measures on a small group of boys at an English preparatory school: a measure of pitch discrimination, a ranking of musical talent, and examination grades in several academic areas--Classics, French, English studies, and Mathematics. Fig. 1.14 represents his two-factor theory, as applied to these data. The letter G at the top of the figure represents the latent variable of general intellectual ability, C, F, E, and M at the bottom represent observed performances in the academic subjects, P stands for pitch discrimination and T for musical talent. General intellectual ability is assumed to contribute to all these performances. Each also involves specific abilities, represented by the residual arrows.

If Spearman's theory provides an adequate explanation of these data, the path diagram implies that the correlation between any two tasks should be equal to the product of the paths connecting them to the general factor: the correlation between Classics and Mathematics should be cm, that between English and French should be ef, between French and musical talent ft, and so on. Because we are attempting to explain $6 \times 5 / 2 = 15$ different observed correlations by means of 6 inferred values--the path coefficients c, f, e, m, p, and t--a good fit to the data is by no means guaranteed. If one is obtained, it is evidence that the theory under consideration has some explanatory power.

Fig. 1.15 gives the correlations for part of Spearman's data: Classics, English, Mathematics, and pitch discrimination.

If the single general-factor model fit the data exactly, we could take the

Intercorrelations				
	C	E	M	P
C	1.00	.78	.70	.66
E		1.00	.64	.54
M			1.00	.45
P				1.00

Fig. 1.15 Data to illustrate the method of triads.

intercorrelations among any three variables and solve for the values of the three respective path coefficients, because they would provide three equations in three unknowns. For example:

$$r_{CE} \times r_{CM} / r_{EM} = cecm / em = c^2 = .78 \text{x} .70 / .64 = .853; \; c = .92$$
$$r_{EM} \times r_{CE} / r_{CM} = emce / cm = e^2 = .64 \text{x} .78 / .70 = .713; \; e = .84$$
$$r_{CM} \times r_{EM} / r_{CE} = cmem / ce = m^2 = .70 \text{x} .64 / .78 = .574; \; m = .76.$$

This procedure has been given a name: It is called the *method of triads*. If the data, as here, only approximately fit a model with a single general factor, one will get slightly different values for a particular path coefficient depending on which triads one uses. For example, we may solve for *m* in two other ways from these data:

$$r_{CM} \times r_{MP} / r_{CP} = cmmp / cp = m^2 = .70 \text{x} .45 / .66 = .477; \; m = .69$$
$$r_{EM} \times r_{MP} / r_{EP} = emmp / ep = m^2 = .64 \text{x} .45 / .54 = .533; \; m = .73.$$

These three values of *m* are not very different. One might consider simply averaging them to obtain a compromise value. A slightly preferable method, one less vulnerable to individual aberrant values, adds together the numerators and denominators of the preceding expressions, and then divides:

$$m^2 = \frac{.70 \text{x} .64 + .70 \text{x} .45 + .64 \text{x} .45}{.78 + .66 + .54} = .531; \; m = .73$$

You may wish to check your understanding of the method by confirming that it yields .97 for *c*, .84 for *e*, and .65 for *p*, for the data of Fig. 1.15.

We may get some sense of how accurately our solution can account for the observed intercorrelations among the four variables, by producing the intercorrelation matrix implied by the paths: that is, *ce, cm, cp*, and so on.

.81	.71	.63
	.61	.55
		.47

As is evident, the implied correlations under the model do not differ much from the observed correlations: The maximum absolute difference is .03. The assumption of a single general factor plus a residual factor for each measure does a reasonable job of accounting for the data.

We may as well go on and estimate the variance accounted for by each of the residual factors. Following the path model, the proportion of the variance of each test accounted for by a factor equals the correlation of that test with itself by way of the factor (the sum of the paths to itself via the factor). In this case these have the value c^2, e^2, etc. The variances due to the general factor are thus .93, .70, .53, and .42 for Classics, English, Mathematics, and pitch discrimination, repectively, and the corresponding residual variances due to specific factors are .07, .30, .47, and .58. In traditional factor analytic terminology, the variance a test shares with other tests in the battery is called its *communality*, symbolized h^2, and the variance not so shared is called its *uniqueness*, symbolized u^2. The communalities of the four measures are thus .93, .70, .53, and .42, and their uniquenesses .07, .30, .47, and .58. Pitch discrimination has the least in common with the other three measures, Classics has the most.

The observant reader will notice that the communality and uniqueness of a variable are just expressions in the factor analytic domain of the general notion of the predicted (R^2) and residual variance of a downstream variable in a path diagram, as discussed earlier in the chapter.

The path coefficients *c, e, m*, and so on, are in factor-analytic writing called the *factor pattern coefficients* (or more simply, the *factor loadings*). The correlations between the tests and the factors, here numerically the same as the pattern coefficients, are collectively known as the *factor structure*.

The centroid method of solving for a general factor

The solution methods we have described can readily be carried out with pencil and hand calculator for small matrices, but the amount of computational labor ascends steeply as the size of the correlation matrix increases. For instance, the four-variable submatrix from Spearman provides 3 triads for each of the four variables, or 12 altogether. The original six-variable matrix yields five times as many, a total of 60 triads.

A more practical way of solving for a single factor underlying a set of intercorrelations was devised by the British factorist Cyril Burt (1917). It is called the *centroid method*. Table 1-1 illustrates its basic logic.

The square array of paired symbols represents the intercorrelation matrix of the six measures; for example, under the path model of Fig. 1.14, the

Table 1-1 Logic of the centroid method, applied to Spearman example

$$
\begin{array}{llllll}
c^2 & fc & ec & mc & pc & tc \\
cf & f^2 & ef & mf & pf & tf \\
ce & fe & e^2 & me & pe & te \\
cm & fm & em & m^2 & pm & tm \\
cp & fp & ep & mp & p^2 & tp \\
\underline{ct} & \underline{ft} & \underline{et} & \underline{mt} & \underline{pt} & t^2
\end{array}
$$

let $\Sigma = c + f + e + m + p + t$

$c\Sigma + f\Sigma + e\Sigma + m\Sigma + p\Sigma + t\Sigma = (c+f+e+m+p+t)\Sigma = \Sigma\Sigma$

$$\Sigma = \sqrt{\Sigma\Sigma}$$

$c = c\Sigma/\Sigma$, $f = f\Sigma/\Sigma$, etc.

correlation between Classics and French is *cf* (or equivalently, *fc*). The main diagonal contains the communalities c^2, f^2, and so on. Now if we take Σ to represent the sum $c + f + e + m + p + t$, the sums of the columns of the table can be given as $c\Sigma$, $f\Sigma$, $e\Sigma$, etc., because each column contains a single term paired in turn with each of the six. The sum of the column totals is then equal to $\Sigma\Sigma$, as shown, and the square root Σ of this quantity can be divided into each of the column totals to solve for c, f, e, m, p, and t, the desired paths.

   This method can readily be applied to an intercorrelation matrix, regardless of size, to obtain the path coefficients for a general factor: One simply sums the columns, and divides each by the square root of the sum of these sums. The only catch is, how does one get the communalities to put in the diagonal of the matrix? The answer is that even a rough estimate will do, especially if the correlation matrix is fairly large. In a later chapter, several different methods of communality estimation will be described, but for the moment, one method we can use is to estimate the communality from two or three triads involving the variable.

Table 1-2 Numerical illustration of the centroid method, applied to the Spearman example

	C	F	E	M	P	T	
C	(.93)	.83	.78	.70	.66	.63	
F	.83	(.77)	.67	.67	.65	.57	
E	.78	.67	(.70)	.64	.54	.51	
M	.70	.67	.64	(.53)	.45	.51	
P	.66	.65	.54	.45	(.42)	.40	
T	.63	.57	.51	.51	.40	(.42)	
	4.53	4.16	3.84	3.50	3.12	3.04	$\Sigma\Sigma$=22.19
							Σ=4.7106
	.962	.883	.815	.743	.662	.645	path coeff.
	.92	.78	.66	.55	.44	.42	h^2

	C	F	E	M	P	T
C		.85	.78	.71	.64	.62
F	-.02		.72	.66	.58	.57
E	.00	-.05		.61	.54	.53
M	-.01	.01	.03		.49	.48
P	.02	.07	.00	-.04		.43
T	.01	.00	-.02	.03	-.03	

Note: Upper matrix--observed intercorrelations; estimated communalities in diagonal. Lower matrix--above diagonal, correlations implied by path coefficients; below diagonal, residual correlations unaccounted for by general factor.

Table 1-2 applies the centroid method to the full Spearman example. For C, E, M, and P we have used the communalities estimated earlier from the four-variable set (three triads each). For F and T we have arbitrarily used the three triads obtained by pairing F and T with C and E, with E and M, and with M and P. The total of the column totals is 22.19. Dividing the column totals by the square root of this, 4.7106, yields the path coefficients as shown, and squaring them gives the communalities. Note that the path coefficients for Classics, English, Mathematics, and pitch discrimination--.96, .82, .74, and .66--do not differ much from the .97, .84, .73, and .65 obtained earlier by the method of triads with the partial data set.

The obtained communalities also do not differ much from the estimated ones--the maximum discrepancy is .04 for E. If we wanted to see how much difference this makes (and incidentally, get slightly improved values for the path coefficients), we could put these obtained communality values in place of the estimates we used originally and repeat the calculations leading to the path coefficients. There is no need to show the calculations. In no case is the resulting difference greater than .01.

The bottom of Table 1-2 shows the correlations implied by the path coefficients. Again, we see that they do a reasonably good--but not a perfect--job of reproducing the original correlations. About half the values are within one or two points of the original in the second decimal place; the largest discrepancy is .07. We return later to the question of just how good a fit is "good enough."

One final point: The centroid method assumes that all variables are scored in the same direction with respect to the general factor, so that their intercorrelations are predominantly positive. Suppose that Spearman had happened to use a measure of pitch discrimination, such as errors or latency, that was scored so that a high score meant that discrimination was poor. Its correlation with all the other measures would then be negative, and this would cause trouble. In such a case one could reverse the scoring of the original measure (say, by subtracting each score from the highest possible score plus 1), or, equivalently, one could simply reverse all the signs of the correlations in the matrix that involve that variable. This is known as *reflecting* the variable and should be carried out if necessary before applying the centroid method. Note that if one were to fail to do this, it would not affect the column total for the variable in question, other than changing its sign, but it would decrease the totals for all the other variables and hence distort the analysis.

More than one common factor

As soon became evident to Spearman's followers and critics, not all observed sets of intercorrelations are well explained by a model containing only one general factor; factor analysts soon moved to models in which more than one latent variable was postulated to account for the observed intercorrelations among measures. Such latent variables came to be called *common* factors, rather than *general* factors, because, although they were common to several of the variables under consideration, they were not general to all. There remained, of course, *specific* factors unique to each measure. Fig. 1.16 gives

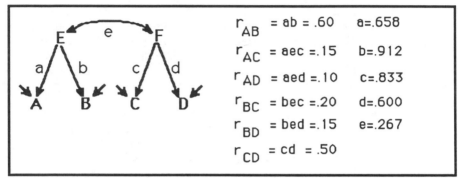

$$r_{AB} = ab = .60 \qquad a=.658$$
$$r_{AC} = aec = .15 \qquad b=.912$$
$$r_{AD} = aed = .10 \qquad c=.833$$
$$r_{BC} = bec = .20 \qquad d=.600$$
$$r_{BD} = bed = .15 \qquad e=.267$$
$$r_{CD} = cd = .50$$

Fig. 1.16 A simple factor model with two factors.

an example of a path diagram in which there are two latent variables, E and F, and four observed variables, A, B, C, and D. E is hypothesized as influencing A and B, and F as influencing C and D. E and F are correlated.

In the path diagram of Fig. 1.16 there are five unknowns, the paths *a, b, c,* and *d,* and the correlation *e* between the two latent variables. There are six equations, shown to the right of the diagram, based on the six intercorrelations between pairs of observed variables. Hypothetical values of the observed correlations are given--.60 for r_{AB}, for example. Because there are more equations than unknowns, one might expect that a single exact solution would not be available, and indeed this is the case. An iterative least squares solution, carried out in a way discussed in the next chapter, yielded the values shown to the far right of Fig. 1.16. Table 1-3 reports a typical factor analysis solution based on these values. The factor pattern represents the values of the paths from factors to variables; i.e., the paths *a* and *b* and two zero paths from E to A, B, C, and D, and the corresponding paths from F. The factor structure presents the correlations of the variables with the factors: for factor E these have the values *a, b, ec,* and *ed,* respectively, and for factor F, *ea, eb, c,* and *d.* The communalities (h^2) are in this case simply a^2, b^2, c^2, and d^2, because each variable is influenced by only one factor. Finally, the correlation between E and F is just *e.*

24

Table 1-3 Factor solution for the two-factor problem of Fig. 1.16

Variable	Factor pattern		Factor structure		h^2
	E	F	E	F	
A	.66	.00	.66	.18	.43
B	.91	.00	.91	.24	.83
C	.00	.83	.22	.83	.69
D	.00	.60	.16	.60	.36

Factor intercorrelations

	E	F
E	1.00	.27
F	.27	1.00

Reproduced and residual correlations

	A	B	C	D
A		.600	.146	.105
B	.000		.203	.146
C	.004	-.003		.500
D	-.005	.004	.000	

The reproduced correlations (those implied by the path values) and the residual correlations (the differences between observed and implied correlations) are shown at the bottom of Table 1-3. The reproduced correlations are obtained by inserting the solved values of *a, b, c,* etc. into the equations of Fig. 1.16: r_{AB} = .658 x .912, r_{AC} = .658 x .267 x .833, and so on.

A more complex model with three factors is shown in Fig. 1.17. Because this model has 10 unknowns and only 6 equations, it is underdetermined

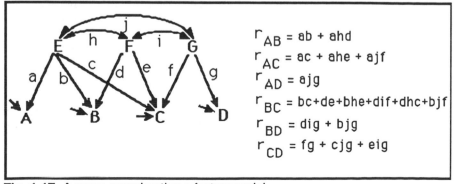

$$r_{AB} = ab + ahd$$
$$r_{AC} = ac + ahe + ajf$$
$$r_{AD} = ajg$$
$$r_{BC} = bc+de+bhe+dif+dhc+bjf$$
$$r_{BD} = dig + bjg$$
$$r_{CD} = fg + cjg + eig$$

Fig. 1.17 A more complex three-factor model.

and cannot be solved as it stands. However, if one were to fix sufficient values by a priori knowledge or assumption, one could solve for the remaining values. The factor solution in symbolic form is given in Table 1-4. By inserting the known and solved-for values in place of the unknowns, one could obtain numerical values for the factor pattern, the factor structure, the communalities, and the factor intercorrelations. Also, one could use the path equations of Fig. 1.17 to obtain the implied correlations and thence the residuals.

Notice that the factor pattern is quite simple in terms of the paths, but that the factor structure (the correlations of factors with variables) and the communalities are more complex functions of the paths and factor intercorrelations.

Table 1-4 Factor solution of Fig. 1.17, in symbolic form

Variable	Factor pattern E	F	G	Factor structure E	F	G	h^2
A	a	0	0	a	ha	ja	a^2
B	b	d	0	b+hd	d+hb	id+jb	b^2+d^2+2bhd
C	c	e	f	c+he +jf	e+hc +if	f+ie +jc	$c^2+e^2+f^2+2che$ $+2eif+2cjf$
D	0	0	g	jg	ig	g	g^2

Factor intercorrelations

	E	F	G
E	1.0	h	j
F	h	1.0	i
G	j	i	1.0

Structural Equations

An alternative way of representing a path diagram is as a set of *structural equations*. Each equation expresses a downstream variable as a function of the causal paths leading into it. There will be as many equations as there are downstream variables. Fig. 1.18 shows one of the path diagrams considered earlier. It has one downstream variable, hence one structural equation: The score of a person on variable C is an additive function of his scores on A, B, and X. If the variables are obtained in standard-score form for a set of subjects, the values of the weights *a, b,* and *d* required to give a best fit to the data in a least squares sense turn out to be just the standardized partial regression coefficients, or path coefficients, we have discussed earlier.

$$C = aA + bB + dX$$

Fig. 1.18 A structural equation based on a path diagram.

Figure 1.19 gives a slightly more complex example, based on the earlier Fig. 1.3. Now there are two downstream variables, A_2 and B_3. A_2 can be expressed as a weighted additive function of the three source variables A_1, B_1, and X, as shown in the first equation, whereas B_3 can be expressed in terms of A_2, B_1, and Y. Note that to construct a structural equation one simply includes a term for every straight arrow leading into the downstream variable. The term consists of the variable at the tail of the arrow times the path coefficient associated with it.

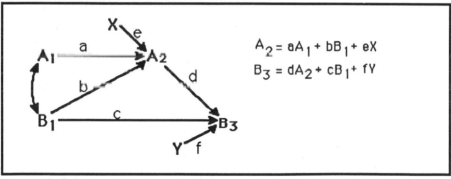

$$A_2 = aA_1 + bB_1 + eX$$
$$B_3 = dA_2 + cB_1 + fY$$

Fig. 1.19 Structural equations based on the path diagram of Fig. 1.3.

For a final example, consider the factor analysis model of Fig. 1.17 in the preceding section. The structural equations are as follows (X_A, X_B, etc. represent the terms involving the residual arrows):

$$A = aE + X_A$$
$$B = bE + dF + X_B$$
$$C = cE + eF + fG + X_C$$
$$D = gG + X_D$$

Notice that the equations are closely related to the rows of the factor pattern matrix (Table 1-4) with residual terms added. The solution of the set of structural equations corresponds essentially to the solution for the paths in the path diagram and would be similarly underdetermined in this instance. Again, by previously defining a sufficient number of the unknowns, the equations could be solved for those remaining.

The structural equation approach to causal models originated in economics and the path approach in biology. For many purposes the two may be regarded simply as alternative representations. Note, however, one difference. Path diagrams explicitly represent the correlations among source variables, whereas structural equations do not. If using the latter, supplementary specifications or assumptions must be made concerning the variances and covariances of the source variables in the model.

Original and Standardized Variables

So far, we have assumed we were dealing with standardized variables. This has simplified the presentation, but is not a necessary restriction. Path, factor, and structural equation analyses can be carried out with variables in their original scale units as well as with standardized variables. In practice, structural equation analysis is usually done in rawscore units, path analysis is done both ways, and factor analysis is usually done with standardized variables. However, this is often simply a matter of tradition or (what amounts to much the same thing) of the particular computer program used. There are occasions on which the standardized and rawscore approach each has definite advantages, so it is important to know that one can convert the results of one to the other and be able to do so when the occasion arises.

Another way of making the distinction between analyses based on standardized and raw units is to say that in the first case one is analyzing correlations, and in the second, covariances. In the first case one decomposes a correlation matrix among observed variables into additive components; in the second case one so decomposes a variance-covariance matrix. The curved arrows in a path diagram are correlations in the first case, covariances in the second. In the first case a straight arrow in a path diagram stands for a standardized partial regression coefficient, in the second case for a rawscore partial regression coefficient. In the first case a .5 beside a straight arrow leading from years of education to annual income means that, other things equal, people in this particular population who are one standard deviation above the mean in education average half a standard deviation above the mean in income. In the second case, if education is measured in years and income in dollars, a 5,000 alongside the straight arrow between them means that, other things equal, an increase of 1 year in education represents an increase of $5,000 in annual income (in this case, .5 would mean 50 cents!). In each case the arrow between A and B refers to how much change in B results from a given change in A, but in the first case change is measured in standard deviation units of the two variables, and in the second case, in the ratio of their rawscore units (dollars of income per year of education).

Standardized regression coefficients are particularly useful when comparisons are to be made across different variables, unstandardized regression coefficients are preferred when comparisons are to be made across different populations.

In the first case, it is difficult to compare the relative importance of education and occupational status in influencing income if the respective rawscore coefficients are 5,000 and 300, based on income in dollars, education in years, and occupational status on a 100-point scale. But if the standardized regression coefficients are .5 and .7, respectively, the greater relative influence of occupational status in this population is more evident.

In the second case, rawscore regression coefficients have the merit of independence of the particular ranges of the two variables involved in the study. If one study happens to have sampled twice as great a range of education as another, a difference in years of education that is, say, one-half a standard deviation in the first study would be a full standard deviation in the second. A standardized regression coefficient of .3 in one study would then describe exactly the same effect of education on income as a standardized regression coefficient of .6 in the other. This is a confusing state of affairs at best and could be seriously misleading if the reader is unaware of the sampling difference between the studies. A rawscore regression coefficient of $2,000 per year of education would, however, have the same meaning across the two studies. If the relevant standard deviations are known, a correlation can readily be transformed into a covariance, or vice versa, or a rawscore into a standardized regression coefficient and back, allowing one freely to report results in either or both ways, or to carry out calculations in one mode and report them in the other, if desired. (I qualify this statement later: Calculational methods can sometimes be sensitive to the scale on which variables are expressed; however, it will do for now.)

The relationships between covariances and correlations are simple:

$$cov_{12} = r_{12}\, s_1 s_2$$
$$r_{12} = cov_{12}/s_1 s_2,$$

where cov_{12} stands for the covariance between variables 1 and 2, r_{12} for their correlation, and s_1 and s_2 for their respective standard deviations.

The relationships between rawscore and standardized path coefficients are equally simple. To convert a standardized path coefficient to its rawscore form, *multiply it by the ratio of the standard deviations of its head to its tail variable.* To convert a rawscore path coefficient to standardized form, invert the process: Multiply by the ratio of the standard deviations of its tail to its head variable.

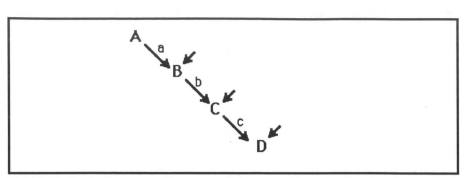

Fig. 1.20 Path diagram to illustrate rawscore and standardized path coefficients.

Table 1-5 Transformation of a sequence of paths from rawscore to standardized form (example of Fig. 1.20)

$$a^* b^* c^* = a(s_B/s_A) \, b(s_C/s_B) \, c(s_D/s_C) = abc(s_D/s_A)$$
$$abc = a^*(s_A/s_B) \, b^*(s_B/s_C) \, c^*(s_C/s_D) = a^*b^*c^*(s_A/s_D)$$

Note: Asterisks designate rawscore path coefficients.

These rules generalize to a series of path coefficients, as illustrated by Fig. 1.20 and Table 1-5. The first line in the table shows, via a process of substituting definitions and cancelling, that the series of rawscore path coefficients *a*b*c** is equal to the series *abc* of standardized path coefficients multiplied by the ratio of standard deviations of its head and tail variables. The second line demonstrates the converse transformation from rawscore to standardized coefficients.

The rule for expressing the value of a compound path between two variables in terms of concrete path coeffcients (stated for a vertically oriented path diagram) is:

The value of a compound path between two variables is equal to the product of the rawscore path coefficients and the topmost variance or covariance in the path.

Tracing of compound paths according to Wright's rules, and adding compound paths together to yield the overall covariance, proceed in just the same way with rawscore as with standardized coefficients. The covariance between two variables in the diagram is equal to the sum of the compound paths between them. If there is just a single path between two variables, the covariance is equal to the value of that path. The two path diagrams in Fig. 1.21 illustrate the rule for compound paths headed by a variance and a covariance respectively. A few examples are given in Table 1-6.

Fig. 1.21 Rawscore paths with (a) a variance and (b) a covariance. (Paths a*, b*, c*, etc. represent rawscore coefficients.)

Table 1-6 Illustrations of rawscore compound path rules, for path diagrams of Fig. 1.21

(a)	(b)
$\text{cov}_{AE} = a^* \, b^* \, s_C^2 \, c^* \, d^*$	$\text{cov}_{AF} = a^* \, b^* \, \text{cov}_{CD} \, d^* \, e^*$
$\text{cov}_{BD} = b^* \, s_C^2 \, c^*$	$\text{cov}_{CF} = \text{cov}_{CD} \, d^* \, e^*$
$\text{cov}_{CE} = s_C^2 \, c^* \, d^*$	$\text{cov}_{DF} = s_D^2 \, d^* \, e^*$

Notice that the rule for evaluating compound paths when using rawscore path coefficients is different from that for standardized coefficients only by the inclusion of one variance or covariance in each path product. Indeed, one can think of the standardized rule as a special case of the rawscore rule, because the variance of a standardized variable is 1, and the covariance between standardized variables is just the correlation coefficient.

Because the rawscore expressions tend to be a bit clumsier to work with, a reasonable way to proceed in many cases is to carry out the analysis using standardized variables, and then to convert path coefficients between measured variables to rawscore form, using the standard deviations of the variables. Both standardized and rawscore coefficients can then be reported. Path coefficients involving latent variables, for which standard deviations will not be available, can be left in their standardized form. An alternative approach, fairly common among those who prefer to work with covariances and rawscore coefficients, is to assign an arbitrary value, usually 1.0, to a path linking the latent variable to an observed variable, thereby implicitly expressing the latent variable in units based on the observed variable. Several examples of this procedure appear in later chapters.

Some Related Topics Not Covered in This Book

We need, also, to be clear about what this book does *not* cover. In this section some related topics, which might easily be confused with latent variable analysis as discussed here, are distinguished from it.

Manifest versus latent variable models

Many multivariate statistical methods, including some of those most familiar to social and behavioral scientists, do not involve latent variables. Instead, they deal solely with linear composites of *observed* variables. In ordinary multiple regression, for example, one seeks an optimally weighted composite of measured independent variables to predict an observed dependent or criterion variable. In discriminant analysis, one seeks composites of measured variables that will optimally distinguish among members of specified groups. In canonical analysis one seeks composites that will maximize correlation across two sets of measured variables.

Path and structural analysis come in both forms: all variables measured or some not. Many of the earlier applications of such methods in economics and sociology were confined to manifest variables. The effort was to fit causal models in situations where all the variables involved were observed. Biology and psychology, dealing with events within the organism, tended to place an earlier emphasis on the latent variable versions of path analysis. As researchers in all the social sciences become increasingly aware of the distorting effects of measurement errors on causal inferences, latent variable methods have increased in popularity, especially in theoretical contexts. In applied situations, where the practitioner must work with existing measures, errors and all, the manifest variable methods retain much of their preeminence.

Factor analysis is usually *defined* as a latent variable method: The factors are unobserved hypothetical variables that underlie and explain the observed correlations. The corresponding manifest variable method is called *component analysis*--or, in its commonest form, the method of *principal components*. Principal components are linear composites of observed variables; the factors of factor analysis are always inferred entities, whose nature is at best consistent with a given set of observations, but never entirely determined by them.

In general, statistical theory is more extensively developed for manifest than for latent variable methods, although there has been a good deal of progress in the latter area in recent years.

Item response theory

A good deal of recent interest among psychometricians has centered on *item reponse theory*, sometimes called *latent trait theory,* in which a latent variable is fit to responses to a series of test items. We do not discuss these methods in this book. They typically focus on fitting a single latent variable (the underlying trait being measured) to the responses of subjects to a set of test items, whereas our principal concern is with fitting models involving multiple latent variables.

More critically, however, the relationships dealt with in item response theory are typically nonlinear: Two- or three-parameter latent curves are fitted, such as the logistic. This book is primarily concerned with methods that assume linear relationships, although we briefly consider some extensions to nonlinear cases in the final chapter.

Latent classes versus latent dimensions

Another substantial topic that this book does not attempt to cover is the modeling of latent classes or categories underlying observed relationships. This topic is often called, for historical reasons, *latent structure analysis* (Lazarsfeld, 1950), although the more restrictive designation *latent class analysis* better avoids confusion with the latent variable methods described in this book. The methods discussed here also are concerned with "latent structure," but it is structure based on relations among continuous variables rather than on the existence of discrete underlying categories.

Chapter 1 Notes

Cause. Mulaik (1987) discusses how this concept is used in causal modoling.

Path analysis. An introductory account, somewhat oriented toward genetics, is Li (1975). The statement of Wright's rules in this chapter is adapted from Li's. Kenny (1979) provides another introductory presentation with a slightly different version of the path-tracing rules: A single rule--a variable entered via an arrowhead cannot be left via an arrowhead--covers rules 2 and 3. The sociologist O. D. Duncan (1966) is usually credited with rediscovering path analysis for social scientists; Werts and Linn (1970) wrote a paper calling psychologists' attention to the method.

RAM. Information about RAM may be found in McArdle (1980,1988), McArdle and McDonald (1984), and McArdle and Epstein (1987). There is also a computer program, RAMpath, for working with RAM path diagrams (McArdle & Boker, 1990). A Ram-based representation is available in CALIS (see Chapter 2), and EzPATH uses a very similar approach (Steiger, 1989).

Factor analysis. Maxwell (1977) has a brief account of some of the early history. Mulaik (1986) brings matters up to the present. See notes to Chapter 5 for books on factor analysis. For an explicit distinction between the exploratory and confirmatory varieties, see Jöreskog and Lawley (1968).

Structural equations. These come from econometrics. For some relationships between econometrics and psychometrics, see Goldberger (1971) and a special issue of the journal *Econometrics,* edited by de Leeuw, Keller, and Wansbeek (1983). A historical perspective is given by Bentler (1986).

Direct and indirect effects. For a discussion of such effects, and the development of matrix methods for their systematic calculation, see Fox (1980, 1985).

Under- and overdetermination in path diagrams. This is discussed as *identification* in the structural equation literature. It is not a simple matter: For an example see Bollen and Jöreskog (1985). As one complication, models may sometimes be identified for some values of their unknown paths, and not for others (Rindskopf, 1984a). In simple cases, an algebraic analysis of the equations can ascertain whether or not all the unknowns are determinate. Jöreskog and Sörbom (1989, section I.9) suggest some approaches for dealing with more complex cases, and Land and Felson (1978) discuss ways of investigating the sensitivity of one's results to arbitrary assumptions made in order to achieve identification.

Original and standardized variables. Their relative merits are debated by Tukey (1954) and Wright (1960). For a more recent discussion, see Kim and Ferree (1981). See Bielby (1986), Williams and Thompson (1986) and several commentators for a discussion of some of the hazards involved in scaling latent variables.

Related topics. Several examples of manifest-variable path and structural analysis may be found in Marsden (1981), especially Part II. Principal component analysis is discussed in most factor analysis texts (see Chapter 5). A number of papers on item response theory comprise a special issue of *Applied Psychological Measurement* (Hambleton & van der Linden, 1982). The basic treatment of latent class analysis is Lazarsfeld and Henry (1968). For a broad treatment of structural models that covers both quantitative and qualitative variables, see Kiiveri and Speed (1982), and for a general review of latent trait and latent class models, see Langeheine and Rost (1988).

Journal sources. Some journals that frequently publish articles on developments in the area of latent variable models include *Psychometrika, Sociological Methods & Research, Multivariate Behavioral Research , The British Journal of Mathematical and Statistical Psychology, Journal of Marketing Research* and *Psychological Bulletin.* See also the annual series *Sociological Methodology.*

Books. Some books dealing with path and structural equation modeling are: Duncan (1975), Heise (1975), Kenny (1979), James, Mulaik, and Brett (1982), Asher (1983), Long (1983a,b), Everitt (1984), Saris and Stronkhorst (1984), Bartholomew (1987), Cuttance and Ecob (1987), Hayduk (1987), Bollen (1989b), and Byrne (1989).

Chapter 1 Exercises

Note: Answers to exercises are in the back of the book, preceding the References.

1. Draw a path diagram of the relationships among impulsivity and hostility at one time and delinquency at a later time, assuming that the first two influence the third but not vice versa.

2. Draw a path diagram of the relationships among ability, motivation, and performance, each measured on two occasions.

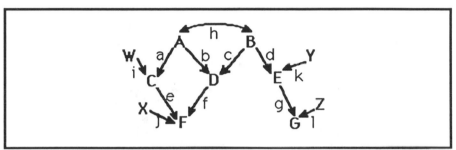

Fig. 1.22 Path diagram for problems 3 to 9. (Assume all variables are in standard-score form unless otherwise specified.)

3. Identify the source and downstream variables in Fig 1.22.

4. What assumption is made about the causation of variable D?

5. Write path equations for the correlations r_{AF}, r_{DG}, r_{CE}, and r_{EF}.

6. Write path equations for the variances of C, D, and F.

7. If variables A, B, F, and G are measured, would you expect the path diagram to be solvable? (Explain why or why not.)

8. Now, assume that the variables in Fig. 1.22 are *not* standardized. Write path equations, using rawscore coefficients, for the covariances c_{CD}, c_{FG}, c_{AG} and the variances s_G^2 and s_D^2.

9. Write structural equations for the variables D, E, and F in Fig. 1.22.

Fig.1.23. Path diagram for problem 10.

10. Redraw Fig. 1.23 above as a RAM path diagram. (E and F are latent variables, A through D are observed.)

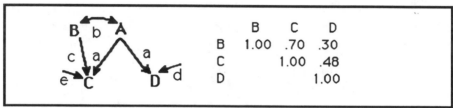

	B	C	D
B	1.00	.70	.30
C		1.00	.48
D			1.00

Fig. 1.24 Path diagram for problem 11.

11. Given the path diagram shown in Fig. 1.24 and the observed correlations given to the right, solve for *a, b, c, d,* and *e*.

12. The following intercorrelations among three variables are observed:

	A	B	C
A	1.00	.42	.12
B		1.00	.14
C			1.00

Solve for the loadings on a single common factor, using the method of triads.

13. Four putative measures of creativity, tests W, X, Y, and Z, are given to a large group of high school students. The intercorrelations among the tests follow:

	W	X	Y	Z
W	1.00	.40	.50	.30
X		1.00	.55	.35
Y			1.00	.40
Z				1.00

Calculate the factor loadings using the centroid method--use an estimate of the communality for each variable based on a triad with its two nearest neighbors in the matrix.

Chapter Two:
Fitting Path Models

In this chapter we consider the processes used in actually fitting path models to data on a realistic scale, and evaluating their goodness of fit. This implies computer-oriented methods. This chapter is somewhat more technical than Chapter 1. Some readers on a first pass through the book might prefer to read carefully only the section on hierarchical χ^2 tests (pp. 65-70) and then go on to Chapters 3 and 4, coming back to Chapter 2 afterward. (You will need additional Chapter 2 material to do the exercises in Chapters 3 and 4.)

Iterative Solution of Path Equations

In simple path diagrams like those we have considered so far, direct algebraic solution of the set of implied equations is often quite practicable. But as the number of observed variables goes up, the number of intercorrelations among them, and hence the number of equations to be solved, increases rapidly. (The number of equations is given by $n(n-1)/2$, where n is the number of observed variables.) Furthermore, path equations by their nature involve product terms, because a compound path is the product of its component arrows. Product terms make the equations recalcitrant to straightforward matrix procedures that can be used to solve sets of linear simultaneous equations. As a result of this, large sets of path equations are in practice usually solved by iterative (= repetitive) trial-and-error procedures, carried out by computers.

The general idea is simple. An arbitrary set of initial values of the paths serves as a starting point. The correlations or covariances implied by these values are calculated and compared to the observed values. Because the initial values are arbitrary, the fit is likely to be poor. So one or more of the initial trial values is changed in a direction that improves the fit, and the process is repeated with this new set of trial values. This cycle is repeated again and again, each time modifying the set of trial values to improve the agreement between the implied and the observed correlations. Eventually, a set of values

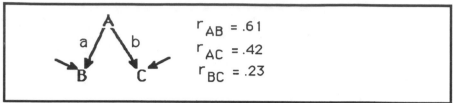

Fig. 2.1 A simple path diagram illustrating an iterative solution.

is reached that cannot be improved on--the process, as the numerical analysts say, has "converged" on a solution. If all has gone well, this will be the optimum solution that is sought.

Let us illustrate this procedure with the example shown in Fig. 2.1. A simple case like this one might be solved in more direct ways, but we use it to demonstrate an iterative solution, as shown in Table 2-1.

We begin in cycle 1 by setting arbitrary trial values of *a* and *b*--for the

Table 2-1 An iterative solution of the path diagram of Fig. 2.1

	Trial values		Correlations			Criterion
	a	b	r_{AB}	r_{AC}	r_{BC}	Σd^2
Observed			.61	.42	.23	
Cycle 1	.5	.5	.50	.50	.25	.018900
1a	.501	.5	.501	.50	.2505	.018701*
1b	.5	.501	.50	.501	.2505	.019081
2	.6	.5	.60	.50	.30	.011400
2a	.601	.5	.601	.50	.3005	.011451
2b	.6	.501	.60	.501	.3006	.011645*
3	.6	.4	.60	.40	.24	.000600
3a	.601	.4	.601	.40	.2404	.000589
3b	.6	.401	.60	.401	.2406	.000573*
4	.6	.41	.60	.41	.246	.000456
4a	.601	.41	.601	.41	.2464	.000450*
4b	.6	.411	.60	.411	.2466	.000457
(5)	.61	.41	.61	.41	.2501	.000504
5	.601	.41	.601	.41	.2464	.0004503
5a	.602	.41	.602	.41	.2468	.0004469*
5b	.601	.411	.601	.411	.2470	.0004514
6	.602	.41	.602	.41	.2468	.0004469
6a	.603	.41	.603	.41	.2472	.0004459
6b	.602	.411	.602	.411	.2474	.0004485*
(7)	.603	.409	.603	.409	.2462	.0004480

*greater change

example we have set each to .5. Then we calculate the values of the correlations r_{AB}, r_{AC}, and r_{BC} that are implied by these path values: They are .50, .50, and .25, respectively. We choose some reasonable criterion of the discrepancy between these and the observed correlations--say, the sum of the squared differences between the corresponding values. In this case this sum is $.11^2 + (-.08)^2 + (-.02)^2$, or .0189.

Next, in steps 1a and 1b, we change each trial value by some small amount (we have used an increase of .001) to see what effect this has on the criterion. Increasing a makes things better and increasing b makes things worse, suggesting that either an increase in a or a decrease in b should improve the fit. Because the change 1a makes a bigger difference than the change 1b does, suggesting that the criterion will improve faster with a change in a, we increase the trial value by 1 in the first decimal place to obtain the new set of trial values in 2. Repeating the process, in lines 2a and 2b, we find that a change in b now has the greater effect; the desirable change is a decrease.

Decreasing b by 1 in the first decimal place gives the line 3 trial values .6 and .4. In line 3a and 3b we find that increasing either would be beneficial, but b more so. However, increasing b in the first decimal place would just undo our last step, yielding no improvement, so we shift to making changes in the second place. (This is not necessarily the numerically most efficient way to proceed, but it will get us there.) Line 4 confirms that the new trial values of .6 and .41 do constitute an improvement. Testing these values in lines 4a and 4b, we find that an increase in a is suggested. We try increasing a in the second decimal place, but this is not an improvement, so we shift to an increase in the third decimal place (line 5). The tests in lines 5a and 5b suggest that a further increase to .602 would be justified, so we use that in line 6. Now it appears that decreasing b might be the best thing to do (line7), but it isn't an improvement. Rather than go on to still smaller changes, we elect to quit at this point, reasonably confident of at least 2-place precision in our answer of .602 and .410 in line 6 (or, slightly better, the .603 and .410 in 6a).

Now, doing this by hand for even two unknowns is fairly tedious, but it is just the kind of repetitious, mechanical process that computers are good at, and many general and special-purpose computer programs exist that can carry out such minimizations. If you were using a typical general-purpose minimization program, you would be expected to supply it with an initial set of trial values of the unknowns, and a subroutine that calculates the function to be minimized, given a set of trial values. That is, you would program a subroutine that will calculate the implied correlations, subtract them from the observed correlations, and sum the squares of the differences between the two. The minimization program would then proceed to adjust the trial values iteratively, in some such fashion as that portrayed in Table 2-1, until an unimprovable minimum value is reached.

A simple computer implementation of iterative path solutions-- IPSOL

The program IPSOL, given in Appendix B, is a simple version of such a computer program written primarily for didactic purposes. It carries out an iterative model-fitting process identical to that we have just done by hand in Table 2-1. IPSOL, which is short for "iterative path solution," is written in the computer language FORTRAN; for readers not familiar with this language, asterisked comment lines have been supplied to provide a general sense of what is going on.

The program consists of three parts. First, there is an executive routine, which reads in problem specifications and data, calls on the minimization routine to do its work, and prints out the results at the end. Next, there is the minimization routine MINIM itself, which makes the trial-and-error changes in the values of the unknown parameters, starting with relatively large steps and shifting to smaller ones as the solution is approached. It evaluates the effect of proposed changes by calling on the third part of the program, the subroutine FUNCT that calculates the implied values and assesses their fit to the observed ones--in this case, as the sum of the squared discrepancies between the two.

Table 2-2 shows the path equations and sample input for solving the path problem of Table 2-1 via IPSOL. The equations, written in the symbolism of the FORTRAN language, express each of the implied, or calculated values, the CV(i)s on the left, in terms of the unknowns, the X(i)s on the right. The equations correspond to the path diagram of Fig. 2.1: The first says that the first correlation (r_{AB}) is equal to the first unknown (*a*); the second says that the second correlation (r_{AC}) is equal to the second unknown; and the third says

Table 2-2 Path equations and input for solving sample problem of Fig. 2.1 and Table 2-1 via IPSOL

Path equations for subroutine FUNCT:
$$CV(1) = X(1)$$
$$CV(2) = X(2)$$
$$CV(3) = X(1)*X(2)$$

Input for sample problem:

```
TRIAL RUN OF IPSOL WITH FIG 2.1 PROBLEM
   3  2  2
     .61      .42      .23
   .5  .5
   .2  .2
```

---

that the third correlation (r_{BC}) is equal to the product of the two unknowns (FORTRAN uses an asterisk to signify multiplication).

The input shown in Table 2-2 supplies the program with the remaining information necessary for carrying out the solution. The first line is a title, which is simply reproduced on the output. The second line gives the problem specifications: 3 observed values, 2 unknowns to be solved for, and 2 runs with different starting values to be carried out. The spacing is important: Each number is right-justified in a 3-digit field (i.e., a 1-digit number is preceded by two blanks; a 2-digit number would be preceded by one blank).

The third line of the input provides the observed values to be fitted, the correlations .61, .42, and .23 (note that they must be in the same order as the equations calculating the corresponding implied values). An 8-digit field is provided for each (to allow space for entering covariances) with a decimal point required. (The location of the number within the 8-digit field is arbitrary.) Ten observed values can be entered per line, in as many lines as necessary.

The final two lines of the input are the starting values to be used in the two trial runs. For the first solution initial values of .5, in 3-digit fields, are assigned to the two paths *a* and *b* at the start of the iteration process; the second solution starts from the trial values .2 and .2.

If one were to run this problem with IPSOL, it would print out .602 and .410 as the final values for the solution on each of the two runs, values corresponding to line 6 in the hand solution in Table 2-1, with a minimum function value (sum of squared differences) of .0004469, again corresponding to the hand solution. Using initial values of .2 and .2 would take a little longer, as it would take six cycles of MINIM to reach trial values of .6 and .4 (reached in two cycles from .5, .5); thereafter the solutions proceed identically.

Geographies of search

For the simple two-variable case of Fig. 2.1 and Table 2-1 we can visualize the solution process as a search of a geographical terrain for its lowest point. Values of *a* and *b* represent spatial coordinates such as latitude and longitude, and values of the criterion Σd^2 represent altitudes above sea level. Fig. 2.2 is a pictorial representation of the situation. A set of starting trial values represents the coordinates of a starting point in the figure. The tests in steps a and b in each cycle represent tests of how the ground slopes each way from the present location, which governs the choice of a promising direction in which to move. In each instance we make the move that takes us downhill most rapidly. Eventually, we reach the low point in the valley, marked by the arrow, from which a step in any direction would lead upward. Then we quit and report our location as the solution.

Note that in simple geographies, such as that represented in this example, it doesn't matter what set of starting values we use: We would reach the same final low point regardless of where we start from. At worst it will take longer from some places than from others. Not all geographies, however, are

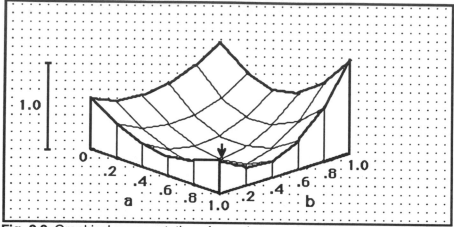

Fig. 2.2 Graphical representation of search space for Fig. 2.1 problem, for values 0 to 1 of both variables.

this simple. Fig. 2.3 shows a cross-section of a more treacherous terrain. A starting point at A on the left of the ridge will lead away from, not toward, the solution--the searcher will wind up against the boundary at B. From a starting point at C, on the right, one will see initial rapid improvement but will be trapped at an apparent solution at D, well short of the optimum at E. Or one might strike a level area, such as F, from which no direction of initial step leads to improvement. Other starting points, such as G and H, will, however, lead satisfactorily to E.

It is ordinarily prudent, particularly when just beginning to explore the landscape implicit in a particular path model, to try at least two or three widely dispersed starting points from which to seek a minimum. If all the solutions converge on the same point and it represents a reasonably good fit to the data,

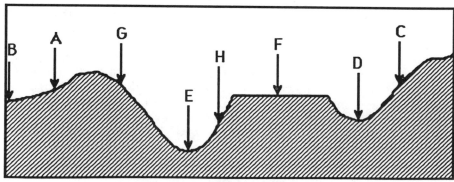

Fig. 2.3 Cross section of a less hospitable search terrain.

it is probably safe to conclude that it is the optimum solution. If some solutions wander off or stop short of the best achieved so far, it is well to suspect that one may be dealing with a less regular landscape and try additional sets of starting values until several converge on the same minimum solution.

The landscapes of Figs. 2.2 and 2.3 are for problems in two unknowns. In the general case of n unknowns, the landscape would be an n-dimensional space with an $n + 1$st dimension for the criterion. Although such spaces are not easily visualizable, they work essentially like the three-dimensional one, with n-dimensional analogues of the valleys, ridges, and hollows of a three-dimensional geography. The iterative procedure of Table 2-1 is easily extended to more dimensions (= more unknowns), although the amount of computation required escalates markedly as the number of unknowns to be solved for increases.

Many fine points of iterative minimization programs have been skipped over in this brief account. Some programs allow the user to place constraints on the trial values (and hence on the ultimate possible solutions), such as specifying that they always be positive, or that they lie between +1 and -1 or other defined limits. Programs differ in how they adjust their step sizes during their search, and in their ability to recover from untoward events (such as a trial value of zero appearing in the denominator of an expression). Some are extremely fast and efficient in certain kinds of friendly terrain but are not well adapted elsewhere. Others are robust, but painfully slow even on easy ground. Some programs allow the user a good deal of control over aspects of the search process and provide a good deal of information on how it proceeds. Others require a minimum of specification from the user and just print out a final answer.

Matrix Formulation of Path Models

Simple path diagrams are readily transformed into sets of simultaneous equations by the use of Wright's rules. We have seen in the preceding section how such sets of equations can be solved iteratively by computer programs. To use such a program, for example, IPSOL, one must give it a subroutine containing the path equations, so that it can calculate the implied values and compare them with the observed values. With three observed values, as in our example, this is simple enough, but with 30 or 40 the preparation of a new subroutine for each problem can get tedious. Furthermore, in tracing paths in more complex diagrams to reduce them to sets of equations, it is easy to make errors--for example, to overlook some indirect path that connects point A and point B, or to include a path twice. Is there any way of mechanizing the construction of path equations, as well as their solution?

In fact, there are such procedures, which allow the expression of the equations of a path diagram as the product of several matrices. Not only does such an approach allow one to turn a path diagram into a set of path equations with less risk of error, but in fact one need not explicitly write down the path equations at all--one can carry out the calculation of implied correlations directly, via operations on the matrices. This does not save effort at the level of actual computation, but it constitutes a major strategic simplification.

The particular procedure we use to illustrate this is one based on a formulation by McArdle and McDonald (1984); an equivalent although different matrix procedure is carried out within the computer program LISREL (of which more later), and still others have been proposed (e.g., Bentler & Weeks, 1980; McArdle, 1980; McDonald, 1978). It is assumed that the reader is familiar with elementary matrix operations; if your skills in this area are rusty or nonexistent, you may wish to consult Appendix A or an introductory textbook in matrix algebra before proceeding.

McArdle and McDonald define three matrices, **A**, **S**, and **F**:

A (for "asymmetric" relations) contains paths.

S (for "symmetric" relations) contains correlations (or covariances) and residual variances.

F (for "filter" matrix) selects out the observed variables from the total set of variables.

If there are a total of t variables (excluding residuals), m of which are measured, the dimensions of these matrices are: **A** = $t \times t$; **S** = $t \times t$; **F** = $m \times t$.

The implied correlation (or covariance) matrix **C** among the measured variables is obtained by the matrix equation:

$$C = F (I - A)^{-1} S (I - A)^{-1\prime} F\prime.$$

I stands for the identity matrix, and $^{-1}$ and $\prime$ refer to the matrix operations of inversion and transposition, respectively.

This is not a very transparent equation. You may wish just to take it on faith, but if you want to get some sense of why it looks like it does, you can turn to Appendix C, where it is shown how this matrix equation can be derived from the structural equation representation of a path diagram. The fact that the equation does what it claims to do is shown by examples in the next two sections of this chapter.

An example with correlations

Figure 2.4 and Tables 2-3 and 2-4 provide an example of the use of the McArdle-McDonald matrix equation. The path diagram in Fig. 2.4 is that of Fig. 1.24, from the exercises of the preceding chapter.

Variables B, C, and D are assumed to be observed; variable A to be latent. All variables are assumed to be standardized--i.e., we are dealing with a correlation matrix. Expressions for the correlations and variances, based on path rules, are given to the right in the figure.

In Table 2-3, Matrix **A** contains the three straight arrows (paths) in the diagram, the two *a*s and the *c*. Each is placed at the intersection of the

$$r_{BC} = ba + c \qquad r_{BD} = ba$$
$$r_{CD} = a^2 + cba \qquad s_D^2 = a^2 + d^2$$
$$s_C^2 = c^2 + a^2 + 2abc + e^2$$

Fig. 2.4 A path diagram for the matrix example of Tables 2-3 and 2-4.

variable it originates from (top) and the variable it points to (side). For example, path c, which goes from B to C, is specified in row C of column B. It is helpful (though not algebraically necessary) to group together source variables and downstream variables--the source variables A and B are given first in the Table 2-3 matrices, with the downstream variables C and D last.

Curved arrows and variances are represented in matrix **S**. The top left-hand part contains the correlation matrix among the source variables, A and B. The diagonal in the lower right-hand part contains the residual variances of the downstream variables C and D, as given by the squares of the residuals paths e and d. (If there were any covariances among residuals, they would be shown by off-diagonal elements in this part of the matrix.)

Finally, matrix **F**, which selects out the observed variables from all the variables, has observed variables listed down the side and all variables along the top. It simply contains a 1 at the row and column corresponding to each observed variable--in this case, B, C, and D.

Table 2-4 demonstrates that multiplying out the matrix equation yields the path equations. First, **A** is subtracted from the identity matrix **I**, and the result inverted, yielding $(I-A)^{-1}$. You can verify that this *is* the required inverse by the

Table 2-3 Matrix formulation of a path diagram by the McArdle- McDonald procedure

A						S				
	A	B	C	D			A	B	C	D
A	0	0	0	0		A	1	b	0	0
B	0	0	0	0		B	b	1	0	0
C	a	c	0	0		C	0	0	e^2	0
D	a	0	0	0		D	0	0	0	d^2

F				
	A	B	C	D
B	0	1	0	0
C	0	0	1	0
D	0	0	0	1

Table 2-4 Solution of the McArdle-McDonald equation, for the matrices of Table 2-3

$(I-A)^{-1}$

	A	B	C	D
A	1	0	0	0
B	0	1	0	0
C	a	c	1	0
D	a	0	0	1

$(I-A)^{-1}S$

	A	B	C	D
A	1	b	0	0
B	b	1	0	0
C	a+bc	ab+c	e^2	0
D	a	ab	0	d^2

$(I-A)^{-1\prime}$

	A	B	C	D
A	1	0	a	a
B	0	1	c	0
C	0	0	1	0
D	0	0	0	1

$(I-A)^{-1}S\,(I-A)^{-1\prime}$

	A	B	C	D
A	1	b	a+bc	a
B	b	1	ab+c	ab
C	a+bc	ab+c	$a^2+c^2+2abc+e^2$	a^2+abc
D	a	ab	a^2+abc	a^2+d^2

$F(I-A)^{-1}S\,(I-A)^{-1\prime}\,F' = C$

	B	C	D
B	1	ab+c	ab
C	ab+c	$a^2+c^2+2abc+e^2$	a^2+abc
D	ab	a^2+abc	a^2+d^2

matrix multiplication $(I-A)^{-1}(I-A) = I$. (If you want to learn a convenient way of obtaining this inverse, see Appendix C.) Pre- and postmultiplying **S** by $(I-A)^{-1}$ and its transpose is done in this and the next row of the table, and the result of pre- and postmultiplying by **F** and **F′** is shown in the last row. This final matrix contains expressions for the correlations among the observed variables. You will see that they agree with the results of applying Wright's rules to the path diagram.

The matrix to the right in the second row, $(I-A)^{-1}S\,(I-A)^{-1\prime}$, contains the correlations among *all* the variables, both latent and observed. The final pre- and postmultiplication by **F** merely selects out the lower right-hand portion of the matrix, the correlations among the observed variables. The upper left-hand portion contains the intercorrelations of the latent variables. The remaining upper right and lower left sections contain the correlations between the latent and observed variables. As you should verify, all these are consistent with those obtainable via path tracing on the diagram. Thus, with particular values of *a, b, c,* etc. inserted in the matrices, the matrix operations of the McArdle-McDonald equation result in exactly the same implied values for the intercorrelations as would putting these same values into expressions derived from the path diagram via Wright's rules.

An example with covariances

The only modification to the procedure that is needed in order to use it with a variance-covariance matrix is to insert variances instead of 1's in the upper diagonal of **S**. The equation will then yield an implied variance-covariance matrix of the observed variables, instead of a correlation matrix, with the path coefficients *a* and *c* in rawscore form.

The procedure is illustrated in Table 2-5. The example is the same as that in Table 2-4, except that variables A, B, C, and D are now assumed to be unstandardized. The table shows the **S** matrix (the **A** and **F** matrices are as in Table 2-3) and the final result. Notice that these expressions conform to the rawscore path rules, by the inclusion of one variance or covariance in each path, involving the variable or variables at its highest point. (The *b*s are, of course, covariances, and the *a*s and *c*s unstandardized path coefficients.) You may wish to check out some of this in detail to make sure you understand the process.

Table 2-5 Solution for covariance matrix, corresponding to Table 2-4

S

	A	B	C	D
A	s_A^2	b	0	0
B	b	s_B^2	0	0
C	0	0	e^2	0
D	0	0	0	d^2

$F(I-A)^{-1} S (I-A)^{-1} {}' F' = C$

	B	C	D
B	s_B^2	$ab + c\, s_B^2$	ab
C	$ab + c\, s_B^2$	$a^2 s_A^2 + c^2 s_B^2 + 2abc + e^2$	$a^2 s_A^2 + abc$
D	ab	$a^2 s_A^2 + abc$	$a^2 s_A^2 + d^2$

Full-Fledged Model-Fitting Programs

Suppose one were to take a search program, such as IPSOL, and replace the path equations in the FUNCT subroutine with a matrix formulation, such as the McArdle-McDonald equation. By describing the matrices **A**, **S**, and **F** in the input to the program, you could avoid the necessity of writing fresh path equations and inserting them in the FUNCT subroutine for each new problem.

You might well dress up such a program with a few additional frills: For example, you could use a more sophisticated search program. You could also offer some additional options in the way of criteria for evaluating goodness of fit. IPSOL minimizes the sum of squared differences between observed and implied correlations. This least squares criterion is one that is easily computed and widely used in statistics, but there are others, such as maximum likelihood, that might be considered and that could be provided as alternatives in subroutine FUNCT. (Some of the relative advantages and disadvantages of different goodness-of-fit criteria are discussed in a later section of this chapter.)

Several programs along these general lines exist and can be used for solving path diagrams. They go by such names as AMOS, CALIS, COSAN, EQS, EzPATH, and LISREL. Several are associated with major statistical packages: LISREL with SPSS, EQS with BMDP, CALIS with SAS, and EzPATH with SYSTAT. The host packages can provide facilities for data management and input, but the programs tend to operate fairly independently of them, and we need not concern ourselves here with details of the interfaces. We begin with the most widely used of the group, LISREL, and then consider EQS and CALIS and the rest more briefly.

LISREL

LISREL stands for LInear Structural RELations. It was devised by the Swedish psychometrician Karl Jöreskog, and has developed through a series of versions. The current version is LISREL 7 (Jöreskog & Sörbom, 1989). LISREL is based on a more elaborate matrix formulation of path diagrams than the McArdle-McDonald equation, although one that works on similar principles and leads to the same end result. The LISREL formulation is more complicated because it subdivides the process, keeping in eight separate matrices various elements that are combined in the three McArdle-McDonald matrices. LISREL makes basic distinctions between independent and dependent variables in addition to latent and manifest variables. The paths connecting latent and manifest variables, and the residual paths for the latter, are collectively called the *measurement model*. There are two measurement submodels, one for the independent variables, and one for the dependent variables. The relationships among and between the corresponding two sets of latent variables are called the *structural model*. This is a formulation within which many problems of interest to social and behavioral scientists can easily and naturally be expressed, and which is flexible enough to handle quite a few others by various

48

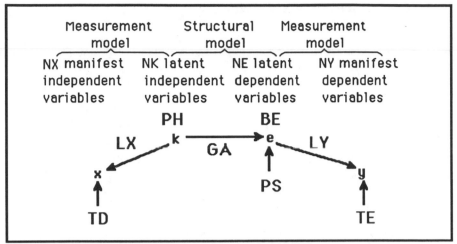

Fig. 2.5 Summary of matrix representation in LISREL.

specializations and equivalences requiring greater or lesser amounts of ingenuity on the part of the user. We consider a number of examples in the next chapter.

Figure 2.5 summarizes the relationships in LISREL. The portions of the diagram to the left and the right constitute the two measurement submodels; the portion in the middle is the structural model. The latent independent variables K are source variables. There are NK of them, in a vector **k**. The latent dependent variables E are downstream variables; there are NE of them, in **e**. There are NX observed independent variables X, and NY observed dependent variables Y. The Xs and Ys are all considered to be downstream variables--fallible observed indexes only imperfectly reflecting the true latent variables lying behind them, whose relationships are our real concern. The vertical upward arrows in Fig. 2.5 represent the residual paths for the three sets of downstream variables--of course, there are none for the Ks, which are source variables. The two-letter symbols next to the arrows in the diagram represent the eight basic LISREL matrices (not all problems need all of these). The matrices **LX** and **LY** represent the paths from latent to observed variables, and **TD** and **TE** the variance-covariance matrices of residuals (diagonal matrices, if the residuals are assumed to be uncorrelated). These four matrices constitute the measurement model. The dimensions of these matrices follow from the numbers of variables involved: **LX** is NX x NK, **LY** is NY x NE, and **TD** and **TE** are square matrices of order NX and NY, respectively.

In the structural model, **GA** contains paths from source to downstream latent variables. **PH** represents the variance-covariance matrix of the source variables, and **BE** any paths between downstream latent variables. **GA** is of dimension NE x NK, and **PH** and **BE** are of order NK and NE, respectively. **PS**, the variance-covariance matrix of the residuals of the downstream latent variables, is also a square matrix of order NE.

The LISREL input sets up the eight matrices with a combination of fixed values (usually 1s and 0s) and unknowns to be solved for. The multiplication of these matrices yields the implied values of the correlations (or covariances) that are used by the minimization part of the program. We need not go into all the details, but to take a simple case, the implied variances and covariances among the independent variables can be obtained by:

LX PH LX′ + TD.

An example is given in Table 2-6 based on the path diagram of Fig. 2.6. The

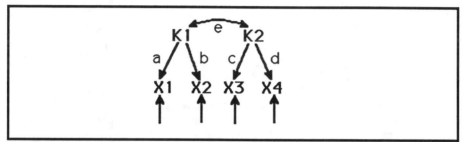

Fig. 2.6 Path diagram for example of Table 2-6.

Table 2-6 Example showing equivalence of path and matrix expressions

					Path expressions for correlations			
						X1	X2	X3	X4
PH					X1	1	ab	aec	aed
		K1	K2		X2	ab	1	bec	bed
	K1	1	e		X3	aec	bec	1	cd
	K2	e	1		X4	aed	bed	cd	1
LX				**TD**					
		K1	K2			X1	X2	X3	X4
	X1	a	0		X1	$1-a^2$	0	0	0
	X2	b	0		X2	0	$1-b^2$	0	0
	X3	0	c		X3	0	0	$1-c^2$	0
	X4	0	d		X4	0	0	0	$1-d^2$
LX PH				**LX PH LX′**					
		a	ae			a^2	ab	aec	aed
		b	be			ab	b^2	bec	bed
		ce	c			aec	bec	c^2	cd
		de	d			aed	bed	cd	d^2

path expressions derived from the diagram by Wright's rules are shown at the top right of Table 2-6; the LISREL matrices **PH, LX**, and **TD** are given to the left and below; and the calculation **LX PH LX′** is shown. The result of this calculation plus **TD** clearly will equal the correlation matrix at the top.

Table 2-7 shows one way of defining input to LISREL for the problem of Fig. 2.6 and Table 2-6. The first line of the input is a title. The second gives data specifications: number of input variables = 4; number of observations (cases) = 100; the matrix to be analyzed is a correlation matrix (CM would mean covariance matrix). The third line specifies that a correlation matrix is to be read, in free-field format (items separated by any number of spaces). If the matrix were to be in other than lower triangular form, or in a fixed format, this would be specified as well. The correlations follow in lines 4 through 7. The lines from MODEL to START define the matrices and starting values of the model.

The general philosophy of LISREL is that things are assumed to be in some typical form by default unless otherwise specified. The MODEL line says that there are 4 X variables and 2 K variables. The "ST" specifies that the **PH** matrix is to be a correlation matrix (symmetrical, with 1s fixed in the diagonal and free values elsewhere--the *e*s of Table 2-6). Because nothing is said about **LX** and **TD**, these matrices are assumed to be in their default forms--respectively, a rectangular matrix with all values fixed to zero, and a diagonal matrix with all diagonal values free. The line beginning FREE specifies exceptions: **LX** locations 1 and 2 of column 1, and locations 3 and 4 of column 2, are to be free values to be solved for (they correspond to *a*, *b* and *c, d* of Table 2-6). The line beginning START sets an initial value of .5 into all free values. The NS in the OUTPUT line tells LISREL to use the starting values we have provided, rather than calculate its own. Because OUTPUT carries no additional specifications the standard output will be produced and the standard fitting criterion will be used (for LISREL this is maximum likelihood).

Table 2-7 An example of LISREL input

```
INPUT FOR FIG 2.6 PROBLEM
DATA NI=4 NO=100 MA=KM
KM
   1.00
    .50 1.00
    .10   .10 1.00
    .20   .30   .20 1.00
MODEL NX=4 NK=2 PH=ST
FREE LX 1 1 LX 2 1 LX 3 2 LX 4 2
START  .5 ALL
OUTPUT NS
```

Fig. 2.7 A different model for the data of Fig. 2.6.

Figure 2.7 shows a different model that might be fit to the same data. In this model, we assume that there are two X variables, the same X1 and X2 as in Fig. 2.6, but now X3 and X4 are considered to be dependent variables, Y1 and Y2, and there is a causal path, labeled *d*, rather than a simple correlation, between the two latent variables. Also, because this makes K2 into E1, a downstream variable, it acquires a residual arrow.

Table 2-8 Example of LISREL matrices and input, for Fig. 2.7 problem

LX	LY	PH	GA	PS	TD		TE	
a	1	1	d	v	w	0	y	0
b	c				0	x	0	z

INPUT FOR FIG 2.7 PROBLEM

[lines 2-7 same as for previous example]

```
SELECT
3 4 1 2
MODEL NX=2 NK=1 NY=2 NE=1 PH=ST LX=FR LY=FR
FIX LY 1 1
START 1.0 LY 1 1
OUTPUT SS  UL
```

Table 2-8 shows the modifications in input required. There are now seven LISREL matrices, as shown above the program. (**BE** is the unused eighth--there are no arrows between downstream latent variables.)

Aside from the title, there are no changes in the first seven lines of the input, through the correlation matrix. The next two lines reorder the input: LISREL requires that dependent variables (the third and the fourth in the correlation matrix as read) precede independent variables (1 and 2). The

MODEL line indicates two X and two Y variables, and one K and one E. **LX** and **LY** are started as FREE matrices, and then, in the next two lines, the first element of **LY** is fixed and set to 1. This illustrates an important LISREL feature: Downstream latent variables cannot be specified as standardized. Instead, they must be given an arbitrary scale in the initial solution by assigning a fixed value to a path leading to an observed variable--in this case, Y1. Afterward, however, LISREL can standardize all the latent variables and will if requested to do so by an SS in the OUTPUT line, for "standardized solution." (*Source* latent variables may be treated either way but not both--that is, the latent variable may be standardized by fixing its variance to 1, *or* one path to an observed variable may be fixed to 1.) The UL in the OUTPUT line requests that fitting be done using an ordinary ("unweighted") least squares criterion. This time LISREL is permitted to calculate its own start values.

Many input variations are possible in LISREL. Matrices specifying the model can be given explicitly, if desired; or one can specify matrices to be all zeroes, diagonal, symmetrical, and so on. Lines of the form EQUAL LX 1 1 LX 2 2 can be used to specify that LX 2 2 is constrained to be equal to LX 1 1. Raw data or matrices can be read in from an external file. Various amounts of detail can be requested in the output.

A serious user of LISREL will need to consult the relevant manuals for details; these illustrations are merely intended to convey something of the flavor of LISREL's style, and to provide models for working simple problems. A number of examples of the use of LISREL in actual research are found in the next two chapters.

A Different Representational Strategy, EQS

A rival program that functions along the same general lines as LISREL is EQS (pronounced "X"; Bentler, 1989). There are a number of differences of detail between LISREL and EQS, but from the point of view of the user, the biggest difference is that he or she will specify path models to EQS in the form of structural equations, rather than matrices; most beginners find this easier to do. Structural equations were described in Chapter 1. Recall that there is one structural equation for each downstream latent or observed variable in a path model, and that variances and any covariances of source variables must also be specified.

Four kinds of variables are specified in EQS: V for observed variables (LISREL Xs or Ys), F for latent variables (LISREL Ks or Es), E for residuals of observed variables, and D for residuals of downstream latent variables. Each variable is designated by a letter followed by numbers. A typical structural equation for a V variable will include Fs and an E; one for an F variable will include Fs and a D.

Table 2-9 Examples of EQS input corresponding to the LISREL programs in Tables 2-7 and 2-8

(a)	(b)
/TITLE	/TITLE
INPUT FOR FIG 2.6 PROGRAM	INPUT FOR FIG 2.7 PROGRAM
/SPECIFICATIONS	/SPEC
VAR=4; CAS=100; MA=COR; ANAL=COR;	VAR=4; CAS=100; MA=COR;
/EQUATIONS	ANAL=COR; ME=LS;
V1 = .5*F1 + E1;	/EQU
V2 = .5*F1 + E2;	V1 = *F1 + E1;
V3 = .5*F2 + E3;	V2 = *F1 + E2;
V4 = .5*F2 + E4;	V3 = F2 + E3;
/VARIANCES	V4 = *F2 + E4;
F1,F2 = 1; E1 TO E4 = .5*;	F2 = *F1 + D2;
/COVARIANCES	/VAR
F1,F2 = .5*;	F1=1; E1 TO E4 = *; D2 = *;
/MATRIX	/MAT
1.00	1.00
.50 1.00	.50 1.00
.10 .10 1.00	.10 .10 1.00
.20 .30 .20 1.00	.20 .30 .20 1.00
/END	/END

    Table 2-9 (a) shows an EQS equivalent of the LISREL program in Table 2-7. In the EQUATIONS section, a structural equation is given for each downstream variable. V1 to V4 stand for the observed variables X1 to X4, F1 and F2 for the two latent source variables K1 and K2, and E1 to E4 for the four residuals. The .5s are starting values for estimating the paths *a, b, c,* and *d* in Fig 2.6 (the asterisks designate free variables to be estimated). In the VARIANCES and COVARIANCES sections, the variances of F1 and F2 are fixed at 1 (no asterisk), and E1 to E4 and the covariance of F1 and F2 are given starting values of .5.

    In example (b), corresponding to Table 2-8, the structural relationship of Fig 2.7 is specified between the two latent variables. A structural equation for F2 is added to the list of equations with a residual D2, the covariance involving the latent variables is dropped, and the path from F2 to V3 is fixed to 1. In the SPEC section, the least squares method is specified by ME = LS (as in the case of LISREL, maximum likelihood is the default method). Finally, EQS will calculate its own starting values, because no numbers precede the asterisks.

    Again, many variations are possible in EQS, as in LISREL. A CONSTRAINTS section can impose equality constraints as LISREL's EQUAL statement does. For example, to require paths *a* and *b* in Fig 2.7 to be equal, one would specify /CONSTRAINTS and (V1, F1) = (V2, F1). EQS goes beyond LISREL in allowing inequality constraints to be directly imposed as well (these can be achieved in LISREL via "phantom variables"--see Chapter 7).

A Third Program, CALIS

LISREL is available as part of the SPSS statistical package. EQS is distributed by BMDP. The SAS statistical package has recently added to its repertoire a program for solving latent variable models called CALIS (SAS Institute, 1990b). CALIS appears to be of comparable scope to LISREL and EQS for single-sample model fitting to correlation or covariance matrices, but does not have facilities for doing multiple-sample analyses. CALIS is unique in providing several different ways of specifying models, including a path representation similar to RAM, and a matrix approach that is different from LISREL's but like COSAN's; we confine our description here to a structural equation method similar to that of EQS. Table 2-10 presents CALIS programs for the same two problems used to illustrate LISREL and EQS in Tables 2-7, 2-8, and 2-9.

The part above the TITLE line sets up an SAS data file containing labels, N, and the correlation matrix. The part between PROC CALIS and RUN sets up the model and starting values. The LINEQS lines are like the EQUations

Table 2-10 Examples of CALIS input for the problems of Fig. 2.6 and 2.7

(a)	(b)

```
DATA EX29 (TYPE=CORR);
   INPUT _TYPE_ $ _NAME_ $ X1 X2 X3 X4;
   CARDS;
N . 100 . . .                                    [same as (a)]
CORR X1  1.0 . . .
CORR X2   .50  1.0 . .
CORR X3   .10   .10  1.0 .
CORR X4   .20   .30   .20  1.0
   ;
```

(a)	(b)
`TITLE 'INPUT FOR FIG 2.6 PROBLEM';`	`TITLE 'INPUT FOR FIG 2.7 PROBLEM';`
`PROC CALIS;`	`PROC CALIS  METHOD=ULS;`
`   LINEQS  X1 = A (.5) F1 + E1,`	`   LINEQS  X1 = A  F1 + E1,`
`           X2 = B (.5) F1 + E2,`	`           X2 = B  F1 + E2,`
`           X3 = C (.5) F2 + E3,`	`           X3 =     F2 + E3,`
`           X4 = D (.5) F2 + E4;`	`           X4 = C  F2 + E4,`
`   STD     F1 F2 = 1,`	`           FK2 = D  F1 + D2;`
`           E1 E2 E3 E4 = RS1: (4*.5);`	`   STD     F1 = 1, D2 = DS2,`
`   COV     F1 F2 = CE (.5);`	`           E1 E2 E3 E4 = RS1:;`
`RUN;`	`RUN;`

55

lines in EQS, except that the starting values are in parentheses following the variables to be solved for rather than preceding them, and asterisks are not used. The STD lines correspond to the VAR lines in EQS, and the COV lines are similar in both programs. The colon following RS1 stands for a series of variables RS1, RS2, etc.--in this case to RS4.

Program (b) makes the same changes that the comparable EQS program does: adds a fifth structural equation for F2, omits the COV, omits the starting values (so CALIS will calculate its own), and specifies a least squares solution.

The convention of using F variables for latent variables, E variables for the residuals of manifest variables, and D variables for the residuals of downstream latent variables, is similar to that in EQS. In the STD and COV sections, variables to be fixed are equated to a numerical value, and variables to be solved for are equated to a name. If two variables are to be constrained to be equal, the same name is simply used for both.

As usual, there are many options concerning solution methods and output; the manual should be consulted for details.

Some other programs for latent variable modeling

EzPATH (Steiger, 1989) is a structural modeling program that is associated with the SYSTAT statistical package. The program's input and output follow directly from a RAM-type path diagram, each line of the input or output corresponding to an arrow in the diagram.

AMOS (Arbuckle, 1989) is similar in flavor to EzPATH, although not part of a particular statistical package. AMOS's input is also a direct translation of a path diagram, essentially a listing of its paths.

A flexible program for structural equation modeling is McDonald's (1978) COSAN, which is available in a FORTRAN version (Fraser & McDonald, 1988). This is a matrix-based program, although the matrices are different from LISREL's. They are more akin to the McArdle-McDonald matrices described earlier in the present chapter. Logically, COSAN can be considered as an elaboration and specialization of the McArdle-McDonald model.

Any of the six programs should be able to fit most of the latent variable models described in Chapters 2, 3, and 4 of this book, except that only LISREL, AMOS, and EQS currently handle model fitting in multiple samples.

Do it yourself?

We might consider one other option that a would-be modeler has: Do it your own way. If you have at least modest computer programming skills, it is quite feasible to build a practical IPSOL-like program by replacing its MINIM routine with a general-purpose search subroutine. As mentioned earlier, there are a number of such search programs around. One serviceable procedure is described in programming-level detail by Davidon (1975); there are several minimization routines in the International Mathematical and Statistical Library of computer subroutines (IMSL, 1987), and other programs exist.

Most users, most of the time, should find LISREL, EQS, or one of their fellows quite satisfactory. However, if you are faced with frequent or extensive model-fitting analyses outside the scope of whatever standard programs you have available to you, it may be feasible to put together a package of your own.

Goodness-of-Fit Criteria

A variety of criteria have been proposed to describe how closely the correlation or covariance matrix implied by a particular set of trial values conforms to the observed data. Four will be described: ordinary least squares (OLS), generalized least squares (GLS), maximum likelihood (ML), and a version of Browne's (1984) asymptotically distribution-free criterion (ADF)--the last is called generally weighted least squares in LISREL and arbitrary distribution generalized least squares in EQS.

Why four criteria? The presence of more than one places the user in the situation described in the proverb: A man with one watch always knows what time it is; a man with two watches never does. The answer is that the different criteria have different advantages and disadvantages, as we see shortly.

The various criteria, also known as *discrepancy functions*, can be considered as different ways of weighting the differences between corresponding elements of the observed and implied covariance matrices. In matrix terms, this may be expressed as:

$$(\mathbf{s} - \mathbf{c})'\ \mathbf{W}\ (\mathbf{s} - \mathbf{c}),$$

where $\mathbf{s}$ and $\mathbf{c}$ refer to the nonduplicated elements of the observed and implied covariance matrices $\mathbf{S}$ and $\mathbf{C}$ arranged as vectors. That is, the lower triangular elements $\begin{matrix} a \\ b\ c \\ d\ e\ f \end{matrix}$ of a 3x3 covariance matrix would become the 6-element vector $(a\ b\ c\ d\ e\ f)'$, and $(\mathbf{s} - \mathbf{c})'$ would contain the differences between such elements of the observed and implied covariance matrices. $\mathbf{W}$ is a weight matrix, and different versions of it yield different criteria. If $\mathbf{W}$ is an identity matrix, the above expression reduces to $(\mathbf{s} - \mathbf{c})'(\mathbf{s} - \mathbf{c})$. This is just the sum of the squared differences between corresponding elements of the observed and implied matrices, an ordinary least squares criterion. If the matrices $\mathbf{S}$ and $\mathbf{C}$ are identical, the value of this expression will be zero. As $\mathbf{S}$ and $\mathbf{C}$ become more different, the squared differences between their elements will increase. The sum of these, call it F, is a discrepancy function: The larger F is, the worse the fit. An iterative model-fitting program will try to minimize F by seeking values for the unknowns that make the implied matrix $\mathbf{C}$ as much like the

57

observed matrix **S** as possible. In general, an ordinary least squares criterion is most meaningful when a correlation matrix is used for **S**, or, in the case of a covariance matrix, when the variables are measured on comparable scales. Otherwise, arbitrary differences in the scales of variables can markedly affect their contributions to F.

For ADF, the matrix **W** is based on the variances and covariances among the elements in **s**. If **s** were the 6-element vector of the previous example, **W** would be derived from the inverse of the 6x6 matrix of covariances among all possible pairs *aa, ab, ac,* etc., from **s**. The elements of the matrix to be inverted are obtained via the calculation $m_{ijkl} - s_{ij}s_{kl}$, where m_{ijkl} is a fourth-order moment, the mean product of the deviation scores of variables *i, j, k,* and *l,* and s_{ij} and s_{kl} are the two covariances in question. This calculation is straightforward; however, as the original covariance matrix **S** gets larger, the vector **s** of its nonduplicated elements increases rapidly in length, and **W**, whose size is the square of that, can become a very large matrix whose storage, inversion, and application to calculations in an iterative procedure are quite demanding of computer resources.

If the observed variables have a distribution that is multivariate normal, the general expression given above can be simplified to:

$$1/2 \ tr \ [(\mathbf{S} - \mathbf{C}) \ \mathbf{V}]^2,$$

where *tr* refers to the trace of a matrix (i.e., the sum of its diagonal elements), and **V** is another weight matrix. This expression involves matrices the size of the original covariance matrix, and hence is computationally more attractive.

The choice of weight matrix **V** defines:

$$\mathbf{V} = \mathbf{I} \qquad \text{OLS, ordinary least squares}$$
$$\mathbf{V} = \mathbf{S}^{-1} \qquad \text{GLS, generalized least squares}$$
$$\mathbf{V} = \mathbf{C}^{-1} \qquad \text{ML, maximum likelihood}$$

(The maximum likelihood criterion is typically defined in a different way, as $ML = \ln|\mathbf{C}| - \ln|\mathbf{S}| + tr\mathbf{SC}^{-1} - n$, which involves the natural logarithms of the determinants of the **C** and **S** matrices, the trace of the product of **S** and $\mathbf{C}^{-1}$, and the number of variables, *n*. While the two definitions are not identical, it has been shown that the estimates that minimize the one also tend to minimize the other.)

In the case of ordinary least squares--as with the general version given earlier--the simplified expression above reduces to a function of the sum of squared differences between corresponding elements of the **S** and **C** matrices. The other criteria, GLS and ML, require successively more computation. GLS uses the inverse of the observed covariance matrix **S** as a weight matrix. This only needs to be obtained once, at the start of the iterative process, because the observed matrix doesn't change. However, the implied matrix **C** changes with each change in trial values, so $\mathbf{C}^{-1}$ needs to be recalculated many times during an iterative ML solution, making ML more costly than GLS.

Both GLS and ML criteria, when the assumption of multivariate normality holds and sample size is reasonably large, will yield an approximate chi square by the multiplication $(N - 1)F_{min}$, where F_{min} is the value of the discrepancy function at the point of best fit and N is the sample size. ADF will do this too, and it does not require the assumption of multivariate normality; however, it needs larger samples for accuracy in estimating the fourth moments, as well as more computational effort because of the bigger matrices involved.

All these criteria have a minimum value of zero when the observed and implied matrices are the same (i.e., when $S = C$), and all become increasingly large as the difference between S and C becomes greater.

Table 2-11 illustrates the calculation of OLS, GLS, and ML criteria for two C matrices departing slightly from S in opposite directions. (The calculations for ADF would require a return to the raw data to obtain the fourth moments.) Note

Table 2-11 Sample calculation of OLS, GLS, and ML criteria for the departure of covariance matrices C_1 and C_2 from S

S		2.00	1.00		
		1.00	4.00		
S⁻¹		.5714286	-.1428571		
		-.1428571	.2857143		
		C₁		**C₂**	
C	2.00	1.00	2.00	1.00	
	1.00	4.01	1.00	3.99	
C⁻¹	.5712251	-.1424501	.5716332	-.1432665	
	-.1424501	.2849003	-.1432665	.2865330	
(S - C)S⁻¹	.0000000	.0000000	.0000000	.0000000	
	.0014286	-.0028571	-.0014286	.0028571	
(S - C)C⁻¹	.0000000	.0000000	.0000000	.0000000	
	.0014245	-.0028490	-.0014327	.0028653	
OLS		.00005000		.00005000	
GLS		.00000408		.00000408	
ML		.00000406		.00000411	

that all the goodness-of-fit criteria are small, reflecting the closeness of **C** to **S**, and that they are positive for either direction of departure from **S**. (OLS is on a different scale from the other two, so its size cannot be directly compared to theirs.) In this example, the ML and GLS criteria are very close in numerical value to each other; as we see later, this is by no means always the case.

Another message of Table 2-11 is that considerable numerical accuracy is required for calculations such as these--one more reason for letting computers do them. In this problem, a difference between **C** and **S** matrices in the second decimal place requires going to the sixth decimal place in the GLS and ML criteria in order to detect its effect. With only, say, 4- or 5-place accuracy in obtaining the inverses, quite misleading results would have been obtained.

Goodness-of-fit criteria serve two purposes in iterative model fitting. First, they guide the search for a best fitting solution. Second, they evaluate the solution when it is obtained. The criteria being considered have somewhat different relative merits for these two tasks.

For the first purpose, guiding a search, a criterion should ideally be cheap to compute, because the function is evaluated repeatedly at each step of a trial-and-error search. Furthermore, the criterion should be a dependable guide to relative distances in the search space, especially at points distant from a perfect fit. For the second purpose, evaluating a best fit solution, the statistical properties of the criterion are a very important consideration, computational cost is a minor issue, and the behavior of the function in remote regions of the search space is not in question.

In computational cost, ordinary least squares is by far the cheapest, GLS comes next, then ML, with ADF the most expensive. As we have seen, the latter three criteria have the statistical advantage that when they are multiplied by N - 1 at the point of best fit, they yield a quantity that is approximately distributed as chi-square, permitting statistical tests of goodness of fit in the manner described later in the chapter. These statistical properties depend on large samples. It is hard to say how large "large" is, because, as usual, things are not all-or-nothing--approximations gradually get rougher as sample size decreases; there is no single value marking a sharp boundary between smooth sailing and disaster. As a rough rule of thumb, one would probably do well to be modest in one's statistical claims if N is less than 100.

Finally, the criteria differ in their ability to provide dependable distance measures, especially at points remote from the point of perfect fit. Figure 2.8 and Table 2-12 provide an example of a case where ML gives an anomalous solution. The data are from Dwyer (1983, p. 258), and they represent the variance-covariance matrix for three versions of an item on a scale measuring authoritarian attitudes. The question Dwyer asked is whether the items satisfy a particular psychometric condition known as "*tau*-equivalence," which implies that they measure a single common factor for which they have equal weights, but possibly different residual variances, as shown in the path diagram of

Implied variance-covariance matrix

$$\begin{array}{ccc} a^2+b^2 & a^2 & a^2 \\ a^2 & a^2+c^2 & a^2 \\ a^2 & a^2 & a^2+d^2 \end{array}$$

Fig. 2.8 Model of single common factor with equal loadings, plus different specifics ("*tau*-equivalent" tests).

Fig.2.8. It is thus a problem with four unknowns, a, b, c, and d. Such a model implies that the off-diagonal elements in **C** must all be equal, and so a should be assigned a value to give a reasonable compromise fit to the three covariances. The unknowns b, c, and d can then be given values to insure a perfect fit to the three observed values in the diagonal.

This is just what an iterative search program using an OLS criterion does, as shown in the left column of Table 2-12. A value of $\sqrt{5.58}$ is found for a, and values of $\sqrt{.55}$, $\sqrt{2.71}$, and $\sqrt{1.77}$ for b, c, and d, respectively, yielding the implied matrix $\mathbf{C_{OLS}}$. Dwyer used an ML criterion (with LISREL) and obtained a solution giving the implied matrix on the right in Table 2-12, labeled $\mathbf{C_{ML}}$. Notice that this matrix has equal off-diagonal values, as it must, but that the

Table 2-12 OLS and ML solutions for Fig. 2.8

S						
	6.13	6.12	4.78			
	6.12	8.29	5.85			
	4.78	5.85	7.35			

	$\mathbf{C_{OLS}}$			$\mathbf{C_{ML}}$		
C	6.13	5.58	5.58	6.46	5.66	5.66
	5.58	8.29	5.58	5.66	7.11	5.66
	5.58	5.58	7.35	5.66	5.66	8.46
S - C	.00	.54	-.80	-.33	.46	-.88
	.54	.00	.27	.46	1.18	.19
	-.80	.27	.00	-.88	.19	-1.11
ML		.32			.10	
OLS		1.00			2.39	

diagonal values are not at all good fits to the variances in **S**, as shown by the matrix **S-C**. The values of the ML criterion for the fit of the two **C** matrices to **S** are given at the bottom of the table. It is clear that the ML goodness-of-fit criterion for C_{ML} is substantially less than that for the solution on the left, which both the eye and OLS judge to be superior.

Table 2-13 gives some further examples to illustrate that the criteria do not always agree on the extent to which one covariance matrix resembles another, and that ML and GLS can sometimes be rather erratic judges of distance when distances are not small.

Table 2-13 How different goodness-of-fit criteria evaluate the distance of two Cs from **S**

S		C_1		C_2		GLS says C_1	C_2	ML says C_1	C_2
2	1	1	2	10	9				
1	4	2	5	9	10	.45	10.29	34.00	.86
5	0	5	3	10	-7				
0	5	3	4	-7	10	.38	2.96	3.00	.47
6	5	6	0	2	-1				
5	6	0	7	-1	1	5.80	.73	.59	404.00

In each row of the table, two different **C** matrices are compared to the **S** matrix shown at the left. In each case, which **C** matrix would you judge to be most different from **S**? The OLS criterion (and most people's intuition) judges C_2 to be much further away from **S** than matrix C_1 is, in all three examples. GLS agrees in the first two cases, but ML does not--in both instances, the ML criterion is decidedly larger for the comparison of C_1 with **S**. The third example shows that the shoe is sometimes on the other foot: In this case, it is ML that agrees with OLS that C_2 is much more different, and it is GLS that disagrees.

This is not to say that GLS or ML will not give accurate assessments of fit when the fit is good, that is, when **C** and **S** are close to each other. Recall that in Table 2-11 the OLS and GLS criteria agreed very well for Cs differing only very slightly from the **S** of the first example. But in the early stages of a search, when **C** is still remote from **S**, or for problems like that of Table 2-12 where the best fit is not a very good fit, eccentric distance judgments can give trouble. After all, if a fitting program were to propose C_1 as an alternative to C_2 in the first row in Table 2-13, OLS and GLS would accept it as a dramatic improvement, but ML would reject it as tending to move away from **S**!

None of this is meant to imply that searches using the ML or GLS criterion are bound to run into difficulties--in fact, studies reviewed in the next section suggest that ML in practice usually works quite well. I do, however, want to emphasize that uncritical acceptance of any solution a computer program happens to produce can be hazardous to one's scientific health. If in doubt, you should try solutions from several starting points with two or three different criteria--if all converge on similar answers, you can then use the ML solution for its favorable statistical properties, or, if you have obvious violation of multivariate normality and a large sample, ADF.

Monte Carlo studies using the maximum likelihood criterion

There have been several studies in which fairly extensive explorations have been made with the program LISREL and a maximum likelihood criterion, studies based on repeated random sampling from artificial populations with known characteristics (Anderson & Gerbing, 1984; Boomsma, 1982, 1985; Gerbing & Anderson, 1985). These studies manipulated model characteristics and sample sizes and studied the effects on accuracy of estimation and the frequency of improper or nonconvergent solutions.

These studies do not address all possible issues, of course. Anderson and Gerbing worked solely with confirmatory factor analysis models, and Boomsma largely did, so the results apply most directly to models of this kind. Both studies sampled from multivariate normal populations, so questions of the robustness of maximum likelihood to departures from multivariate normality are not addressed. For the most part, both studies used optimum starting values for the iteration, namely, the true population values; thus, the behavior of the maximum likelihood criterion in regions distant from the solution is not at issue. (In one part of Boomsma's study, alternative starting points were compared.)

Within these limitations, a variety of models and sample sizes were used in the two studies combined. The number of latent variables (factors) ranged from 2 to 4, and the correlations between them were .0, .3, or .5. The number of observed indicators per latent variable ranged from 2 to 4, and the sizes of nonzero factor pattern coefficients from .4 to .9, in various combinations. Sample sizes of 25, 50, 75, 100, 150, 200, 300, and 400 were employed.

The main tendencies of the results can be summarized briefly, although there were some complexities of detail for which the reader may wish to consult the original articles.

First, *convergence failures.* These occurred quite frequently with small samples and few indicators per factor. In fact, with samples of less than 100 cases and only two indicators per factor, such failures occurred on almost half the trials under some conditions (moderate loadings and low interfactor correlations). With three or more indicators per factor and 150 or more cases, failures of convergence rarely occurred.

Second, *improper solutions* (negative estimates of residual variance--so-called "Heywood cases"). Again, with samples of less than 100 and only two indicators per factor, these cases were very common. With three or more indicators per factor and sample sizes of 200 or more, they were pretty much eliminated.

Third, *accuracy.* With smaller samples, naturally, estimates of the population values were less precise--that is, there was more sample-to-sample variation in repeated sampling under a given condition. However, with some exceptions for the very smallest sample sizes (25 and 50 cases), the standard error estimates provided by the LISREL program appeared to be dependable--that is, a 95% confidence interval included the population value somewhere near 95% of the time.

Finally, *starting points.* As mentioned, in part of Boomsma's study the effect of using alternative starting values was investigated. This aspect of the study was confined to otherwise favorable conditions--samples of 100 or more cases with three or more indicators per factor--and the departures from the ideal starting values were not *very* drastic. Under these circumstances, the solutions usually converged, and when they did it was nearly always to essentially identical final values; differences were mostly in the third decimal place or beyond.

In summary, then, these studies suggest that for the class of problems investigated--confirmatory factor analyses with two to four factors--one should plan on sample sizes of at least 100 cases (200 is better) and use at least three indicators per factor. Using a combination of two indicators per factor and 50 cases or less is just inviting trouble. In between there are tradeoffs. If you are stuck with a small sample, use more indicators per factor if you can and plan toward replication in another sample.

The results reported were obtained using LISREL and multivariate normal distributions, but presumably they would serve as guidelines for other similar programs, and distributions more or less approximating multivariate normality.

We encounter here, of course, the usual dilemma confronting the individual who would like to be both statistical purist and practical researcher. Few, if any, users of chi-square tests or standard error estimates with maximum likelihood estimation are in a position to fully justify the probability values they report. Nearly always, the strongest appropriate claim would be something like: "To the extent that the underlying assumptions hold, we can conclude that. . . . " Or, perhaps more frankly: "The statistical tests and probability values in this paper are reported in a mainly descriptive spirit, to help orient the reader among the various models we present."

Some such statement should be taken as appended to every substantive study described in this book. I have not ordinarily made it explicitly. To do it only on occasion would be invidious. To do it every time would be an unkindness to the reader.

Hierarchical χ^2 Tests

As noted earlier, for GLS or ML or AGF (but not for OLS) one can multiply the criterion at the point of best fit by N -1 to obtain an approximate χ^2 in large samples. This can be used to test the fit of the implied **C** to **S**. The degrees of freedom for the comparison are the number of independent values in **S** less the number of unknowns used in generating **C**.

For example, in the problem of *tau*-equivalence discussed earlier in the chapter (Fig. 2.8), there were $n(n+1)/2 = 6$ independent values in **S** (the three variances in the diagonal and the three covariances on one side of it), and there were four unknowns being estimated, *a, b, c,* and *d.* So there are two degrees of freedom for a χ^2 test. The minimum value of the ML criterion is .0993 (Table 2-12). As it happens, the data were gathered from 109 subjects, so $\chi^2 = 108 \times .0993 = 10.7$. From a χ^2 table (see Appendix G), the χ^2 with 2 df required to reject the null hypothesis at the .05 level is 5.99. The obtained χ^2 of 10.7 is larger than this, so we would reject the null hypothesis and conclude that the model of *tau*-equivalence did not fit these data; that is, that the difference between **C** and **S** is too great to readily be attributed to sampling error. Notice that the χ^2 test is used to conclude that a particular model *does not* fit the data. Suppose that χ^2 in the preceding example had been less than 5.99, what could we then have concluded? We could not conclude that the model is correct, but merely that our test had not shown it to be incorrect. How impressive this statement is depends very much on how powerful a test we have applied. By using a sufficiently small sample, for instance, we could fail to reject models that are grossly discrepant from the data. On the other hand, if our sample is extremely large, a failure to reject the model would imply a near-exact fit between **C** and **S**. Indeed, with very large samples we run into the opposite embarrassment, in that we may obtain highly significant χ^2s and hence reject models in cases where the discrepancies between model and data, although presumably not due to chance, are not large enough to be of any practical concern. It is prudent always to examine the residuals **S - C**, in addition to carrying out a χ^2 test, before coming to a conclusion about the fit of a model.

It is also prudent to look at alternative models. The fact that one model fits the data reasonably well does not mean that there could not be other, different models that fit better. At best, a given model represents a tentative explanation of the data. The confidence with which one accepts such an explanation depends, in part, on whether other, rival explanations have been tested and found wanting.

Fig. 2.9 Path models for the χ^2 comparisons of Table 2-14.

Table 2-14 Comparing two models with χ^2

	S			
	1.00	.30	.20	.10
	.30	1.00	.20	.20
	.20	.20	1.00	.30
	.10	.20	.30	1.00

	Model		
	(a)	(b)	(diff)
χ^2, N = 120	4.64	.75	3.89
χ^2, N = 240	9.31	1.51	7.80
df	2	1	1
$\chi^2_{.05}$	5.99	3.84	3.84

Figure 2.9 and Table 2-14 provide an example of testing two models for fit to an observed set of intercorrelations, given as **S** at the top of the table. Model (a) is a Spearmanian model with a single general factor G. Model (b) has two correlated common factors, E and F. Fits to the data, using an iterative solution with a maximum likelihood criterion, are shown for both models. If we assume that the correlations in **S** are based on 120 subjects, what do we conclude?

As the individual χ^2s for the two models indicate, we can reject neither. The correlation matrix **S** could represent the kind of chance fluctuation to be expected in random samples of 120 cases drawn from populations where the true underlying situation was that described by either model (a) or model (b).

Suppose that the correlations had instead been based on 240 subjects. Now what conclusions would be drawn?

In this case, we could reject model (a) because its χ^2 exceeds the 5.99 required to reject the null hypothesis at the .05 level with 2 df. Model (b), however, remains a plausible fit to the data.

Does this mean that we can conclude that model (b) fits significantly better than model (a)? Not as such--the fact that one result is significant and another is nonsignificant is *not* the same as demonstrating that there is a significant difference between the two, although, regrettably, one sees this error made fairly often. (If you have any lingering doubts about this, consider the case where one result is just a hairsbreadth below the .05 level and the other just a hairsbreadth above--one result is nominally significant and the other not, but the difference between the two is of a kind that could very easily have arisen by chance.)

There is, however, a direct comparison that can be made in the case of Table 2-14 because the two models stand in a *nested*, or hierarchical, relationship. That is, the model with the smaller number of free variables can be obtained from the model with the larger number of free variables by fixing one or more of the latter. In this case, model (a) can be obtained from model (b) by fixing the value of the the interfactor correlation *e* at 1.00--if E and F are standardized and perfectly correlated, they can be replaced by a single G.

Two such nested models can be compared very simply by a χ^2 test: The χ^2 for this test is just the difference between the separate χ^2s of the two models, and the df is just the difference between their dfs (which is equivalent to the number of parameters fixed in going from the one to the other).

In the example of Table 2-14, the difference between the two models turns out, in fact, to be statistically significant, as shown in the rightmost column at the bottom of the table. Interestingly, this is true for either sample size. In both cases, the χ^2 for the difference exceeds the 3.84 required for significance (at the .05 level, for 1 df). Thus, in this instance, with N = 120 either model represents an acceptable explanation of the data, but model (b) provides a significantly better one than does model (a). With the larger N of 240, the results are straightforward: Model (b) is acceptable, model (a) can be rejected, and the difference between the two is itself significant.

67

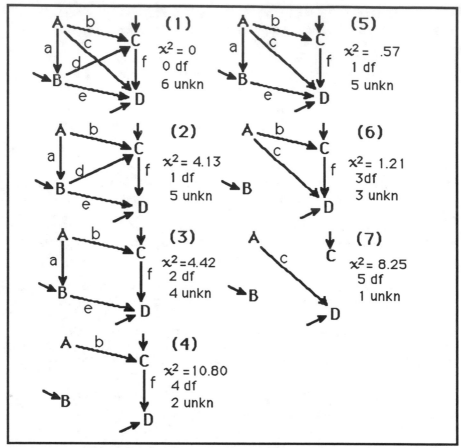

Fig. 2.10 Hierarchical series of path models (χ^2s hypothetical).

Figure 2.10 further illustrates the notion of nested models. Models 1, 2, 3, and 4 represent such a hierarchical series because 2 can be obtained from 1 by setting path *c* to the fixed value of zero, 3 from 2 by similarly fixing *d*, and 4 from 3 by fixing *a* and *e* to zero. Obviously, in such a series any lower model can be obtained from any higher one by fixing paths--e.g., model 4 can be obtained from model 1 by setting paths *a*, *c*, *d*, and *e* to zero. Thus tests based on differences in χ^2 can be used to compare the fit of any two models in such a nested series. In the last described case, such a test would have four degrees of freedom, corresponding to the four paths fixed in going from model 1 to model 4.

However, models 5, 6, and 7 in Fig. 2.10, although hierarchically related to model 1 and each other, are not in the same series as 2, 3, and 4. Thus, model 6 could not be compared with model 3 by taking the difference in their respective χ^2s. Although model 6 has fewer paths than model 3, they are not included within those of model 3--model 6 has path c as an unknown to be solved for, whereas model 3 does not.

Assuming that the four variables A, B, C, and D are all measured, model 1 is a case with $n(n-1)/2 = 6$ observed correlations and 6 unknowns to be solved for. A perfect fit will in general be achievable, χ^2 will be 0, and there will be 0 df. Obviously, such a model can never be rejected, but then, because it can be guaranteed to fit perfectly, its fit provides no special indication of its merit. The other models in Fig. 2.10 do have degrees of freedom and hence can potentially be rejected. Notice that the direct χ^2 tests of these models can be considered as special cases of the χ^2 test of differences between nested models because they are equivalent to the test of differences between these models and model 1.

Table 2-15 gives some examples of nested χ^2 tests based on the models of Fig. 2.10. The test in the first line of the table, comparing models 2 and 1, can be considered to be a test of the significance of path c. Does constraining path c to be zero significantly worsen the fit to the data? The answer, based on $\chi^2 = 4.13$ with 1 df, is yes. Path c makes a difference; the model fits significantly better with it included. Another test of the significance of a single path is provided in line 6 of the table, model 5 versus model 1. Here it is a test of the path d. In this case, the data do not demonstrate that path d makes a significant contribution: $\chi^2 = .57$ with 1 df, not significant. A comparison of model 3 with model 1 (line 2) is an interesting case. Model 2, remember, did differ significantly from model 1. But model 3, with one less

Table 2-15 Some χ^2 tests for hierarchical model comparisons based on Fig. 2.10

	Model comparison	χ^2 1st	χ^2 2nd	df 1st	df 2nd	χ^2_{diff}	df_{diff}	p
1.	2 vs 1	4.13	0	1	0	4.13	1	<.05
2.	3 vs 1	4.42	0	2	0	4.42	2	ns
3.	3 vs 2	4.42	4.13	2	1	.29	1	ns
4.	4 vs 3	10.80	4.42	4	2	6.38	2	<.05
5.	4 vs 1	10.80	0	4	0	10.80	4	<.05
6.	5 vs 1	.57	0	1	0	.57	1	ns
7.	6 vs 1	1.21	0	3	0	1.21	3	ns
8.	7 vs 6	8.25	1.21	5	3	7.04	2	<.05

unknown, cannot be judged significantly worse than model 1 ($\chi^2 = 4.42$, 2 df, ns). This mildly paradoxical situation arises occasionally in such χ^2 comparisons. It occurs because the increase in χ^2 in going from model 2 to model 3 is more than offset by the increase in degrees of freedom. Thus whereas the additional restriction on model 3 caused by setting path *d* to zero makes it fit worse than model 2 in an absolute sense, relative to the degrees of freedom one is less confident that the difference from model 1 is real.

Eliminating paths *a* and *e* in addition to *d* and *c* (model 4) is clearly going too far, whether the comparison is made with the full model (line 5), or with a model with *c* and *d* removed (line 4). However, if *c* is present *a* and *e* can be dispensed with--or at any rate, they cannot be demonstrated to be essential (line 7). Nevertheless, as line 8 indicates, *c* alone cannot do the job--deleting *b* and *f* leads to a significant worsening of fit ($\chi^2 = 7.04$, 2 df, $p < .05$).

Figure 2.10 also illustrates that the fact that a given model cannot be rejected does not mean that one should conclude that it represents the truth. Consider model 3. One cannot reject it as a plausible explanation of the data ($\chi^2 = 4.42$, 2 df, $p > .10$--line 2). But this does not mean that other models might not do at least as well. Indeed, we have one in model 6, that with fewer parameters actually achieves a smaller χ^2. To be sure, we cannot carry out a direct statistical test of the relative goodness of fit of models 3 and 6 because they are not nested, but one would hardly wish to cheer very loudly about model 3 if one were aware that model 6 was lurking in the wings. The moral is that it pays to do some exploring of alternative models before going too far out on a limb on the basis of a significance test of any one. Otherwise, one risks the embarrassment of an unsuspected model 6 turning up.

Standard errors

Model-fitting programs usually provide approximate standard errors for path and variance estimates, either routinely or on request. This saves having to carry out χ^2 difference tests to assess the significance of individual paths, a fact that is particularly helpful if one is scanning a large model with a view to dropping a number of possibly superfluous paths. A single χ^2 difference test can then be carried out to see if the selected paths are jointly dispensable. (In EQS, a test called the Wald test is available for this.)

Because at this point one is in an exploratory mode, one should treat the reported standard errors as helpful guidelines, and not be very serious in the assignment of probability values based on them. If many tests are being made, some may well be "significant" merely by chance. Nor should one feel compelled to drop every path that is nonsignificant, especially when the sample size is small. With small samples, a path that is numerically appreciable may not exceed twice its standard error, yet its removal may materially affect the solution. If the path was theoretically justified in the first place, it is often wiser to leave it in the model until cross-validation confirms that it is negligible.

Descriptive Criteria of Model Fits

A goodness-of-fit χ^2 provides a useful basis for making decisions about the fit of a model, or the relative fits of different models. Moreover, for reasonable sample sizes, a χ^2 roughly equal to its degrees of freedom is an instant definition of satisfactory fit. A glance at Appendix G will show that $\chi^2 \approx df$ means $p \approx .50$, for df not too small (and even for small df, $p > .30$). Nevertheless, χ^2 has limitations as a descriptive index of model fit.

For one thing, χ^2 is sensitive to sample size. With large enough samples, substantively trivial discrepancies can lead to rejection of an otherwise highly satisfactory model; with small enough samples, χ^2 can be nonsignificant even in the face of gross mis-fits. As a consequence, a variety of proposals have been made as to how one might derive an index, perhaps on a scale of 0 to 1, that would describe how well, in a qualitative rather than in a statistical sense, a given model accounts for the data.

This area is in a state of flux. There have been numerous articles in the past few years criticizing existing indices and proposing new ones. The only strong recommendation that seems justified at present is to treat the indications of any one such index with caution until experience and Monte Carlo studies demonstrate that it can be relied on in the sorts of situations in which you wish to employ it.

In the meantime, there is one method of evaluating the fit of a model that can always be employed, and usually should be--the direct inspection of the residuals **S - C**. Not only does the smallness of these residuals give an absolute sense of the goodness of the fit, but the location of the larger residuals can suggest which aspects of the data are least well captured by the model. Model-fitting programs typically provide such residual matrices either routinely or on request. Residuals from analyzing correlation matrices are relatively easy to evaluate, because all variables are on comparable scales. Those from analyzing covariance matrices, especially if the variables are on quite different scales, can be harder to interpret, but most programs also provide standardized residuals that facilitate comparisons across variables on different scales.

The various overall fit indices that have been proposed tend to fall into two categories: those that simply describe goodness of fit, and those that involve considerations of parsimony--i.e., that take into account the number of unknowns used to achieve that fit. A model reaching a particular level of fit while solving for fewer free parameters would show up well on an index of the latter kind.

Examples of each kind of index will be described. First, for historical

71

reasons, and because they express the basic ideas simply, we consider the Bentler-Bonett normed fit index and a df-adjusted version of it, James, Mulaik, and Brett's parsimonious fit index. Then we describe briefly a fairly widely used alternative, Akaike's information criterion, and LISREL's goodness-of-fit indices. Finally, we look at a general approach to fit indices described by Tanaka and Huba, which includes LISREL's goodness-of-fit indices as special cases.

Bentler and Bonett's normed fit index

Bentler and Bonett (1980) suggest that the goodness of fit of a particular model may be usefully assessed by placing it on a scale running from a perfect fit to the fit of some baseline "null model." Such a null model would be an arbitrary, highly restricted model--say, that all correlations are zero, or that all correlations are equal, or some such--that would represent a baseline level that any realistic model would be expected to exceed. The index would then represent the point at which the model being evaluated falls on a scale running from this null model to perfect fit. The normed fit index may be formally defined as:

$$nfi = (\chi_0^2 - \chi_k^2)/ \chi_0^2,$$

where the subscripts k and 0 refer to the model in question and the null model, respectively.

An example is given in Table 2-16, based on the model comparisons of Fig. 2.10. The first column in the righthand part of the table gives values of the normed fit index for the models. Within a series of nested models, such as 1, 2, 3, 4 or 1, 5, 6, 7, the fit always gets poorer as fewer unknowns are fitted and the degrees of freedom increase. But the normed fit index gives some idea of how relatively good or poor the fit of a particular model might be. Thus, models

Table 2-16 Comparison of three χ^2-based descriptive criteria of model fits, for models of Fig. 2.10

Model	χ^2	Unknowns	df	Three criteria		
				nfi	pfi	AIC
1	0.00	6	0	1.00	.00	12.00
2	4.13	5	1	.74	.12	14.13
3	4.42	4	2	.72	.24	12.42
4	10.80	2	4	.32	.21	14.80
5	.57	5	1	.96	.16	10.57
6	1.21	3	3	.92	.46	7.21
7	8.25	1	5	.48	.40	10.25
null	16.00	0	6	.00	.00	16.00

5 and 6 fit quite well, but models 4 or 7 are not much better than the null model.

James, Mulaik, and Brett's parsimonious fit index

James, Mulaik, and Brett (1982) suggested a modification of Bentler and Bonett's normed fit index, which they called the *parsimonious fit index*. This takes into account the number of degrees of freedom given up in order to arrive at any particular level of goodness of fit. Other things being equal, a good fit attained by a parsimonious model, one with few unknowns (and hence more df), should represent the scientific ideal. James et al. suggested that if one were to modify Bentler and Bonett's index by multiplying it by the ratio of the degrees of freedom of the model under consideration to those of the null model, this would have the desired effect; that is:

$$pfi = (df_k/df_o) \; nfi.$$

Values of the parsimonious fit index for the models of F.j. 2.10 are shown in the second column in the righthand part of Table 2-16. Notice that within a nested series, such as 1, 2, 3, 4, null, or 1, 5, 6, 7, null, instead of always increasing, as nfi does, the values of pfi tend to increase and then decrease. The models with maximum values of pfi are the ones that best describe the data with the fewest unknowns to be solved for. The best model in this sense is model 6. Note that it scores much higher on pfi than does model 5. The latter has a slightly better overall level of fit (nfi of .96 vs. .92), but the fact that model 5 requires us to solve for 5 unknowns whereas model 6 gets by with only 3 gives the latter a decided advantage in its pfi. In fact, model 7, with only one unknown, comes out very well on the pfi; its overall level of fit is not especially good (nfi = .48), but it consitutes a highly parsimonious explanation of the data.

Akaike's information criterion

Akaike (1987) has proposed an index of goodness of fit derived from information theory, known as Akaike's Information Criterion (AIC), which is given in various forms, but most commonly as:

$$AIC = \chi^2 + 2q \; ,$$

where χ^2 is the goodness-of-fit χ^2, and q represents the number of unknown parameters solved for in the model being fitted. A minimum value of AIC represents an optimum fit. The best-fitting model is one in which a good fit (small χ^2) is obtained with a small number of unknowns. AIC is thus a parsimonious goodness-of-fit index: With models of equal χ^2, the one involving the fewest unknowns will be favored. Akaike's criterion is not on a simple normed scale and is also sensitive to sample size, so it is more useful in comparing a series of alternative models fit to the same data than in making comparisons of goodness of fit across studies.

The rightmost column of Table 2-16 shows the AIC values for the models of Fig. 2.10. Observe that AIC has a rough, though not perfect, inverse correspondence with pfi; in particular, both criteria agree on model 6 as the most parsimonious fit to the data.

LISREL's indices of fit

Jöreskog and Sörbom (1989) provide several goodness-of-fit indices for LISREL that are based more or less directly on discrepancies between the observed covariance matrix **S** and the implied matrix **C**, rather than proceeding by way of χ^2 as do the indices so far described.

The simplest of their measures is just the square root of the mean of the squared discrepancies between **S** and **C**, the root-mean-square residual, abbreviated RMR. This represents a kind of average of the absolute discrepancies between the observed and implied matrices; it is most easily interpretable when these are on a familiar scale, as would be the case if they were correlation matrices.

A more sophisticated goodness-of-fit index GFI is based on a ratio of squared discrepancies to observed variances, thus allowing for scale. Finally, an adjusted index AGFI adjusts GFI by a ratio of the degrees of freedom of the restricted to the null matrix, much in the spirit of the James, Mulaik, and Brett parsimonious fit index.

A general approach to fit indices

As just noted, LISREL provides a fit index called GFI (Goodness-of-Fit Index) as well as a parsimonious fit index AGFI (Adjusted Goodness-of-Fit Index). Tanaka and Huba (1985) have shown that GFI is a special case of a general formulation introduced by Bentler (1983). This is, for a fitted model:

$$1 \ - \ \frac{(s - c)' \ W \ (s - c)}{s' W \ s} \ .$$

The symbols are as identified in the previous section on goodness-of-fit criteria. For the various criteria discussed in that section, suitable variations on the general formula can be used. Note that if the best we can do for **c** is a null vector, **s - c** becomes just **s**, the righthand part of the expression will have a value of one, and the whole expression will equal zero. As the fit gets better the residuals **s - c** get smaller, and the value of the expression as a whole increases from zero toward one. As the fit becomes perfect (**c = s**), the numerator expression becomes zero and the index has a value of one.

For ordinary least squares, where **W** is an identity matrix, the numerator of the righthand part is simply the sum of the squared residuals, and the denominator is the sum of squares of the observed values. Thus, in this case the goodness-of-fit index can be interpreted as the proportion of the sum of squares of the observed covariances that is explained by the model. Analogous interpretations hold for the other cases, where these become weighted sums (see Tanaka & Huba, 1989).

This goodness-of-fit index can be converted to the parsimonious goodness-of-fit index AGFI by adjusting it for degrees of freedom. This can be done by multiplying the righthand part by the ratio of the the number of elements in **s** to the df of the fitted model. As the number of unknowns decreases, these values approach equality, and AGFI approaches GFI. On the other hand, as the number of unknowns increases, the divisor of the multiplier shrinks, and AGFI can go to zero or even negative values. Thus a good fit achieved with few unknowns will yield relatively high values for both indices, whereas a good fit achieved by solving for many unknowns, leaving few degrees of freedom, will produce a high GFI but a low AGFI.

Choice among the criteria

Here we are in the position of a person with six watches--we may not know exactly what time it is, either, but if we consult all our watches and get a consensus, we should be pretty close. Actually, the situation is not quite analogous because not all the criteria are intended to measure exactly the same thing, but it is still the case that by consulting several we should have a more accurate picture of the situation.

Three of the criteria, nfi, GFI, and RMR are measures of goodness of fit per se. The other three, AIC, pfi, and AGFI, are indices of parsimonious goodness of fit, taking into account the number of free parameters required in order to achieve a given level of fit. As all are easily computed or available in program output, it is perfectly feasible to obtain and consider several of them in making interpretations and decisions during exploratory model fitting.

Correlations Versus Covariances in Model Fitting

Earlier, in discussing the use of standardized versus unstandardized variables in path models, it was noted that one often had a choice as to which scaling was used. What are some of the considerations in making such a choice, apart from the greater familiarity of correlations to many readers?

A fairly obvious point is that if one is comparing different groups, different times, etc., and one wants to take variance differences into account, one should analyze a covariance matrix; if one wishes to ignore variance differences, one should analyze standardized variables, i.e., a correlation matrix.

A related consideration involves the inadvertent changes in scale that the calculation of correlations may bring about. Suppose that the effect of education, in years, on income, in dollars, is being compared in two populations in which these variables differ in variance. (If an added year of education is worth $5000 in income in both populations, the unstandardized regression coefficients obtained in an analysis using covariances will be equal, but the standardized regression coefficients obtained in an analysis of correlations will not be.) In the latter case, if one believes rawscore-based parameters in a model should be equal across groups or across time, the automatic changes of scale involved in the calculation of correlations separately in the different groups or for the different times will defeat one's purpose. One should specify the equality on the scale for which it is expected to hold--in this case the rawscore scale--and thus should analyze covariances. If one elects to standardize variables for other reasons, the standardization should be across the combined groups to preserve the uniformity of scale.

This may not always be the case. If one's theory indicates that equality should be defined relative to the variability in each population--that an extra year of education has more effect on income in a group where education tends not to vary much--then standard score regressions may be more nearly constant than raw score regressions, and correlation matrices calculated within groups will be the better choice for analysis. Or if one is equating factor loadings or residual variances across variables within a sample, standardization may often make sense. The important thing is that one think about where the equality is expected, and make sure that one's constraints are imposed as intended.

In addition, there are some technical issues. First, the statistical theory underlying maximum likelihood and generalized least squares solutions has mostly been developed for the case of covariance matrices rather than correlation matrices. While workers in the area rather freely assume in practice that correlation matrices can be substituted for covariance matrices without serious risk, statistical purists are happier with covariance matrices. Because correlation matrices *are* covariance matrices--of standardized variables--one might wonder why a problem arises. The answer is that statistical constraints are introduced when the same sample is used both to standardize the variables and to calculate the covariances. However, if one is dealing with large samples, as is highly desirable on other grounds, the loss of a degree of freedom in using the sample standard deviation to determine the rescaling of a variable will probably not have serious statistical consequences (assuming that such rescaling is substantively appropriate). More complicated issues of statistical constraint arise if one insists that values of the parameters be restricted to those that yield a proper correlation matrix, i.e., one with exact unities in the diagonal. The typical practice, however, is not to do this, but simply to analyze correlation matrices as covariance matrices that have been calculated using standardized variables. This is what usually happens by default when one inputs a correlation matrix to a model-fitting program.

To summarize, model-fitting to covariance matrices is technically the

76

standard procedure, but the substitution of correlation matrices often yields satisfactory results, and in some cases may have real advantages. However, in instances where one is equating parameters across groups or over time, and variance changes are involved, one should probably be analyzing covariances unless one has clear theoretical justification to the contrary.

Chapter 2 Notes

Search methods. Various procedures go by such names as steepest descent, Fletcher-Powell, Gauss-Newton, Newton-Raphson, the Fisher scoring method, the EM algorithm, etc. LISREL uses a Fletcher-Powell variant, but offers other options; EQS uses a Gauss-Newton algorithm. Schoenberg and Richtand (1984) discuss the use of the EM method for estimating factor analysis and measurement models.

IPSOL. For serious use, one would probably want to change the .001s in subroutine MINIM at least to .0001s, use double precision for calculations, and increase MAXFN.

Matrix formulations. McArdle and McDonald (1984) discuss some relationships among such formulations, and Bentler and Weeks (1985) comment on their article.

Assumptions. Browne (1987), Huba and Harlow (1987), and Sharma et al. (1989) discuss the robustness of model-fitting methods to departures from multivariate normality. Babakus et al. (1987) and Muthén (1984; Muthén & Kaplan, 1985) consider the effects of categorical and ordinal data in structural modeling. The statistical implications of sample size are discussed by Tanaka (1987). There seems to be some consensus that parameter estimates are often quite robust in the face of departures from assumptions that have severe consequences for chi-squares and standard errors.

In addition to ADF, other approaches avoiding normality assumptions, such as bootstrapping, are beginning to be explored for latent variable problems--see Bone et al. (1989) for an example. Chatterjee (1984) gives an application to exploratory factor analysis (actually, in his example, component analysis).

The effects of selection are considered by Muthén and Jöreskog (1983) and Muthén (1989). Lee (1986) and Muthén et al. (1987) discuss the handling of missing data in structural modeling.

Browne's ADF. For examples of applications see Huba and Harlow (1983), Tanaka and Huba (1987), and Windle et al. (1989).

Descriptive fit indices. Anyone interested in exploring current trends in goodness-of-fit indices can get a good start with Akaike (1987), Bentler (1990), Bollen (1989a, 1990), Bollen and Liang (1988), Bozdogan (1987), Cudeck and Henly (1991), La Du and Tanaka (1989), Maiti and Mukherjee (1990), Marsh et al. (1988), McDonald (1989), McDonald and Marsh (1990), and Mulaik et al. (1989).

EQS vs LISREL. Comparisons of ease of use are made by Brown (1986) and Brecht et al. (1986).

Other model-fitting approaches. As a variation on do-it-yourself, Lee and Jennrich (1984) point out how one can use a general nonlinear least squares program, PAR in the BMDP series, to achieve very flexible model fitting. The procedure runs somewhat more slowly than LISREL and requires a modest amount of FORTRAN-type programming, but it is much more general in the kind of constraints that may be imposed on the variables being solved for.

Correlations and covariances. See Lee (1985) and Cudeck (1989) for discussions.

Chapter 2 Exercises

In problems 1, 5, and 8, at the instructor's discretion, other programs may be used, or you may be asked merely to set up the problem, not to solve it numerically.

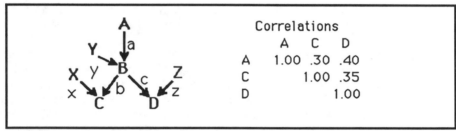

Fig. 2.17 Path model and correlations for Problem 1.

1. Use IPSOL to solve the path model of Fig. 2.17, with the correlations shown to its right. Reproduce the implied correlations from your solution as a check. Solve also for the residual paths.

2. Draw a cross-section of a perverse terrain in which very good solutions exist but a search program along the lines of IPSOL would have almost no chance of finding them.

3. Set up the three McArdle-McDonald matrices for the path diagram of problem 1.

4. An investigator believes that ambition, of which he has three measures, is a cause of achievement, for which he has two measures. If he sets this up as a normal LISREL problem, what would be the dimensions of the following matrices: **PH, BE, PS, LX, GA, LY, TD,** and **TE**?

5. In the study of problem 4, which used 60 subjects, the following correlations were observed. Use LISREL or another program to solve for the (standardized) path values, with a maximum likelihood criterion. Interpret the results.

	Ach1	Ach2	Amb1	Amb2	Amb3
Ach1	1.00				
Ach2	.60	1.00			
Amb1	.30	.20	1.00		
Amb2	.20	.30	.70	1.00	
Amb3	.20	.10	.60	.50	1.00

6. Four nested models based on a 4 x 4 variance-covariance matrix have 3, 5, 6, and 9 unknowns and yield χ^2s of 16.21, 8.12, 2.50, and 0.08, respectively. What conclusions about models or the differences between models could you draw at the .05 level of significance?

7. Compute the three χ^2-based criteria for exploratory model fitting for the data of problem 6, assuming a null model with no free parameters and $\chi^2 =$ 25.00. What interpretation would you make?

8. Solve problem 13 of Chapter 1 using LISREL or another program, and a least squares criterion. Fix one path to 1.0 and free the variance of the latent variable. Obtain a standardized as well as the unstandardized solution. Compare to the Chapter 1 result.

9. Convert the unstandardized solution of problem 8 by hand to a standardized solution, using the rules for standardized and unstandardized path coefficients from Chapter 1. Compare the results to those obtained in problem 8.

Chapter Three:
Varieties of Path and Structural Models--I

In this chapter and the next we consider a number of different applications of path and structural models. This serves two purposes. First, it gives some sense of various ways in which these methods can be employed, as well as practice in applying and interpreting them. Second, it introduces some additional concepts and techniques useful in dealing with path and structural models, both in general and in some important special cases.

Structural and Measurement Models

As we have seen, Jöreskog makes a useful distinction between two conceptually distinct parts of many complex path models, namely, a *structural* part and a *measurement* part. The structural part of a model specifies the relationships among the latent variables, and the measurement part specifies the relationship of the latent to the observed variables.

An example from a desegregation study

Figure 3.1 gives an example. This is a path diagram of part of a study of school desegregation. The diagram adopts the convention of representing latent variables by circles or ovals, and observed variables by squares or rectangles. This is helpful in keeping things straight in complicated models.

There are five latent variables, listed beside the diagram. Each is indexed by two or three observed variables, identified below the diagram. Collectively, these constitute the measurement model, shown in the top part of the next figure, Fig. 3.2. The structural model consists of the relationships among the five latent variables, shown at the bottom of Fig. 3.2.

Note that the structural and measurement models play rather distinct roles in the overall path model. One could very easily alter either without changing the other. Thus, one might maintain the same structural model of relationships among the latent variables but change the measurement model by using

80

Latent variables
SES = socioeconomic
status
ABL = ability
ASA = acceptance by
adults
ACH = academic
achievement
APR = acceptance by
peers

Observed variables
SEI = socioeconomic index
EDHH = education of head of household
R/P = rooms per person in house
VACH = verbal achievement score
VGR = verbal grades
RAV = Raven's Progressive Matrices Test
PEA = Peabody Picture Vocabulary Test
FEV = father's evaluation
MEV = mother's evaluation
TEV = teacher's evaluation
SPOP = seating popularity
PPOP = playground popularity
WPOP = schoolwork popularity

Fig. 3.1 Path model used in a desegregation study (Maruyama & McGarvey,
1980).

different tests or measurements to index the latent variables. Alternatively, one
could keep the same measures but change the structural model by making
different assumptions about the relationships among the latent variables--one
could assume, say, that the child's academic achievement influences peer
approval but not vice versa, or that acceptance by adults is affected by the
child's academic achievement.

The measurement model is a variant of confirmatory factor analysis. One
could consider the top part of Fig. 3.2 to consist of five small Spearman

Fig. 3.2 Measurement and structural components of path model of Fig. 3.1.

general-factor problems: In each case the latent variable can be seen as a factor general to the tests that measure it, with the residual arrows--shown here below the squares--representing influences specific to the tests. This would not, however, be an altogether satisfactory way to proceed, because it is not only the correlations of, say, SEI, EDHH, and R/P among themselves that provide information concerning the paths between them and SES; such information is also supplied in the relative correlations of these variables with others in the model. In fact, a direct Spearman approach would not work at all for the latent variables with only two indicators, which require at least some additional correlations in order to obtain a unique solution. It is perhaps more appropriate, therefore, to think of the measurement model as a single, multiple-factor confirmatory factor analysis. So far as the measurement model is concerned, the relationships among these factors are unanalyzed correlations. It is the structural model that interprets these correlations as resulting from a particular set of causal relationships among the latent variables.

In practice, the usual procedure is to solve the measurement and structural models simultaneously because, in so doing, one brings to bear all information available about each path. In Chapter 7 we discuss situations in which one might wish to solve them separately.

A solution of the model

Maruyama and McGarvey presented correlations among the 13 observed variables for a sample of 249 children--the correlations given in Table 3-1. One could, in principle, write path expressions for each of these 78 correlations in terms of the unknown paths and solve them for the path values, but Maruyama and McGarvey preferred to set up the appropriate LISREL matrices and let the program handle the details.

Table 3-1 Correlations among observed variables in desegregation study (data from Maruyama & McGarvey, 1980), N = 249

	SEI	EDH	R/P	VACH	VGR	RAV	PEA	FEV	MEV	TEV	SP	PP	WP
SEI	1.00												
EDHH	.56	1.00											
R/P	.17	.10	1.00										
VACH	.17	.30	.19	1.00									
VGR	.16	.21	-.04	.50	1.00								
RAV	.06	.15	-.00	.29	.28	1.00							
PEA	.16	.21	.28	.40	.19	.32	1.00						
FEV	.01	-.04	-.04	.01	.12	.10	-.06	1.00					
MEV	-.07	-.05	.00	.13	.27	.16	-.07	.42	1.00				
TEV	-.02	-.01	.04	.21	.27	.14	.08	.18	.31	1.00			
SPOP	.05	.04	.02	.28	.24	.08	.13	.07	.15	.25	1.00		
PPOP	.10	.10	-.04	.23	.18	.09	.17	.02	.08	.08	.59	1.00	
WPOP	.10	.17	-.03	.32	.40	.14	.17	.08	.17	.33	.55	.49	1.00

The results are shown in Fig. 3.3, in which all latent variables are standardized, so that these numbers are ordinary path coefficients and correlations. Residual variances are shown at the ends of the residual arrows.

The χ^2 for testing the goodness of fit of the model is 140.30, based on 59 degrees of freedom. A χ^2 of 140.30 based on 59 df is unlikely (p < .001) to occur with a sample of this size if the model of Fig. 3.1 truly holds in the population. Thus, we may reject the model. The sample size of 249 is not so huge that any trivial departure from the model would lead to its rejection, so we should probably take the negative outcome seriously. Further exploration might yield a better fitting version of the model; however, Maruyama and McGarvey did not pursue matters further at this point.

One feature of this model, the reciprocal paths between ACH and APR, represents a step beyond the models that we have so far considered. We look further at such looped models in the next chapter; for the moment we need merely note that with adequate data their solution in LISREL presents no

Fig. 3.3 Standardized solution to path diagram of Fig. 3.1 from correlations of Table 3-1.

special problems.

We need not go into all the details of Maruyama and McGarvey's solution procedure, but a few points may be helpful. First, as is usual with LISREL, the correlation matrix was treated as if it were a variance-covariance matrix, with $n(n + 1)/2 = 91$ distinct observed values--the 13 variances plus the 78 covariances on one side of the diagonal. Maruyama and McGarvey employed a mixed technique for scaling the latent variables. On the independent variable side they specified standardized latent variables, leaving 16 unknowns to be solved for in the measurement model: the $3 + 2 + 3 = 8$ paths from the latent variables SES, ABL, and ASA to the eight manifest variables measuring them, plus the corresponding 8 residual paths. On the dependent variable side of the measurement model, they fixed one path from each of the latent variables to 1.0, leaving only $1 + 2 = 3$ paths to be solved, plus the 5 residual paths, or 8 unknowns. Altogether, then, there are a total of $16 + 8 = 24$ unknown paths to be solved for in the measurement model.

In the structural model there are a total of 8 unknowns: 1 correlation among independent latent variables, 3 paths from independent to dependent latent variables, 2 reciprocal paths between the latter, and 2 residuals for the downstream latent variables. Thus, there are altogether $24 + 8 = 32$ unknowns to be solved for; and 91 observed values minus 32 unknowns yields the 59 df.

The initial solution provided by LISREL (using a maximum likelihood criterion) is thus standardized on the independent variable side but not on the dependent variable side; however, one can also request a fully standardized solution, and it is that which is reported in Fig. 3.3.

Confirmatory Factor Analysis

Traditionally, a latent variable analysis that is called a *confirmatory factor analysis* is one in which a hypothesized model is fit to a correlation matrix, the model being mainly a measurement model with the structural model confined to simple correlations among the latent variables. The restriction to correlation matrices, though usual, is not essential--covariance matrices can be factor analyzed, and sometimes are.

The main result of a factor analysis, as noted in Chapter 1, is a table showing the *factor pattern*, or values of the paths between the latent and observed variables. If the latent variables are correlated, there will also be a table of their intercorrelations (*factor intercorrelation matrix*). In the case of correlated factors, there may also be reported a table of the correlations between observed and latent variables (*factor structure matrix*).

A study of attitudes toward police

In Chapter 1 we considered some simple artificial examples of confirmatory factor analysis. Here we look at a case (McIver, Carmines, & Zeller, 1980) in which several hypotheses were fit to correlations based on a large real-life data set.

The correlations, from a study of attitudes toward police, are given in Table 3-2. They are based on telephone interviews with a total of some 11,000

Table 3-2 Correlations among nine items in police survey (data from McIver, Carmines, & Zeller, 1980)

	1	2	3	4	5	6	7	8	9
1. Police service	1.00	.50	.41	.33	.28	.30	-.24	-.23	-.20
2. Responsiveness	.48	1.00	.35	.29	.26	.27	-.19	-.19	-.18
3. Response time	.42	.37	1.00	.30	.27	.29	-.17	-.16	-.14
4. Honesty	.34	.30	.26	1.00	.52	.48	-.13	-.11	-.15
5. Courtesy	.31	.27	.24	.51	1.00	.44	-.11	-.09	-.10
6. Equal treatment	.29	.26	.23	.48	.44	1.00	-.15	-.13	-.13
7. Burglary	-.24	-.21	-.19	-.14	-.13	-.13	1.00	.58	.47
8. Vandalism	-.22	-.19	-.17	-.13	-.12	-.11	.58	1.00	.42
9. Robbery	-.18	-.16	-.14	-.11	-.10	-.09	.47	.42	1.00

Note: Original correlations are above diagonal; those implied by 3-factor solution are below it.

respondents in 60 neighborhoods in three U.S. metropolitan areas. Included in the table are the intercorrelations among six items reflecting attitudes toward the quality of police services, plus three items having to do with the likelihood of burglary, vandalism, and robbery in the neighborhood.

The authors had originally surmised that the six attitude items might form a single general dimension of attitude toward police, and indeed they are all mutually positively intercorrelated in Table 3-2. But inspection of the table suggested that there might be two distinct subclasses of attitude items, judging from somewhat higher correlations within than across item subsets. The first three items, having to do with the general quality of police services, their responsiveness to citizen needs, and the rapidity with which the police answered a call, seemed to go together, as did the second three, having to do with the personal qualities of the police--their honesty, courtesy, and fairness. The three items concerning the likelihood of various kinds of crime also seemed to group together and to be mildly negatively correlated with the first six items having to do with the perceived quality of the police service.

Consequently, a hypothesis of three correlated factors was fit to the data. (The fact that this hypothesis was arrived at on the basis of preliminary inspection of the data means that the chi-square tests should not be regarded as yielding strict probabilities, but rather as more informal indices of goodness of fit.)

Table 3-3 gives the results of fitting the hypothetical three-factor model shown in Fig. 3.4. Each item has a substantial loading on its corresponding factor. The first two factors of police attitudes are substantially correlated (r = .62), and the third, crime factor, is negatively correlated with both, more highly with the first factor (police service) than with the second (personal qualities of the police). The communalities (h^2), which in this case are simply

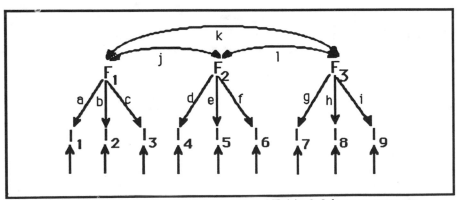

Fig. 3.4 Simple three-factor model for data of Table 3-2 from survey on attitudes toward police (McIver et al., 1980).

equal to the squares of the individual paths *a, b, c,* and so forth (see Fig. 3.4 for the reason), suggest that only about half the item variance is being accounted for by the common factors, with the rest presumably due to specific factors and error.

The three common factors were assumed to be in standard-score form. Forty-five observed variances and covariances (9 x 10 / 2) were fit using 21 unknowns (*a* through *l*, in Fig. 3.4, plus the 9 residuals), leaving 24 df for the χ^2 test. The obtained χ^2, with this huge sample, is a highly significant 225.10. Nevertheless, the solution does a fairly good job of accounting for the data. Correlations implied by the solution of Table 3-3 are shown in Table 3-2, below the principal diagonal. The largest discrepancy between observed and expected correlations is .06, and the bulk of the differences are .02 or less. For many purposes one might be perfectly content with this good a fit.

However, the discrepancies of .04, .03, and .06 of item 3 (police response time) with items 4 through 6 (personal qualities) suggest that the fit might be improved a little if F_2 as well as F_1 were allowed to influence item 3. Such a

Table 3-3 Factor pattern and factor intercorrelations for model of Fig. 3.4 (McIver et al., 1980)

	Factor pattern			
Item	F_1	F_2	F_3	h^2
1. Police service	.74	.00	.00	.55
2. Responsiveness	.65	.00	.00	.42
3. Response time	.57	.00	.00	.32
4. Honesty	.00	.75	.00	.56
5. Courtesy	.00	.68	.00	.46
6. Equal treatment	.00	.64	.00	.41
7. Burglary	.00	.00	.80	.64
8. Vandalism	.00	.00	.72	.52
9. Robbery	.00	.00	.59	.35

	Factor intercorrelations		
	F_1	F_2	F_3
F_1	1.00	.62	-.41
F_2		1.00	-.24
F_3			1.00

$\chi^2 = 225.10$, 24 df, p < .001

solution yielded a reduction of χ^2 from 225.10 to 128.00, at the cost of one degree of freedom--a very substantial improvement in goodness of fit. Substantively, however, the change makes little difference except in the paths to item 3 (the path from F_1 drops from .57 to .45 as that from F_2 rises from 0 to .15; the estimated correlation of F_1 and F_2 also drops slightly, from .62 to .59).

The authors went on to test models allowing the residuals to be correlated for a couple of pairs of variables, 4 and 9, and 2 and 7, further reducing the χ^2 to 90.33. This is still a highly significant improvement, if one takes the χ^2s seriously, but as this amounts to introducing new factors to explain the discrepancies of single correlations, it is not very helpful from the point of view of parsimony.

The overall χ^2 is still highly significant with 21 df, despite the fact that at this stage the data are being fit very much ad hoc. With very large samples one needs to be careful not to confuse statistical with practical significance. Some of the small deviations of the data from the model may indeed not be due to chance, but to introduce a hypothetical variable to account for each one of them is unlikely to be of much value for either science or practice.

Some Psychometric Applications of Path and Structural Models

A number of problems in psychometrics lend themselves to latent variable methods. We considered an example involving test reliability in Chapter 1. In the present section, we look at examples involving parallel and congeneric tests, and the separation of trait and method variance.

Parallel and congeneric tests

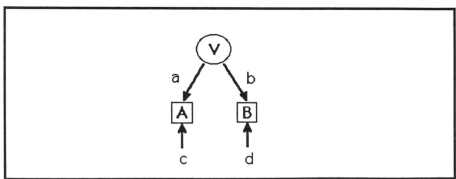

Fig. 3.5 Parallel or congeneric tests.

st, some definitions: Two tests are said by psychometricians to be *parallel* if
y share equal amounts of a common factor, and each also has the same
ount of specific variance. Consider Fig. 3.5. If tests A and B are parallel, *a*
d *b* would be equal, and so would *c* and *d*. V would represent the common
tor the two tests share.

Tests are said to be *congeneric* if they share a common factor, but not
cessarily to the same degree. Tests A and B would still be congeneric--
cause they share V--even if *a* were not equal to *b*, nor *c* to *d*. (We
countered also in Chapter 2 a third, intermediate condition, *tau-equivalence*,
which *a =b*, but *c ≠d*; however, this will not be involved in the present
ample.)

Jöreskog provided a structural analysis of some data gathered by
A. Lord on four vocabulary tests. Tests A and B were short tests given under
surely conditions, whereas C and D were longer tests given under time
essure. The variance-covariance matrix of the four tests is given in Table 3-4.

Jöreskog carried out tests of four hypotheses, which can be expressed in
ms of Fig. 3.6 by imposing the conditions noted in parentheses:

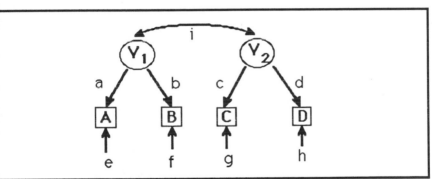

g. **3.6** Hypotheses about parallel and congeneric tests.

H1: Tests A and B are parallel, as are C and D, and all four tests are congeneric
=*b*, *e =f*; *c =d*, *g =h*; the correlation *i* =1.0--that is, V_1 and V_2 are identical except
ssibly for scale).

H2: Both test pairs are parallel, as in H1, but the two pairs are not
cessarily congeneric (*a =b*, *e =f*; *c =d*, *g =h*).

H3: All four tests are congeneric but are not necessarily parallel (*i* =1.0).

H4: A and B are congeneric, as are C and D, but the two pairs need not be
ngeneric with each other (Fig. 3.6 as it stands).

Note that these hypotheses form two nested series, H1, H2, H4, and H1, H3, H4,
thin which χ^2 comparisons may be made.

Table 3-4 Covariance matrix for four vocabulary tests (Jöreskog & Sörbom, 1979, p. 55; data from Lord), N = 649

Test	A	B	C	D
A	86.40			
B	57.78	86.26		
C	56.87	59.32	97.28	
D	58.90	59.67	73.82	97.82

Table 3-5 Hypothesis tests for problem of Fig. 3.5 with data of Table 3-4 (after Jöreskog & Sörbom, 1979, p. 55)

Model	Unknowns	χ^2	df	p
H1	4	37.33	6	<.01
H2	5	1.93	5	.86
H3	8	36.21	2	<.01
H4	9	.70	1	.70

Model comparison	χ^2_{diff}	df	p
H2 vs H1	35.40	1	<.01
H4 vs H3	35.51	1	<.01
H3 vs H1	1.12	4	>.80
H4 vs H2	1.23	4	>.80

Table 3-5 shows the results of several χ^2 tests. In the upper part of the table the models representing the four hypotheses are tested individually. Models H1 and H3 can be rejected; models H2 and H4 cannot. The rejected models H1 and H3 contain the assumption that all four tests are congeneric, whereas models H2 and H4 do not contain this assumption.

The specific comparisons of H2 versus H1 and H4 versus H3 (bottom part of Table 3-5) represent pairs of models that are equivalent except for the assumption that tests A and B are congeneric with tests C and D. Both comparisons show that this assumption is not tenable. The other two comparisons shown, H3 versus H1, and H4 versus H2, test whether A is parallel to B and C is parallel to D. These assumptions remain quite tenable.

Note that the sample size is fairly large (N = 649). Although A and B have been shown to be noncongeneric with C and D by large χ^2s, the two pairs of tests are not in fact *very* different. The correlation *i* was estimated in the solution to model H2 as approximately .90, suggesting that although the speeded and unspeeded vocabulary tests are not measuring quite the same thing, what they measure does not differ much for practical purposes.

Fitting one of these psychometric models is equivalent to carrying out a confirmatory factor analysis. Another psychometric model that shares this character is the multitrait-multimethod model, to which we now turn.

Multitrait-multimethod models

The *multitrait-multimethod model* (Campbell & Fiske,1959) is an approach to psychological measurement that attempts to separate out true variance on psychological traits from variance due to measurement methods. The basic strategy is to measure each of several traits by each of several methods. Correlations among these measurements are arranged in a multitrait-multimethod matrix that enables one to assess *convergent validity*, the tendency for different measurement operations to converge on the same underlying trait, and *discriminant validity*, the ability to discriminate among different traits.

Table 3-6 is an example of a multitrait-multimethod correlation matrix. It is based on part of a study by Bentler and McClain (1976) in which 68 fifth-grade girls were measured in each of three ways on four personality variables: impulsivity, extraversion, academic achievement motivation, and test anxiety.

For the self-rating measure, each of the girls filled out four standard personality questionnaires, one for each trait. For the teacher ratings, teachers were asked to rank the children in their class on each of the four variables under consideration. Their ratings were converted to scores using a normalizing transformation.

The peer ratings were obtained by a sociometric procedure, in which children in the class were asked to write the names of children who fit various descriptions. Four to eight items were used per trait. An example of an item for extraversion was: "Which children like to be with other children a lot?"

The off-diagonal elements in a multitrait-multimethod matrix such as Table 3-6 can be classified into three groups. In the triangles adjacent to the main diagonal are *within-method, cross-trait* correlations. They are underlined in Table 3-6. An example would be the .42 at the start of the third row, the correlation between extraversion and impulsivity, both measured by peer ratings. In the diagonals of the square blocks in the rest of the table, given in boldface type, are the *within-trait, cross-method* correlations, also known as the *validity diagonals*. An example would be the .64 at the start of the fifth row, the correlation between peer and trait assessments of extraversion. The remaining, unmarked off-diagonal elements are the *cross-trait, cross-method* correlations.

Table 3-6 Multitrait-multimethod correlation matrix for four traits measured by peer, teacher, and self-ratings (data from Bentler & Lee, 1979), N = 68

Trait and method of measurement

	Ep	Ap	Ip	Mp	Et	At	It	Mt	Es	As	Is	Ms
Ep	1.00											
Ap	-.38	1.00										
Ip	.42	-.21	1.00									
Mp	-.25	.54	-.54	1.00								
Et	**.64**	-.15	.26	-.05	1.00							
At	-.29	**.66**	-.19	.44	-.25	1.00						
It	.38	-.09	**.56**	-.19	.59	-.14	1.00					
Mt	-.22	.51	-.33	**.66**	.06	.62	-.05	1.00				
Es	**.45**	-.05	.12	.10	**.50**	-.05	.36	.17	1.00			
As	.04	**.38**	-.03	.14	.08	**.30**	.09	.16	.02	1.00		
Is	.33	-.13	**.35**	-.18	.41	-.14	**.45**	-.13	.43	.16	1.00	
Ms	-.21	.37	-.44	**.58**	-.01	.41	-.10	**.62**	.06	.04	-.37	1.00

Note: Trait: E = extraversion, A = test anxiety, I = impulsivity, M = academic achievement motivation. Rater: p = peer, t = teacher, s = self. Correlations: underlined = within-method, cross-trait; boldface = within-trait, cross-method.

High correlations in the validity diagonals are evidence of *convergent validity*, the agreement of different methods of measuring the same trait. Low correlations elsewhere provide evidence of *discriminant validity*, that the putatively different traits really are distinct. Within-method, cross-trait correlations in excess of cross-method, cross-trait correlations are evidence of the presence of *method variance*, associations among measures stemming from properties of the measurement methods used.

In Table 3-6 the correlations in the validity diagonals are generally positive and appreciable in size (.30 to .66, with a mean of .51), suggesting reasonable convergent validity. They tend to be decidedly higher than the cross-method, cross-trait correlations (mean absolute value of .20), indicating some degree of discriminant validity. However, the latter correlations are by no means always negligible (they range up to about .50), suggesting some overlap among the traits. The within-method, cross-trait correlations (mean absolute value of .28) are slightly higher than the cross-method, cross-trait correlations; thus, there appears to be some method variance.

Such a multitrait-multimethod matrix can be represented by a path model in the manner shown in Fig. 3.7. The 12 observed variables are shown in the center row of the figure. Four latent variables representing true scores on

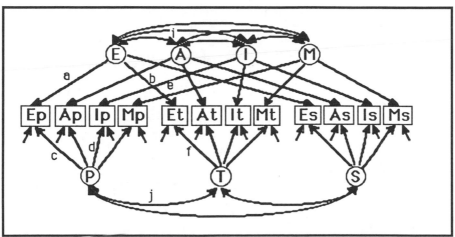

Fig. 3.7 Path model of multitrait-multimethod matrix of Table 3-6.

the four traits are shown in the circles at the top of the diagram. Three latent variables representing the effects of the three methods are shown in the circles at the bottom. Each observed measurement is determined by a trait and a method (e.g., arrows *a* and *c* for Ep), plus a residual. The traits may be intercorrelated--for example, extraversion and impulsivity might be related (arrow *i*). So might the methods--for example, peer and teacher ratings (arrow *j*). However, it is assumed in this particular diagram that the design of the experiment has insured that there will be no systematic correlations between methods and traits (no curved arrows connecting the top and bottom circles).

Within-trait, cross-method correlations are produced by direct paths via the trait in question, and possibly by indirect paths via the correlations among methods. For example, the correlation between peer and teacher ratings of extraversion may be expressed as:

$$r_{EpEt} = ab + cjf.$$

Within-method, cross-trait correlations are the other way around--direct paths via methods and indirect paths via possible correlations among traits. For example, the correlation between peer ratings of extraversion and impulsivity may be expressed as:

$$r_{EpIp} = cd + aie.$$

Cross-method, cross-trait correlations are produced only via indirect paths of both kinds. For example:

$$r_{IpEt} = eib + djf.$$

The model of Fig. 3.7 involves 12 paths from traits to measures, 12 paths from methods to measures, 12 residuals, 6 intercorrelations among traits, and 3 intercorrelations among measures, a total of 45 unknowns to be estimated from 78 observed variances and covariances (12 x 13 / 2), leaving 33 degrees of freedom for a χ^2 goodness-of-fit test. (This assumes standardized factors: Alternatively, one could set seven paths, one per factor, to 1.0, and solve instead for the seven factor variances, leaving the number of df unchanged at 33.)

A solution of the path model by Bentler and Lee (1979) is given in Table 3-7. The values of the 12 paths from the trait factors to the measurements are given in the first subtable. Obviously, the measurements are substantially determined by the traits--somewhat more so for the peer and teacher ratings than for the self-ratings.

Determination of the measurements by the methods is shown in the second subtable. On the whole, these numbers are a bit lower than those in the first part of the table, but they are by no means all low--measurements of impulsivity, for example, seem to be about as much determined by methods (third column of second table) as by the trait (third row of first table).

The trait factors are substantially interrelated (third subtable). Test anxiety and academic achievement motivation tend to go together, as do extraversion and impulsivity, with the two pairs negatively related to each other. The method factors (fourth subtable) are fairly independent of one another, except for a modest correlation betwen teacher and self-ratings.

Bentler and Lee fit their model using a generalized least squares criterion, obtaining a χ^2 of 43.88 with 35 df, indicating a tolerable fit (p > .10). They had 35 df rather than 33 because they additionally set the unique variances of two variables, Mp and Is, to zero. (This was done to forestall a tendency for these variances to go negative during the solution, an awkward event known in factor analytic circles as a "Heywood case.") Negative variances of any kind are, of course, not possible in the real world. Empirical measures with no unique variance are also implausible, because this implies, among other things, the absence of errors of measurement. Thus, the present solution, although an adequate fit statistically, cannot be regarded as completely satisfactory. (Actually, Bentler and Lee fit several other hypothetical models to these data as well--the interested reader can consult their article for details.)

Table 3-7 Solution to model of Fig. 3.7 for data of Table 3-6 (after Bentler & Lee, 1979, Table 7)

Trait factors	Peer	Ratings Teacher	Self	
Extraversion	.98	.62	.42	
Anxiety	.77	.91	.35	
Impulsivity	.78	.64	.42	
Motivation	.72	.90	.66	
Method factors	E	Traits A	I	M
Peer ratings	.15	-.25	.32	-.68
Teacher ratings	.74	-.19	.49	.13
Self ratings	.34	.17	.89	-.22

Trait factor intercorrelations

	E	A	I	M
Extraversion	1.00	-.35	.52	-.24
Anxiety		1.00	-.26	.74
Impulsivity			1.00	-.48
Motivation				1.00

Method factor intercorrelations

	P	T	S
Peer ratings	1.00	.08	.04
Teacher ratings		1.00	.32
Self ratings			1.00

Testing the relationship between trait and method variance

The previous section, on multitrait-multimethod matrices, showed how latent variable analysis could be used to assess the relative contribution of trait scores and measurement methods to observed scores. In this section we consider a related problem: whether, for a particular questionnaire scale, a certain artifact occurs, and if it does, whether it tends to be correlated with the true score.

The particular questionnaire scale considered is the Psychasthenia (*Pt*) scale of the MMPI. This is a scale that purports to measure certain tendencies toward anxiety, obsessive worrying, and lack of confidence. It happens, however, that most of the items on this scale are expressed in such a way that agreeing with them gives one a high score on *Pt*, and disagreeing with them gives one a low score. This raises an alternative possibility. Suppose there are people who are just generally inclined to agree to anything--call them "acquiescent." Given the nature of the *Pt* items, individuals with a strong general tendency toward acquiescence would also get high *Pt* scores. So what, in fact, does *Pt* measure--a trait of psychasthenia, a trait of acquiescence, or both?

One method that has been used to study this question is to reverse the wording of items and see how this affects responses. If a person says "true" to an item like "I worry a great deal," you don't know whether he is a worrier or an agreer. But if you later give him the item "I worry very little," his response will give you a clue. If he says "true" again, you judge him to be an agreer. If he says "false," you judge him to be a worrier.

Bramble and Wiley (1974) used a latent variable approach to address this question, analyzing data from original and reversed versions of the *Pt* scale that had been gathered earlier by Bock, Dicken, and Van Pelt (1969). A group of 81 undergraduates had taken the *Pt* items in their original and reversed forms on two occasions. Figure 3.8 gives a path model representing this situation. Three latent variables are postulated: the true trait of psychasthenia, the trait of acquiescence, and a third latent variable representing change between occasions of testing.

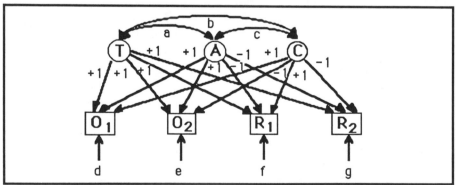

Fig. 3.8 Path model for original and reversed versions of an MMPI scale administered on two occasions. T = trait, A = acquiescence, C = temporal change; O = original items, R = reversed items; 1,2 = two occasions of testing.

As seen in the figure, Bramble and Wiley adopted a slightly different strategy than has been used in the examples so far, although it is still a variant of confirmatory factor analysis.

They set the paths from the latent to observed variables at fixed values to reflect the theoretical design of the experiment and solved for the variances of the latent variables T, A, and C, the covariances *a, b,* and *c* among them, and the specific variances *d, e, f,* and *g,* under various hypotheses.

The scales are assumed all to be keyed to measure the trait, so that a large amount of the true trait will always contribute positively to the obtained score: hence the positive signs on all the paths from T. A tendency toward acquiescence would work in the same direction for the original scales (paths of +1.0 from A to O_1 and O_2) but would work in the opposite direction for scales with reversed items (paths of -1.0 from A to R_1 and R_2). The signs of the paths from C are taken so that tests given on the same occasion will tend to have an increment in correlation (O_1 and R_1, O_2, and R_2), whereas tests given on different occasions will have lowered correlations (O_1 with R_2, O_2 with R_1).

Bramble and Wiley considered four models, based on the following hypotheses:

H1: T, A, and C are uncorrelated, and all residual variances are equal ($a = b = c = 0$, $d = e = f = g$; 4 unknowns--variances T, A, C, and the residual variance; 6 df).

H2: T, A, and C are uncorrelated, but residual variances may be unequal ($a = b = c = 0$; 7 unknowns, 3 df).

H3: Residual variances equal, but T, A, and C may be correlated ($d = e = f = g$; 7 unknowns, 3 df).

H4: T, A, and C correlated and unequal residual variances (Fig. 3.8 as it stands; 10 unknowns, 0 df).

Table 3-8 shows the results for *Pt,* based on the data of Bock et al. given

Table 3-8 χ^2 tests of various hypotheses, based on path model of Fig. 3.8 and data of Table 3-9

Model	Unknowns	χ^2	df	p
H1	4	14.46	6	<.05
H2	7	10.70	3	<.02
H3	7	2.61	3	>.30
H4	10	0.00	0	1.00
Comparisons		χ^2_{diff}	df	p
H1 vs H2		3.76	3	>.10
H1 vs H3		11.85	3	<.01

Table 3-9 Observed variance-covariance matrix for *Pt* scale, for path model of Fig. 3.8 (data from Bock, Dicken, & Van Pelt, 1969), N = 81

Scale version	O_1	O_2	R_1	R_2
Original, time 1	34.82			
Original, time 2	30.52	35.00		
Reversed, time 1	28.18	24.84	29.38	
Reversed, time 2	25.52	27.61	22.32	26.78

in Table 3-9. Models H1 and H2, which assume uncorrelated T, A, and C, do not fit the data; model H3, which assumes equal residual variances, does fit. (Model H4, with as many unknowns as observations, also fits the data, of course.)

The direct comparison of H3 and H1, identical except for the presence or absence of correlation among T, A, and C, shows that allowing T, A, and C to be correlated yields a statistically significant improvement in fit (p < .01).

Table 3-10 shows the values of the unknowns that gave the best fit for model H3, using a maximum likelihood criterion. Also shown is the

Table 3-10 Fitted values for model H3, and implied covariance matrix

Unknown	Estimate	Standardized
s^2_T	27.16	1.00
s^2_A	.62	1.00
s^2_C	1.36	1.00
cov_{TA}	1.88	.46
cov_{AC}	-.26	-.28
cov_{TC}	.22	.04
s^2_{resid}	2.36	

Implied variance-covariance matrix

	O_1	O_2	R_1	R_2
O_1	35.18			
O_2	30.18	35.32		
R_1	28.34	24.66	28.70	
R_2	25.70	27.45	22.66	26.78

standardized version of the solution, which provides the correlations among the three latent variables. At the bottom of the table is the variance-covariance matrix implied by the solution under H3.

From the implied variance-covariance matrix, we see that the model does a reasonable job of fitting the data--the largest absolute discrepancy from the observed data is .68 and the median is .25. From the standardized solution we see that there is a modest positive correlation of .46 estimated between the trait factor *Pt* and the method factor of acquiescence; that is, scores on psychasthenia could be mildly inflated by a tendency for those high on the trait also to be acquiescent. However, if one compares the estimated trait variance with the variance of O_1, which would represent the typical single administration of the original test, one finds that 77% of the variance (27.16/35.18) appears to be due to the trait, with only about 11% (2 x 1.88 / 35.18) due to the covariation of *Pt* and acquiescence, and 2% (.62/35.18) attributable to acquiescence as such.

Structural Models--Controlling Extraneous Variables

The technique of partial correlation, and the related method of analysis of covariance, are often used by social scientists to examine relationships between certain variables when other, potentially distorting variables are held statistically constant. Users of these methods sometimes do not realize that the partialled variable or covariate is assumed to be measured without error, and that if this is not the case, very misleading conclusions may be drawn.

Figure 3.9 provides a simple example. A correlation between latent variables A and B is assumed in the model to be due wholly to a third variable C that influences them both; removing the effect of this third variable should,

Latent variables A, B, C:
r_{AB} = .64
$r_{AB \cdot C}$ = .00

Observed variables X, Y, Z:
r_{XY} = .5184
$r_{XZ} = r_{YZ}$ = .504

$$r_{XY \cdot Z} = \frac{r_{XY} - r_{XZ} \cdot r_{YZ}}{\sqrt{(1 - r_{XZ}^2)(1 - r_{YZ}^2)}} = .3544$$

Fig. 3.9 Example of misleading partial correlation when partialled variable C is imperfectly measured by Z.

therefore, result in a partial correlation $r_{AB \cdot C} = 0$. But see what happens when C is measured with considerable error, and one applies the traditional formula for partial correlation. An observed correlation of .52 between A and B is reduced only to .35, perhaps leading an unsuspecting reader to believe that A and B are connected in other ways than through C. A structural analysis based on an appropriate path model, even with quite rough estimates of the reliabilities of measurement of A, B, and C, should provide a much less misleading picture.

Analyzing a quasi-experiment--the effect of Head Start

Table 3-11 presents some data from a study on the effects of a Head Start program on children's cognitive skills. Two measures of the latter were used--the Illinois Test of Psycholinguistic Abilities and the Metropolitan Readiness Test, both taken after completion of the Head Start program; they were also given to a control group of nonparticipants.

As you can see from Table 3-11, the correlations between participating in Head Start and scores on the two tests assessing cognitive ability are on the face of it a little embarrassing to proponents of Head Start--although they are small, they are in the wrong direction: Participants in the program did a little worse than members of the control group.

Table 3-11 Correlations among variables in Head Start evaluation (data from Bentler & Woodward, 1978), N = 303

	MEd	FEd	FOc	Inc	HS	ITPA	MRT
Mother's education	1.00	.47	.24	.30	-.12	.26	.28
Father's education	.47	1.00	.28	.21	-.08	.25	.22
Father's occupation	.27	.24	1.00	.41	-.22	.22	.26
Income	.29	.23	.41	1.00	-.18	.12	.19
Head Start participation	-.10	-.11	-.21	-.18	1.00	-.10	-.09
ITPA score	.26	.24	.25	.15	-.10	1.00	.65
MRT score	.26	.24	.25	.15	-.10	.65	1.00

Note: ITPA = Illinois Test of Psycholinguistic Abilities, MRT = Metropolitan Readiness Test. Original correlations are above diagonal, correlations predicted by fitted model are below it.

But there were also negative correlations between Head Start participation and various parental educational and economic measures-- apparently the control group members were selected from families somewhat better off than those from which the Head Start children came. Could this account for the results?

Figure 3.10 represents a path model proposed by Bentler and Woodward (1978). (It is actually only one of several considered in their article, but we confine ourselves to this one.) The model involves five latent variables. The four main source variables include the independent variable, Head Start participation, and three variables describing family background--a general socioeconomic status variable (SES) common to all four of the observed socioeconomic indicators, and two variables capturing specific aspects of education and economic circumstances. (As the diagram indicates, Bentler and Woodward assumed that these latter two might be correlated with each other, and that all three might be correlated with Head Start participation.)

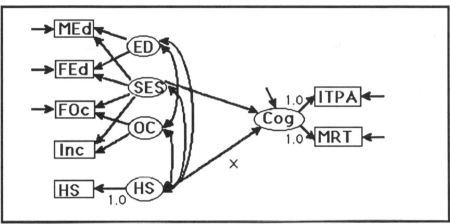

Fig. 3.10 Path diagram of a Head Start evaluation. *x* = path showing effect of Head Start participation on cognitive skills.

Other assumptions made in the diagram were that general SES and Head Start participation were the avenues of any influence of the source variables on cognitive skills, that cognitive skills were equally well measured by the two tests, and that Head Start participation and family income were measured without error. (One could certainly argue with some of these assumptions, but we proceed with the example. You might find it instructive to try fitting some other variations of the model to the data.)

The latent variables were taken as standardized except for Cognitive Skills (Cog), which was assigned arbitrary paths of 1.0 to the observed variables (themselves standardized).

The crucial path, marked *x* in the diagram, describes the direct influence of Head Start on cognitive skills when the other variables are held constant. Is it positive (Head Start helps) or negative (Head Start hinders), and--in either case--does it differ significantly from zero?

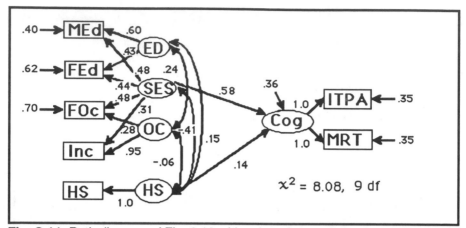

Fig. 3.11 Path diagram of Fig. 3.10 with values from solution including Head Start effect.

Figure 3.11 shows the values of the paths and the variance of the latent variable Cognitive Skills that were obtained in a solution using LISREL with the data of Table 3-11. Observe that when the socioeconomic statuses of the participants and the controls are taken into account, the estimate of the effect of Head Start participation on cognitive skills is slightly positive (.14).

The obtained χ^2 of 8.08 with 9 degrees of freedom represents a reasonably good fit to the data for the model as a whole, a fact that is also indicated by the reproduced correlations (shown below the diagonal in Table 3-11). However, Bentler and Woodward quite properly went on to test whether the particular path representing Head Start effects differed significantly from zero, by comparing the result with it included to that from a model that was identical except that this path was set to zero. The obtained χ^2 for the latter model is 9.93. The difference between the two χ^2s, 1.85, when tested as a χ^2 with 1 df, is well short of conventional levels of statistical significance (p > .10). Bentler and Woodward concluded, accordingly, that these data could not be said to demonstrate any effect of Head Start, positive or negative.

A note on degrees of freedom may be helpful. The model was treated as a covariance model with standardized latent independent variables. Twenty-eight (7 x 8 / 2) observed variances and covariances were fitted. Nineteen unknowns were solved for: 4 correlations among the source variables; 2 paths from source variables to Cog and 8 to the observed variables; the residual to Cog; and 4 different residuals to observed variables (those to ITPA and MRT are forced by the model to be the same). Twenty-eight data points minus 19 unknowns equals 9 degrees of freedom. In the second model, with one less path to be solved for, there are 10 df.

Chapter 3 Notes

You might like to look at other published examples from the literature involving models like those in this chapter. Here is a sampling of some model-fitting studies on assorted topics (full citations are given in the reference list at the back of the book). If you want still more examples, a list of 72 structural modeling studies in personality and social psychology appearing between 1977 and 1987 is given in Breckler (1990).

A. J. Fredericks & D. L. Dossett (1983)--a paper exploring attitude-behavior relationships.

J. E. Hunter, D. W. Gerbing, & F. J. Boster (1982)--Machiavellian beliefs and personality.

G. Donaldson (1983)--models of information-processing stages.

W. M. Mason, J. S. House, & S. S. Martin (1985)--dimensions of political alienation.

M. D. Newcomb & P. M. Bentler (1983)--dimensions of the female orgasmic experience.

R. L. Baker, B. Mednick, & W. Brock (1984)--health problems in early infancy.

H. W. Marsh & D. Hocevar (1983)--a multitrait-multimethod analysis of university teaching evaluations.

P. M. Homer & L. R. Kahle (1988)--attitudes, values, and behaviors concerning natural foods.

R. G. Walters & S. B. MacKenzie (1988)--the effect of special promotions on supermarket sales.

A. R. McIntosh & F. Gonzalez-Lima (1991)--modeling neural systems in the brains of rats.

C. E. Lance (1991)--Job satisfaction, organizational commitment and turnover.

Caution: Numerical results given in this and the following chapter sometimes differ slightly from those reported in the original sources, presumably because of differences in rounding, slight convergence discrepancies, minor misprints in correlation tables, or the like. I have not recomputed everything, but if a study forms the basis of an exercise, I have tried to provide consistent figures.

Maruyama-McGarvey study. There is some inconsistency in the labeling of variables in the original paper. I have followed the identifications in their Table 2, which according to Maruyama (personal communication) are the correct ones.

Bramble-Wiley analysis. They actually used paths of ± 1/2 rather than ±1, which I have preferred for simplicity of presentation. This only affects the scale of the rawscore estimates, not the fit of the models or the standardized solution.

Multitrait-multimethod models. K. F. Widaman (1985) discusses hierarchically nested models for MTMM data, and Schmitt and Stults (1986) review different methods of analyzing MTMM matrices. Marsh and Hocevar (1988) suggest the use of second-order confirmatory factor analysis to allow the separation of error and uniqueness in MTMM analyses. There has been recent interest in MTMM models that multiply the effects of traits and methods instead of adding them (e.g., Cudeck, 1988; Wothke & Browne, 1990; Verhees & Wansbeek, 1990). Wothke and Browne show how multiplicative models can be fit using standard programs such as LISREL. Although such models are attractive in theory, there is some evidence that in practice additive ones are more often successful (Bagozzi & Yi, 1990).

Chapter 3 Exercises

As before, other programs may be used for model-fitting, at the discretion of the instructor.

1. Can you conclude that tests T1 to T3, whose covariance matrix is given below, are not parallel tests? (N = 35) How about *tau* -equivalent?

	T1	T2	T3
T1	54.85		
T2	60.21	99.24	
T3	48.42	67.00	63.81

2. Solve McIver et al.'s police survey model (Fig. 3.4) using IPSOL, and compare to the results of Table 3-3. (Yes, it will require writing 36 equations.)

3. Part of Campbell and Fiske's original multitrait-multimethod matrix is given in Table 3-12. These are ratings of clinical psychology trainees by staff members, fellow trainees, and themselves. Tabulate and compare the correlations in the three principal categories (within trait, across method; within method, across trait; and across both method and trait).

4. Estimate a multitrait-multimethod model for the data of Table 3-12, using LISREL or another program (in LISREL 7 you may need to set AD=OFF to obtain a solution). Assume that the methods are uncorrelated, and that the traits are uncorrelated with the methods. Compare to the results of models using trait factors only and method factors only.

Table 3-12 Multitrait-multimethod matrix (data from Campbell & Fiske, 1959), N = 124

	As	Cs	Ss	At	Ct	St	Ao	Co	So
				Trait and method					
Ratings:									
Staff									
Assertive	1.00								
Cheerful	.37	1.00							
Serious	-.24	-.14	1.00						
Trainee									
Assertive	.71	.35	-.18	1.00					
Cheerful	.39	.53	-.15	.37	1.00				
Serious	-.27	-.31	.43	-.15	-.19	1.00			
Self									
Assertive	.48	.31	-.22	.46	.36	-.15	1.00		
Cheerful	.17	.42	-.10	.09	.24	-.25	.23	1.00	
Serious	-.04	-.13	.22	-.04	-.11	.31	-.05	-.12	1.00

5. Estimate a null model (all correlations zero) for the data of Table 3-12. Calculate goodness-of-fit and parsimonious goodness-of-fit indices for the various solutions of problem 4. Discuss your results.

6. For the Bock et al. data (Table 3-9), use LISREL or another program to test the hypothesis that the trait and acquiescence variances are equal. (Assume equal residual variances.)

7. Calculate the original and partial correlations r_{XY} and $r_{XY \cdot Z}$--see Fig. 3.9--for the following additional values of the path from C to Z: .9, 1.0, .5, .0. Comment on the results.

8. Keep the measurement model from Maruyama and McGarvey's desegregation study but make one or more plausible changes in the structural model. Fit your model, using LISREL or another program, and compare the results to those in Fig. 3.3.

9. Construct a different path model for the Head Start evaluation data (Table 3-11), with different latent variables and hypothesized relations among them. Retain in your model the dependent latent variable of Cognitive Skills and a path x to it from Head Start participation. Fit your model and make a χ^2 test for the significance of path x.

Chapter Four:
Varieties of Path and Structural Models--II

In this chapter we continue our survey of a variety of applications of path and structural models. The models considered introduce some additional features over those discussed in Chapter 3. We begin by looking at a model containing reciprocal influences and correlated errors. Then we consider several models dealing with events over time. Finally, we consider models fitted across different groups.

Models With Reciprocal Influences and Correlated Errors

Most of the models considered so far have been unlooped, that is, they have no causal sequences that loop back on themselves either remotely (A causes B causes C causes A) or immediately (A causes B causes A). The latter are usually described as models with reciprocal influences, because A influences B and B influences A. Also, most of the models considered so far have uncorrelated residuals; that is, the miscellaneous unspecified residual causes that influence a given variable are assumed uncorrelated with any other specific or residual causes in the diagram.

Violations of either of these conditions create problems for Wright's rules and for path analyses carried out by ordinary regression methods, although it is possible to deal with them by various special techniques, such as two-stage least squares (e.g., James & Singh, 1978). However, these conditions do not present any special difficulties for the general iterative model-fitting procedures described in this book provided the models are adequately identified, that is, are sufficently well-rooted in data to yield definite solutions. In practice, such models often give trouble--assuring identification is sometimes not easy when loops or correlated errors are present, and convergence on a solution may be more difficult to attain--but in principle one simply specifies the model in the usual way and presents it to the iterative program. If the program can't solve the model, it responds in the same manner as it would for any other underspecified model or unsatisfactory set of starting values.

A study of career aspirations

Table 4-1 presents a set of data from a classic and much analyzed study by Duncan, Haller, and Portes (1968), in which both reciprocal influences and correlated residuals are involved. The original data were gathered in a study of career aspirations (Haller & Butterworth, 1960) in which 442 seventeen-year-old boys in a southern Michigan county were given tests and questionnaires. There were 329 boys in the sample naming at least one other boy also in the sample as one of their best friends. Thus, there were 329 instances of a boy and a close friend, on both of whom similar data on abilities, background, and career aspirations were available. (There are some statistical issues raised by taking both boys and friends from the same sample, but we ignore them here.)

Table 4-1 Correlations among variables related to career aspirations of boys and their friends (data from Duncan, Haller, & Portes, 1968), N = 329

Respondent	Respondent					Friend				
	PA	IQ	SES	EA	OA	PA	IQ	SES	EA	OA
Parent aspiration	1.00	.18	.05	.27	.21	.11	.08	.02	.11	.08
Intelligence		1.00	.22	.40	.41	.10	.34	.19	.29	.26
Family SES			1.00	.40	.32	.09	.23	.27	.31	.28
Educ. aspiration				1.00	.62	.07	.29	.24	.37	.33
Occup. aspiration					1.00	.08	.30	.29	.33	.42
Friend										
Parent aspiration						1.00	.21	-.04	.28	.20
Intelligence							1.00	.30	.52	.50
Family SES								1.00	.41	.36
Educ. aspiration									1.00	.64
Occup. aspiration										1.00

Five variables were measured for each boy: (1) his perception of what his parents' aspirations were for his further education and occupational status; (2) his intelligence (measured by his score on a nonverbal IQ test); (3) his family's socioeconomic status (as measured by parental income and material possessions); (4) the amount of further education that he expected to obtain; and (5) the level of occupation to which he aspired.

Figure 4.1 shows a version of one model proposed by Duncan, Haller and Portes. In the left-hand part of the diagram are six source variables. Three represent the respondent's intelligence, his family's socioeconomic status, and his perception of his parents' aspirations for him; the other three represent the same measures for the respondent's friend. To the right in the diagram are two downstream latent variables representing the level of ambition of the respondent and his friend. It is assumed that an individual's ambition for

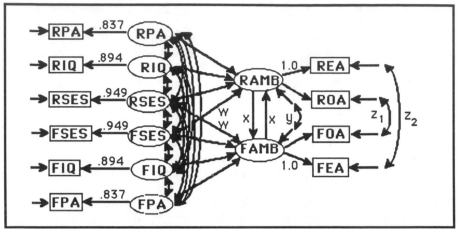

Fig. 4.1 Path model for study of career aspirations. R = respondent,
F = friend; PA = parental aspirations; IQ = intelligence; SES = socioeconomic
status; AMB = ambition; EA = educational aspirations; OA = occupational
aspirations. *w, x, y, z* = paths tested. Path values fixed by assumption are
shown.

educational and economic success will be influenced by his parents'
aspirations for him, by his intelligence, and by his family's socioeconomic
status. It is also assumed (path marked *w*) that his friend's family's
socioeconomic status might affect the level of education and occupation to
which he himself aspires, but that his friend's intelligence and parental
aspirations will not, except by way of the effect they might have on the friend's
own ambition.

The latent variable of ambition is indexed by the two observed variables
of educational aspiration and occupational aspiration, for both the respondent
and his friend.

Several additional possibilities are considered, as shown on the path
diagram:

1. Reciprocal influence, as indicated in Fig. 4.1 by the paths marked *x*.
Does one's boy's ambition regarding educational and occupational
achievement influence the ambition of his friend?

2. Correlated residual influences on the two friends' ambition, as
indicated by the path marked *y*. It is possible that factors not included in the
diagram that are shared in common by the two friends might influence their
levels of ambition (in addition to whatever direct influence the boys have on
each other). These might include, for example, the effect of teachers, or of other
peers.

3. Correlated errors of measurement, as indicated by the paths marked *z*.
There might be shared effects on the specifics of a particular measurement
instrument, in addition to the true correlations of the common factors being

measured. For example, two friends might have discussed particular colleges and jobs, in addition to whatever general resemblance there was in their overall levels of ambition.

Previous analyses of these data have usually omitted the extreme left-hand part of the path diagram, i.e., the paths from the latent variables intelligence, SES, and so on, to the measures of them. This is equivalent to assuming that these variables are perfectly measured--an unlikely assumption. If the reliabilities of the measurements were known, the square roots of these reliabilities could be entered as the values of the paths from the latent variables representing the true scores to the fallible observed scores (compare the example of Fig. 1.10, Chapter 1). For the purpose of illustration, we will arbitrarily assume that the reliabilities of measurement of parental aspiration, intelligence, and socioeconomic status are .7, .8, and .9, respectively, in this population, and hence that the square roots of these numbers, .837, .894, and .949, are the values of the corresponding paths in the measurement model.

A preliminary question we may ask is whether we need maintain a distinction between corresponding paths for respondents and their friends. After all, these are drawn from the same population, and it would not be at all surprising if they would agree within sampling error. If so, we need only solve for a single unknown value for each such set of paired paths, increasing the number of degrees of freedom and the general robustness of the analysis.

The first χ^2 test shown in Table 4-2 investigates this possibility. The first row of the table shows a χ^2 of 11.60, with 13 degrees of freedom, for the full model of Fig. 4.1. The second shows the results of assuming 15 equalities between respondent and friend: 3 in the correlations among the source variables for each individual (e.g., $r_{RPA,RIQ} = r_{FPA,FIQ}$); 3 in the correlations across pairs (e.g., $r_{RPA,FIQ} = r_{FPA,RIQ}$); 4 in the paths from source variables to Ambition (e.g., RPA to RAMB = FPA to FAMB); 1 in the reciprocal paths (RAMB to FAMB = FAMB to RAMB); 1 in the paths from the latent to the

Table 4-2. Tests of hypotheses for the Duncan-Haller-Portes career aspiration model (Fig. 4.1)

	χ^2	df	χ^2_{diff}	df	p
1. Unconstrained model	11.60	13			
2. Equality constraints only	18.89	28	7.29	15	>.90
3. No SES path (*w*)	23.07	29	4.18	1	<.05
4. No reciprocal influence (*x*)	20.81	29	1.92	1	>.10
5. No AMB residual correlation (*y*)	18.89	29	.00	1	>.95
6. No correlated errors (*z*)	32.21	30	13.32	2	<.01
7. Both 4 and 5 (no *x* or *y*)	25.67	30	6.78	2	<.05

Note: 2 tested against 1, and 3 to 7 against 2.

observed variables (RAMB to ROA = FAMB to FOA); and 3 in the residuals from occupational and educational aspirations and ambition.

The difference in χ^2 between the model with and without these equality constraints is 7.29; with 15 degrees of freedom, this does not come remotely close to statistical significance. Thus, we might as well simplify matters by making the symmetry assumptions, which we do in the remainder of the analysis.

Line 3 asks whether we really need a path *w*. Is it necessary to postulate a direct influence of his friend's family's status on a boy's ambition? The result of the test is that the model fits significantly better with such a path than without it (χ^2 = 4.18, 1 df, p < .05). However, the estimated value of the path (.08--see Table 4-3, model 2) suggests that it is not a major contributor to the determination of ambition. Line 4 asks the same question about reciprocal influences, the paths *x* in the figure. The model is judged not to fit significantly worse when they are omitted (χ^2 = 1.92, 1 df, p > .10). The same conclusion can be drawn in line 5 about a possible correlation *y* between the residual factors lying back of the two latent dependent variables (χ^2 = .00, 1 df, p > .95). Thus, we cannot show that either of these features of the model--the influence of one friend's ambition on the other, or shared influences among the unmeasured variables affecting each--is necessary to explain the data. If, however, we exclude both of these simultaneously (the analysis of line 7) we *do* get a significant χ^2 (6.78, 2 df, p < .05), suggesting that the two may represent alternative ways of interpreting the similarity between friends' aspirations that our design is not sufficiently powerful to distinguish. As can be seen in Table 4-3, when both are fit, the residual correlation *y* is neglible (model 2), but when the reciprocal paths are set to zero (model 4), the correlation *y* becomes appreciable (.26). Setting *y* to zero (model 5) has little effect, as one would expect from its small previous value.

Finally, the analysis in line 6 of Table 4-2 asks about the possibility that the specific measures of educational and occupational aspirations might have errors that are correlated for the two friends. The substantial χ^2 (13.32, 2 df, p < .01) suggests that it is, indeed, a plausible assumption that such correlated errors exist.

This example, then, illustrates the application of a path diagram with somewhat more complex features than most of those we have considered previously. It is clear that further testable hypotheses could be stated for this model: For just one example, the diagram assumes that the respondent's own aspiration level and his estimate of his parents' aspirations for him are not subject to correlated errors. (Is this a reasonable assumption? How would you test it?) This case also suggests that tests of different hypotheses may not be independent of one another. In addition, if many hypotheses are tested, particularly if some are suggested by inspection of the data, one should remember that the nominal probability levels can no longer be taken literally,

Table 4-3 Estimated values of the paths and correlations for three models from Table 4-2

Paths	Model 2	Model 4	Model 5
PA to AMB	.19	.19	.19
IQ to AMB	.35	.38	.35
SES to AMB	.24	.26	.24
FSES to AMB (w)	.08	.12	.09
AMB to AMB (x)	.12	.00	.12
AMB to OA	.91	.91	.91
Correlations			
AMB residuals (y)	-.00	.26	.00
OA residuals (z_1)	.26	.26	.26
EA residuals (z_2)	.07	.06	.07

Note: Paths are unstandardized, but covariances have been standardized to correlations. Models correspond to the lines in Table 4-2.

though the differential χ^2s may still serve as a general guide to the relative merits of competing hypotheses.

Another point worth noting about this example is that *none* of the overall models tested In Table 4-2 can be rejected; that is, if one had begun with any one of them and tested only it, the conclusion would have been that it represented a tolerable fit to the data. It is only in the comparisons among the models that one begins to learn something of their relative merits.

Models of Events Over Time

As noted earlier, latent variable causal models are often used to analyze situations in which variables are measured over a period of time. Such situations have the advantage of permitting a fairly unambiguous direction of causal arrows: If event A precedes event B and there is a direct causal connection between them, it is A that causes B and not vice versa. If, on the other hand, A and B were measured more or less contemporaneously, a distinction between the hypotheses "A causes B" and "B causes A" must be made on other grounds--not always a simple matter.

This is not to say that variables sequenced in time never give trouble in assigning cause. In the preceding example in which B follows A, it is always possible that B might be a delayed indicator of some third variable C that precedes and is a cause of A, and therefore one might be less wrong in calling B a cause of A than the reverse. Of course, one would be still better off with C in the model as a cause of both A and B, with no causal arrow between A and B at all. Nevertheless, there are many situations in which the presence of temporal ordering lends itself naturally to causal modeling; we examine some examples in the next few sections.

A minitheory of love

Tesser and Paulhus (1976) carried out a study in which 202 college students filled out a 10-minute questionnaire on attitudes toward dating. The questionnaire contained several subscales having to do with attitudes and behavior toward a particular member of the opposite sex "where there is some romantic interest involved on somebody's part." Four measures were obtained: (T) how much the respondent thought about the other person during the last 2 weeks; (L) a 9-item love scale; (C) to what extent the respondent's expectations concerning the other person were confirmed by new information during the past 2 weeks; and (D) the number of dates with the other person during the same 2-week period.

Two weeks later the subjects filled out the questionnaire again, with respect to the same person, for events during the 2 weeks between the two questionnaire administrations. Table 4-4 presents Tesser and Paulhus' basic results, which they subjected to a simple path analysis and which were later reanalyzed by Bentler and Huba (1979) using several different latent variable models.

Table 4-4 Correlations among four measures of "love" on two occasions (data from Tesser & Paulhus, 1976), N = 202

	T1	L1	C1	D1	T2	L2	C2	D2
Occasion 1								
Thought	1.000	.728	.129	.430	.741	.612	-.027	.464
Love		1.000	.224	.451	.748	.830	.094	.495
Confirmation			1.000	.086	.154	.279	.242	.104
Dating				1.000	.414	.404	.108	.806
Occasion 2								
Thought					1.000	.764	.161	.503
Love						1.000	.103	.505
Confirmation							1.000	.070
Dating								1.000
Mean	9.83	50.66	5.08	3.07	9.20	49.27	4.98	2.95
SD	3.59	19.49	1.80	2.87	3.75	20.67	1.72	3.16

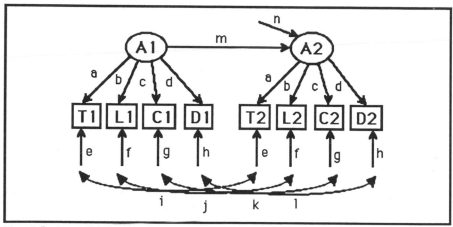

Fig. 4.2 A model for the "love" data of Tesser and Paulhus (Table 4-4). A = general attraction; T, L, C, D = four measures of specific attitudes and behavior (see text); 1, 2 = two occasions.

Figure 4.2 shows a slightly modified version of one of Bentler and Huba's models. Basically, the four scales are shown as reflecting a common factor of attraction at each time period; attraction at the second period is explainable by a persistence of attraction from the first (path *m*) plus possible new events (path *n*). It is assumed that the measurement model (*a, b, c, d ; e, f, g, h*) is the same on both occasions of measurement. It is also assumed that the specifics of a particular behavior or attitude may show correlation across the two occasions. For example, an individual's frequency of dating a particular person is influenced by a variety of factors other than general attraction, and these might well be similar at both times--as might also be various measurement artifacts, such as the tendency of a person to define "dates" more or less broadly, or to brag when filling out questionnaires.

Table 4-5 shows the results of fitting the model of Fig. 4.2 to the correlations in Table 4-4. The paths reported are from an unstandardized solution (using LISREL); however, the measured variables are implicitly standardized by the use of correlations, the variance of the latent variable A1 is set to 1.0, and that of A2 does not differ much from 1.0, so the results in the table can pretty much be interpreted as though they were from a standardized path model. Thinking about a person and the love questionnaire are strong measures of the general attraction variable, dating is a moderate one, and confirmation of expectations is a very weak one. The residual variances, of course, reflect these inversely--the love score is least affected by other things, and the confirmation score is nearly all due to other factors. The general factor of attraction toward a particular person shows a strong persistence over the 2 weeks (*m* = .94, standardized, .92). The residual covariances suggest that for thought and love the correlation between the two occasions of measurement is

Table 4-5 Solution of path model of Fig. 4.2 for data of Table 4-4: Tesser and Paulhus study

Variable	Paths		Residual variances		Residual covariances	
Thought	a	.83	e^2	.31	i	.11
Love	b	.88	f^2	.20	j	.09
Confirmation	c	.17	g^2	.97	k	.21
Dating	d	.53	h^2	.70	l	.53
Attraction	m	.94	n^2	.15		

Note: Paths unstandardized; variance of A1 set at 1.0, variance of A2 = 1.043. χ^2 = 45.87, 22 df, p < .01. Residual variances are squares of path values *e, f, g,* etc.

mostly determined by the persistence of the general factor, whereas for dating there is a large cross-occasion correlation produced by specific factors. On the whole, the measure of confirmation of expectations does not relate to much of anything else within occasions, and only quite moderately to itself across occasions. It was based on only one item, so one might speculate that it would not be a very reliable measure. The measure of dating frequency may suffer from some psychometric problems as well--it appears to be markedly skewed (SD ≈ Mean in Table 4-4). One might wish in such a case to consider preliminary transformation of the scale (say to logarithms or some such), before embarking on an analysis that assumes multivariate normality. Or at any rate, one should hedge one's probability statements.

As a matter of fact, based on the obtained χ^2 of 45.87 with 22 degrees of freedom, if one takes the statistics seriously one would conclude that the present model does not fit the data (a conclusion that Bentler and Huba also arrived at from an analysis based on covariances using a similar model). If one calculates the correlations implied by the solution of Table 4-5 and compares them to the observed correlations, the largest discrepancies are for the correlation between T1 and C2, which the model predicts to be about .13 but which was observed as -.03, and for the correlation between C1 and L2, which was predicted as .14 but observed as .28. If one includes ad hoc paths for these in the model, the fit becomes statistically acceptable (χ^2 = 26.34, 20 df, p > .15)--Bentler and Huba obtained a similar result in their analysis. Because in doing this one is likely to be at least in part fitting the model to the idiosyncracies of the present data set, the revised probability value should be taken even less seriously than the first. The prudent stance is that paths between T1 and C2 and C1 and L2 represent hypotheses that might be worth exploring in future studies but should not be regarded as established in this one.

Should one analyze correlations or covariances? As we have seen, in the present example, the results come out pretty much the same whether correlations were analyzed, as described, or whether covariances were, as in Bentler and Huba's analysis of these data. Both methods have their advantages. It is easier to see from the .83 and .88 in Table 4-5 that paths *a* and *b* are roughly comparable, than to make the same judgment from the values of 3.18 and 16.16 in Bentler and Huba's Table 1. On the other hand, the statistical theory underlying maximum likelihood and generalized least squares model fitting is based on covariance matrices, and application of these methods to correlation matrices, although widely practiced, means that the resulting χ^2s will contain one more step of approximation than they already do.

One further consideration, of minor concern in the present study, will sometimes prove decisive. If the variances of variables are changing markedly over time, one should be wary of analyzing correlations because this, in effect, restandardizes all variables at each time period. If one does not want to do this, but does wish to retain the advantages of standardization for comparing different variables, one should standardize the variables once, either for the initial period or across all time periods combined, and compute and analyze the covariance matrix of these standardized variables.

The simplex--growth over time

Suppose you have a variable on which growth tends to occur over time, such as height or vocabulary size among schoolchildren. You take measurements of this variable once a year, say, for a large sample of children. You can then calculate a covariance or correlation matrix of these measurements across time: grade 1 versus grade 2, grade 1 versus grade 3, grade 2 versus grade 3, and so on.

In general, you might expect that measurements made closer together in time would be more highly correlated--that a person's relative standing on, say, vocabulary size would tend to be less different on measures taken in grades 4 and 5 than in grades 1 and 8. Such a tendency will result in a correlation matrix that has its highest values close to the principal diagonal and tapers off to its lowest values in the upper right and lower left corners. A matrix of this pattern is called a simplex (Guttman, 1954).

Table 4-6 provides illustrative data from a study by Bracht and Hopkins (1972). They obtained scores on standardized tests of academic achievement at each grade from 1 to 7. As you can see in the table, the correlations tend to show the simplex pattern by decreasing from the main diagonal toward the upper right-hand corner of the matrix. The correlations tend to decrease as one moves from left to right along any row, or upward along any column. The standard deviations at the bottom of Table 4-6 show another feature often found with growth data: The variance increases over time.

Figure 4.3 represents a path diagram of a model fit by Werts, Linn, and

Table 4-6 Correlations and standard deviations across grades 1-7 for academic achievement (Bracht & Hopkins, 1972), Ns = 300 to 1240

				Correlations			
Grade	1	2	3	4	5	6	7
1	1.00	.73	.74	.72	.68	.68	.66
2		1.00	.86	.79	.78	.76	.74
3			1.00	.87	.86	.84	.81
4				1.00	.93	.91	.87
5					1.00	.93	.90
6						1.00	.94
7							1.00
SD	.51	.69	.89	1.01	1.20	1.26	1.38

Jöreskog (1977) to these data. Such a model represents one possible way of interpreting growth. It supposes that the achievement test score (T) at each grade level is a fallible measure of a latent variable, academic achievement (A). Achievement at any grade level is partly a function of achievement at the previous grade, via a path w, and partly determined by other factors, z. Test score partly reflects actual achievement, via path x, and partly random errors, u. Because variance is changing, it is appropriate to analyze a covariance rather than a correlation matrix. Covariances may be obtained by multiplying each correlation by the standard deviations of the two variables involved.

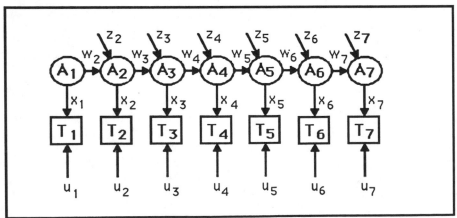

Fig. 4.3 Path model of growth over time. A = academic achievement; T = test score; 1 to 7 = grades.

Figure 4.3 has 7 xs, 7 us, 6 ws, and 6 zs, or a total of 26 unknowns. There are 7 x 8 / 2 = 28 variances and covariances to fit. However, as Werts et al. point out, not all 26 unknowns can be solved for: There is a dependency at each end of the chain so that two unknowns--e.g., two us--must be fixed by assumption. Also, they defined the scale of the latent variables by setting the xs to 1.0, reducing the number of unknowns to 18--5 us, 6 ws, and 7 zs--leaving 10 degrees of freedom. (Seven zs because A_1 is solved for as z_1 in the **PS** matrix.)

Table 4-7. Solution of path diagram of Fig. 4.3 for data of Table 4-6 (growth over time)

Grade	w	z	A	u
1			.184	.076[a]
2	1.398	.041	.400	.076
3	1.318	.049	.743	.049
4	1.054	.137	.962	.058
5	1.172	.051	1.372	.068
6	1.026	.104	1.548	.040
7	1.056	.138	1.864	.040[a]

Note: w, z, A, u as in Fig. 4.3. Values u^a set equal to adjacent value of u. A, z, u expressed as variances, w as an unstandardized path coefficient. If N taken as 300, χ^2 = 10.76, 10 df, p > .30. $A_n = V_n - u_n$, where V_n is the variance of test at grade n.

Table 4-7 shows estimates of the unknown values. The simplex model provides a reasonable fit to the data (χ^2 = 10.76, 10 df, p > .30), at least if N is taken equal to the lower end of its range. The variance of academic achievement, A, increases steadily and substantially over the grades, whereas trends for w, z, and u are much less marked, especially if one discounts the first 2 or 3 years.

A point of mild interest in this solution is that the w parameters, which represent the effect of academic achievement in one grade on that in the next, are slightly greater than 1.0. Does this mean that academic skill persists without loss from one year to the next, indeed with enhancement? Are students who think they forget things over the summer really mistaken? Alas, more likely it means that what happens to a student between one year's measurement and the next is correlated with his standing the preceding year, so that the academically rich get richer and the poor lag further behind them. A suitable latent variable analysis taking additional variables into account would provide a way to clarify this issue.

Finally, could we fit an even simpler model to these data, one that has w,

117

z, and *u* constant, and only A varying? The answer can be obtained by fitting a model with just a single *z, w,* and *u.* The resulting χ^2 of 75.66 with 25 degrees of freedom says, No, we cannot. The grade-to-grade differences in these parameters are too large to be attributable merely to chance.

Liberal-conservative attitudes at three time periods

Judd and Milburn (1980) used a latent variable analysis to examine attitudes in a nationwide sample of individuals who were surveyed on three occasions, in 1972, 1974, and 1976. Table 4-8 shows a portion of their data, based on three topics related to a liberal-conservative dimension of attitude (actually, Judd and Milburn studied five such topics). These particular data are from a subsample of 143 respondents who had attended 4 or more years of college. The numbers in the table mean, for example, that these respondents' attitudes toward busing in the 1972 and 1974 surveys were correlated .79, and their attitude toward busing in 1972 was correlated .39 with their attitude toward criminal rights in 1974.

The authors postulated that the interrelationships among these attitude measurements would largely be accounted for by a general factor of liberalism-conservatism, to which all three of the attitudes would be related at each of the

Table 4-8. Correlations among attitudes at three time periods (Judd & Milburn, 1980), N = 143, 4 years college

		B_{72}	C_{72}	J_{72}	B_{74}	C_{74}	J_{74}	B_{76}	C_{76}	J_{76}
1972	Busing	1.00	.43	.47	.79	.39	.50	.71	.27	.47
	Criminals		1.00	.29	.43	.54	.28	.37	.53	.29
	Jobs			1.00	.48	.38	.56	.49	.18	.49
1974	Busing				1.00	.46	.56	.78	.35	.48
	Criminals					1.00	.35	.44	.60	.32
	Jobs						1.00	.59	.20	.61
1976	Busing							1.00	.34	.53
	Criminals								1.00	.28
	Jobs									1.00
	SD	2.03	1.84	1.67	1.76	1.68	1.48	1.74	1.83	1.54

Note: Busing = bus to achieve school integration; criminals = protect legal rights of those accused of crimes; jobs = government should guarantee jobs and standard of living.

three time periods, plus a specific factor for each attitude that would persist across time. (Actually, the main focus of Judd and Milburn's interest was to compare these features of attitude in a relatively elite group, the present sample, with those in a non-elite group, consisting of respondents who had not attended college. We look at this aspect of the study in the next section of this chapter, which considers cross-group comparisons.)

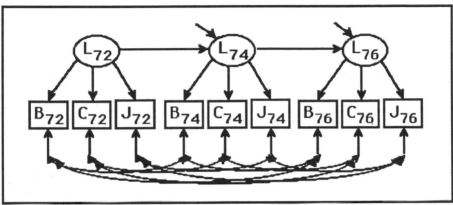

Fig. 4.4 Path model for attitudes measured in 1972, 1974, and 1976.
L = general, B,C,J = specific attitudes; 72,74,76 = years.

Figure 4.4 represents their hypothesis. Liberalism in 1974 is partly predictable from liberalism in 1972, and partly by unrelated events; and similarly for 1976. The general degree of a person's liberalism in any year is reflected in his or her specific attitudes toward busing, the rights of criminals, and guaranteed jobs. A person's attitudes on one of these specific topics in one survey is related to his or her attitude on this same topic in another survey, but not with specific attitudes on other subjects, except by way of the common liberalism-conservatism factor. (Actually, Judd and Milburn worked with a slightly different, but essentially equivalent, model.)
    A word about setting up models of events over time in LISREL may be helpful. Such models, like the present one, often have correlated errors for a given variable measured on different occasions. Such a variable cannot easily be represented on both the X and Y sides of the model because LISREL only permits correlations of residuals within the separate sets of X and Y variables. The model should, then, be set up only on one side--normally the Y side, to allow the paths connecting latent variables over time to be represented in the BE matrix. The PS matrix will then contain the residuals of the latent variables. (The source latent variable or variables at the initial time period can be regarded as having their total variance "residual" because it comes from causal sources outside those represented in the diagram.) Programs such as EQS and CALIS, which do not explicitly distinguish X and Y variables, do not

Table 4-9 Solution of path model of Fig. 4.4 representing liberal/conservative attitudes at three time periods

		Path from L	Residual variance	Specific covariance with 1974	Specific covariance with 1976
1972	Busing	1.00[a]	1.51	.58	.29
	Criminals	.58	2.52	.88	1.21
	Jobs	.63	1.74	.41	.37
1974	Busing	1.00[a]	.92		.23
	Criminals	.62	2.00		1.22
	Jobs	.68	1.18		.48
1976	Busing	1.00[a]	.72		
	Criminals	.49	2.82		
	Jobs	.61	1.49		

Note: Unstandardized coefficients. Paths marked[a] arbitrarily set at 1.00. χ^2 =11.65, 16 df, p > .70. Additional paths: L_{72} to L_{74} = .86, L_{74} to L_{76} = .99; L_{72} variance = 2.60; residual variances, L_{74} = .24, L_{76} = .18.

require special handling in such situations.

Table 4-9 presents an analysis of the Judd and Milburn data using LISREL and a covariance matrix based on Table 4-8. On the whole, the model fits very well $(\chi^2$ = 11.65, 16 df, p > .70). Liberalism is most strongly defined by attitudes toward busing, with attitudes toward guaranteed jobs ranking slightly ahead of attitudes toward justice for accused criminals. Not surprisingly, the three attitudes tend to fall in the reverse order with respect to unexplained variance, as well as the amount of specific association with the same attitude in other years.

A question one might ask is whether liberal-conservative attitudes in 1972 would have any effect on those in 1976 except via 1974; i.e., could there be a delayed or sleeper effect of earlier on later attitudes? This can be tested by fitting a model with an additional direct path from L_{72} to L_{76}. This yields a χ^2 of 11.56 for 15 df. The difference, a χ^2 of .09 with 1 df, is far short of statistical significance. There is, thus, no evidence of such a sleeper effect in these data.

Models Comparing Different Groups

The general approaches described in this and the preceding chapter are readily extended to the case of model fitting in several independent groups of subjects. In the fitting process, one combines the goodness-of-fit criteria from the separate groups and minimizes the total. For statistical tests, one obtains an overall χ^2 for the combined groups, with an appropriate *df* that is the difference between the number of empirical values being fitted and the number of unknowns being solved for, taking into account any constraints being imposed within or across groups.

Again, differences in χ^2s for different nested solutions can be compared, using the differences between the associated degrees of freedom. Thus, for example, if one were solving for five unknowns in each of three groups, one could compare a solution that allowed them all to differ in each group with a solution that required four to be constant across groups and allowed one to vary. There would be 15 unknowns to be solved for in the first case, and only $4 + 3 = 7$ in the second. So the increase in χ^2 between the two would be tested as a χ^2 with $15 - 7 = 8$ df.

Attitudes in elite and non-elite groups

Earlier in this chapter we discussed a set of data by Judd and Milburn involving the structuring of attitudes with respect to a dimension of liberalism-conservatism. These attitudes were measured in three different years for a sample of 143 college-educated respondents. Responses were also available from the same nationwide surveys for a group of 203 individuals who had not attended college. (An intermediate group who had attended college, but for less than 4 years, were excluded in order to sharpen the contrast between the "elite" and "non-elite" groups.) Table 4-10 shows the data for the noncollege group, corresponding to Table 4-8 for the college group.

As we have seen, a model of a general attitude at each time period and specific attitudes correlated across time periods fits the data for college graduates quite well. Would it do as well for a less elite group? If it did, would there be quantitative differences between the groups in the various parameters of the model?

One can fit the model of Fig. 4.4 simultaneously to the data from both groups. If the same model fits in both, but with different values for the paths, one can conclude that the same general sort of explanation is applicable in both groups although with differences in quantitative detail. Or one can go further and ask if the same model with the same values will fit both sets of data. And, of course, one can take intermediate positions and constrain the values of certain paths to be the same in both groups, but allow others to vary.

If one fits the path model of Fig. 4.4 to the data of both the college and noncollege groups, without additional cross-group constraints, one obtains a χ^2 of 24.56 with 32 df, representing an excellent fit to the data (p > .80). (This, in effect, represents a separate solution for the same model in each group, and one can indeed do the solutions separately and add the χ^2s and dfs: Fitting the

Table 4-10 Correlations among attitudes at three time periods (Judd & Milburn, 1980), N = 203, no college

		B_{72}	C_{72}	J_{72}	B_{74}	C_{74}	J_{74}	B_{76}	C_{76}	J_{76}
1972	Busing	1.00	.24	.39	.44	.20	.31	.54	.14	.30
	Criminals		1.00	.25	.22	.53	.21	.21	.40	.25
	Jobs			1.00	.22	.16	.52	.22	.13	.48
1974	Busing				1.00	.25	.30	.58	.13	.33
	Criminals					1.00	.21	.25	.44	.16
	Jobs						1.00	.21	.23	.41
1976	Busing							1.00	.17	.28
	Criminals								1.00	.14
	Jobs									1.00
	SD	1.25	2.11	1.90	1.31	1.97	1.82	1.34	2.00	1.79

Note: Busing = bus to achieve school integration; criminals = protect legal rights of those accused of crimes; jobs = government should guarantee jobs and standard of living.

model separately in the noncollege group gives a χ^2 of 12.91 with 16 df; 11.65 + 12.91 = 24.56 and 16 + 16 = 32. Such simple additivity will not hold if there are cross-group constraints.)

If one goes to the opposite extreme and requires that both the model and quantitative values be the same in both groups, one obtains a χ^2 of 153.98 with 61 df, $p < .001$--thus, one can confidently reject the hypothesis of no quantitative differences between the samples.

One particular intermediate hypothesis, that quantities in the structural model are the same in both groups but the measurement models may be different, leads to a χ^2 of 27.05 with 37 degrees of freedom. This does not represent a significant worsening of fit from the original solution, in which both structural and measurement models were allowed to vary $(\chi^2_{diff} = 2.49, 5$ df, $p > .70)$. Thus, the difference between the two groups appears to lie in the measurement rather than the structural model.

Table 4-11 compares the solutions for the college and noncollege groups. The absolute values of paths from the latent variables to the observed variables are different for the two samples, but this is primarily a matter of the arbitrary scaling: Attitude toward busing happens to be a relatively strong indicator of liberalism for the college group and a relatively weak one for the noncollege

Table 4-11 Solution for the paths from liberalism to specific attitudes, for college and noncollege groups

		Unstandardized		Standardized	
		College	Noncollege	College	Noncollege
1972	Busing	1.00[a]	1.00[a]	.80	.63
	Criminals	.58	1.12	.51	.42
	Jobs	.63	1.40	.61	.58
1974	Busing	1.00[a]	1.00[a]	.84	.55
	Criminals	.62	.96	.54	.35
	Jobs	.68	1.44	.68	.58
1976	Busing	1.00[a]	1.00[a]	.87	.47
	Criminals	.49	.90	.41	.28
	Jobs	.61	1.65	.60	.58

Note: Paths marked[a] fixed at 1.0. Standard deviation for latent variable of liberalism from fitted solution: college--72 = 1.614, 74 = 1.475, 76 = 1.519; noncollege--72 = .789, 74 = .727, 76 = .633.

group, so that scalings based on this attitude will look quite different in the two cases. The standardized paths in the right-hand part of Table 4-11, obtained by multiplying the unstandardized paths by the ratio of standard deviations of their tail to their head variables (see Chapter 1) provide a better comparison. Because the two samples are not very different in the overall level of variance of the observed variables (median SD across the 9 scales is 1.74 for college and 1.82 for noncollege), these values suggest a lesser relative contribution of the general liberalism-conservatism factor in the noncollege group.

Table 4-12 compares the paths between the latent variables across time. For both groups the analysis suggests a relatively high degree of persistence of liberal-conservative position, particularly between the 1974 and 1976 surveys.

Table 4-12 Solution for the paths connecting liberalism across years, for college and noncollege groups

	Unstandardized		Standardized	
	College	Noncollege	College	Noncollege
1972 to 1974	.86	.77	.94	.84
1974 to 1976	.99	.86	.96	.99

The genetics of numerical ability

Some problems in behavior genetics can be treated as straightforward intercorrelation or covariance problems involving multiple groups, and solved with programs such as LISREL, although more typically, explicit models are written and solved with general fitting programs. We will consider an example of each approach.

Table 4-13 gives correlations for three subscales of the Number factor in Thurstone's Primary Mental Abilities battery, in male and female identical and fraternal twin pairs. Correlations for male twins are shown above the diagonal in each matrix, and those for female twins are shown below. The data are from studies by S. G. Vandenberg and his colleagues in Ann Arbor, Michigan, and Louisville, Kentucky; the studies and samples are described briefly in Loehlin and Vandenberg (1968).

Table 4-13 Within-individual and cross-pair correlations for three subtests of numerical ability, in male and female identical and fraternal twin pairs (Ns: identicals 63, 59; fraternals 29, 46)

	Ad1	Mu1	3H1	Ad2	Mu2	3H2
Identical twins						
Addition 1	1.000	.670	.489	.598	.627	.456
Multiplication 1	.611	1.000	.555	.499	.697	.567
3-Higher 1	.754	.676	1.000	.526	.560	.725
Addition 2	.673	.464	.521	1.000	.784	.576
Multiplication 2	.622	.786	.635	.599	1.000	.540
3-Higher 2	.614	.636	.650	.574	.634	1.000
Fraternal twins						
Addition 1	1.000	.664	.673	.073	.194	.379
Multiplication 1	.779	1.000	.766	.313	.380	.361
3-Higher 1	.674	.679	1.000	.239	.347	.545
Addition 2	.462	.412	.500	1.000	.739	.645
Multiplication 2	.562	.537	.636	.620	1.000	.751
3-Higher 2	.392	.359	.565	.745	.603	1.000
Standard deviations						
Identicals, male	7.37	13.81	16.93	8.17	13.33	17.56
Identicals, female	8.00	12.37	15.19	6.85	11.78	14.76
Fraternals, male	9.12	16.51	17.20	7.70	14.52	14.74
Fraternals, female	8.99	15.44	16.98	7.65	14.59	18.56

Note: In the correlation tables, males are shown above and females below the diagonal. 1 and 2 refer to scores of the first and second twin of a pair.

Figure 4.5 gives a path model for genetic influences on the correlations (or covariances) within and across twins. The latent variable N refers to a general genetic predisposition to do well on numerical tests. It is assumed to affect performance on all three tests, but perhaps to different degrees, as represented by paths *a*, *b*, *c*. These are assumed to be the same for both twins of a pair (designated 1 and 2). The genetic predispositions N are assumed to be perfectly correlated for identical twins, who have identical genotypes, but to be correlated .5 for fraternal twins, who are, genetically, ordinary siblings.

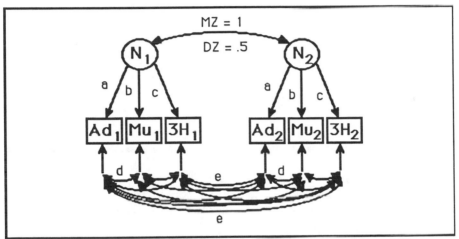

Fig. 4.5 Twin correlations on three subscales of numerical ability. MZ = identical twins, DZ = fraternal twins; N – genetic component of numerical ability; Ad, Mu, 3H = subscales; 1,2 =1st and 2nd twin of a pair.

The bottom part of Fig. 4.5 allows for nongenetic sources of correlation among abilities within individuals and across pairs. Again, corresponding correlations are assumed to be equal--not all of these are marked on the figure, but two examples are given. The residual correlation *d* between the addition and multiplication scales is assumed to be the same in those individuals designated "twin 2" as it is in those individuals designated "twin 1," and a correlation such as *e* between twin 1's score on "3-Higher" and twin 2's score on "Addition" is assumed to be the same as the correlation between twin 2's "3-Higher" score and twin 1's "Addition."

Altogether, there are 15 unknowns to be solved for: the 3 paths *a*, *b*, *c*, 3 residual variances, 3 within-person correlations across traits (*d* is an example), 3 different across-person correlations across traits (*e* is an example), and 3 across-person correlations for the same trait. There are $4 \times 6 \times 7 / 2 = 84$ data points (treating correlations as covariances), leaving $84 - 15 = 69$ df for testing the fit of the model to the data from the four groups at once. The obtained value of χ^2 (using LISREL) is 74.83, indicating that the model provides

Table 4-14 Solution of model of Fig. 4.5 with data of Table 4-13, for genetics of numerical ability

	Genetic path	Residual variance	Residual same-trait cross-person covariance
Addition	.680	.540	.138
Multiplication	.732	.468	.208
3-Higher	.575	.673	.378

	Other residual covariances	
	Within-person	Cross-person
Ad-Mu	.185	.092
Ad-3H	.244	.165
Mu-3H	.215	.204

a reasonable explanation of the data (p > .20).

Could we improve things by fitting the model for the males and females separately? This would involve 30 unknowns and 84 - 30 = 54 df. The obtained χ^2 is 56.40, so the difference in χ^2 is 18.34 for 15 df, which does not represent a statistically significant improvement in fit (p >.20). We may as well go with the same result for both sexes.

Table 4-14 shows this result. The genetic paths have values from .58 to .73; the squares of these represent the proportion of variance attributable to genetic factors (if the model is correct), namely, from 33% to 54% for these three measures. The rest, the residual variances, are attributable to non-genetic factors, including errors of measurement. Whereas the trait variances include a component due to errors of measurement, the trait covariances do not. Here the genes show up more strongly, although the environmental contributions are still evident. The genetic contributions to the within-person correlations among the tests are .50, .39, and .42 (calculated from the path diagram as, for example, .680 x .732 = .50). The environmental contributions are .18, .24, and .22 (bottom of Table 4-14). The genes are estimated as contributing 63-74% to the correlations among the measures, as against 33-54% of their variance--reflecting the contribution of measurement error and specific environmental effects to the latter.

Heredity, environment, and sociability

In the last section we discussed fitting a model of genetic and environmental influences on numerical ability, treated as a LISREL problem involving multiple groups--namely, male and female identical and fraternal twins. In this section we consider a model-fitting problem in which data from two twin samples and a study of adoptive families are fit using a more general model-fitting program--in this case, a variant of IPSOL.

The data to be used are provided in Table 4-15. They are correlations on the scale Sociable of the Thurstone Temperament Schedule. The correlations are between pairs of individuals in the specified relationships. The first four pairings are for identical (MZ) and like-sexed fraternal (DZ) twins from two twin

Table 4-15. Correlations for the trait Sociable from the Thurstone Temperament Schedule in two twin studies and an adoption study

	Pairing	Correlation	Number of pairs
1.	MZ twins: Michigan	.47	45
2.	DZ twins: Michigan	.00	34
3.	MZ twins: Veterans	.45	102
4.	DZ twins: Veterans	.08	119
5.	Father-adopted child	.07	257
6.	Mother-adopted child	-.03	271
7.	Father-natural child	.22	56
8.	Mother-natural child	.13	54
9.	Adopted-natural child	-.05	48
10.	Two adopted children	-.21	80

Note: Michigan twin study described in Vandenberg (1962), and Veterans twin study in Rahe, Hervig, & Rosenman (1978); correlations recomputed from original data. Adoption data from Loehlin, Willerman, & Horn (1985).

studies. The first study, done at the University of Michigan, involved highschool-age pairs, both males and females (see Vandenberg, 1962, for details). The second study was of adult pairs, all males, who had served in the U.S. armed forces during World War II and were located through Veterans Administration records (Rahe, Hervig, & Rosenman, 1978). The remaining pairings in the table are from a study of adoptive families in Texas (Loehlin, Willerman, & Horn, 1985).

Figure 4.6 shows a generalized path diagram of the causal paths that might underlie correlations such as those in Table 4-15. A trait S is measured in each of two individuals, 1 and 2, by a test T. Correlation on the trait is presumed to be due to three independent sources: additive effects of the genes, G; nonadditive effects of the genes, D; and the environment common to pair members, C. A residual arrow allows for effects of the environment unique to each individual and--in all but the MZ pairs--for genetic differences as well.

Table 4-16 shows equations for the correlation $r_{T_1T_2}$ between the test scores of members of various kinds of pairs. The equations are derived from

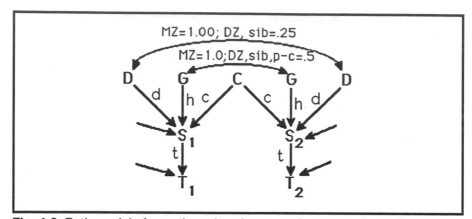

Fig. 4.6 Path model of genetic and environmental sources of correlation between two individuals. G = additive genes, D = nonadditive genetic effect, C = shared environment; S = sociability, T = test score; 1,2 = two individuals.

the path model of Fig. 4.6. The assumptions inherent in the genetic correlations at the top of Fig. 4.6 are that mating is random with respect to the trait, that all nonadditive genetic variance is due to genetic dominance, and that there is no selective placement for the trait in adoptions. Doubtless none of these is exactly true (e.g., the spouse correlation in the adoptive familes for sociability was .16, which is significantly different from zero with 192 pairs but is certainly not very large). However, minor departures from the assumptions should not seriously compromise the model. The Table 4-16 equations allow (via c_1, c_2, c_3) for differentiating among the degrees of shared environment in the cases of identical twins, ordinary siblings, and parents and their children. The equations do not attempt to discriminate between the environmental relationships of parents and adopted or natural children, or of DZ twins and other siblings;

Table 4-16 Equations for correlations between pairs of individuals in different relationships

Relationship	Table 4-15 pairings	Equation for correlation
MZ twins	1,3	$(h^2 + d^2 + c_1^2) t^2$
DZ twins	2,4	$(.5h^2 + .25d^2 + c_2^2) t^2$
Parent, adopted child	5,6	$(c_3^2) t^2$
Parent, natural child	7,8	$(.5h^2 + c_3^2) t^2$
Adoptive siblings	9,10	$(c_2^2) t^2$

Note: h, c, d, t as in Fig. 4.6.

obviously, one might construct models that do, and even--with suitable data--solve them.

The path *t* in Fig. 4.6 is taken as the square root of the reliability of test T (the residual represents error variance). The reliability (Cronbach's alpha) of the TTS Sociable scale in the Veterans sample, .76, was assumed to hold for all samples. Thus, *t* was taken as √.76 = .87 in solving the equations. A variant of IPSOL was used for the solution, modified to yield an approximate generalized least squares fit (for details, see Appendix B).

There are 10 observed correlations in Table 4-15; models with 1 to 4 unknowns were tested, allowing 6 to 9 df for the χ^2 tests.

Table 4-17 Solutions of Table 4-16 equations for various combinations of parameters

Model	χ^2	df	nfi	pfi	AIC
1. all rs equal (null)	36.02	9			38.02
2. h^2 only	9.09	9	.75	.75	11.09
3. $h^2 + c^2$	8.47	8	.76	.68	12.47
4. $h^2 + d^2$	7.60	8	.79	.70	11.60
5. $h^2 + c_1^2 + c_2^2$	6.18	7	.83	.64	12.18
6. $h^2 + c_1^2 + c_2^2 + c_3^2$	2.60	6	.93	.62	10.60

Table 4-17 gives χ^2s from several models based on the Table 4-16 equations. The first row contains a "null model"--that all correlations are equal. It can be rejected with confidence ($p < .001$). The models in the remaining lines of the table all constitute acceptable fits to the data ($p > .30$). We may still, however, compare them to see if some might be better than others. Adding a single environmental or nonadditive genetic parameter to h^2 (lines 3 or 4) does not yield a significant improvement in fit; nor does breaking down the environmental parameter into MZ twins versus others (line 5). A three-way breakdown of environment (line 6), into that for parent and child, siblings and MZ twins, does somewhat better, although the improvement is not statistically significant (χ^2_{diff} of 6.49 from line 2, 5.87 from line 3, and 3.58 from line 5, all $p > .05$).

The parsimonious fit index and Akaike's information criterion agree that solutions 3, 4, and 5 are inferior to the one-parameter simple genetic model of line 2, but they disagree on the four-parameter line 6 solution. AIC evaluates it as the best of the lot, but the pfi judges it to be the poorest.

Table 4-18 gives parameter estimates for the two solutions that seem to deserve the most serious consideration, the one-parameter genetic model of line 2 and the four-parameter model of line 6.

The simple one-parameter genetic model estimates that approximately half of the variance of sociability (52%) is genetic in origin--the rest is presumably attributable to environment; this is not, however, the environment shared by family members, but that unique to the individual.

The model of line 6 allows for a more complex view of the effects of family environment, suggesting that the environmental effects on sociability are almost independent for parents and children, positively shared by identical twins, and negatively related for other siblings. If this last is correct, it suggests also that our model of a shared influence of environment, C in Fig. 4.6, is not altogether appropriate, at least in the case of siblings, because a variance should not be negative. Perhaps direct reciprocal negative paths between the individuals might provide a more satisfactory representation in this case. However, given that differentiating among the various environments does not produce a statistically significant improvement over the simpler model, such further elaborations are not pursued here.

Table 4-18 Parameter estimates for Table 4-17 solutions

line 2	$h^2 = .524$			
line 6	$h^2 = .449$	$c_{p-c}^2 = .022$	$c_{sib}^2 = -.167$	$c_{MZ}^2 = .153$

A Concluding Comment

The examples we have considered in this and the preceding chapter represent some typical applications of path and structural analysis to empirical data in the social and behavioral sciences. Most of these models were originally fit using LISREL, but as we noted earlier, this fact reflects the widespread availability of this particular program rather than any inherent feature of these kinds of problems.

In the next two chapters we turn temporarily away from models like these to consider the important class of latent variable methods known as *exploratory factor analysis*. In the final chapter we return to consider some further elaborations and refinements of path and structural models, and some other latent variable models sharing some of their features.

Chapter 4 Notes

Again, here is a sampling of empirical papers involving some of the kinds of models discussed in this chapter. See also a special section of *Child Development* (Connell & Tanaka, 1987) dealing with structural modeling over time, and an issue of *Behavior Genetics* (Boomsma, Martin, & Neale, 1989) devoted to the fitting of LISREL models to behavior-genetic data.

G. W. Bohrnstedt & R. B. Felson (1983)--modeling self-esteem in the sixth to eighth grades.

J. M. LaRocco (1983)--predicting who re-enlists in the Navy.

N. Schmitt (1982)--modeling different kinds of change in the attitudes of people who have lost jobs.

P. Lindsay & W. E. Knox (1984)--values related to work, at the time of highschool graduation and 7 years later.

E. S. Wellhofer (1984)--modeling political realignments in Great Britain between 1885 and 1950; illustrates and compares to LISREL a different "soft modeling" approach called *partial least squares*--see, e.g., Wold (1982), Fornell & Bookstein (1982), Dijkstra (1983), and Lohmöller (1988).

R. R. Newton et al. (1984)--comparing the structure of anxiety in male and female college students.

S.-O. Brenner & R. Bartell (1984)--Is teacher stress the same in Canada and Sweden?

H. W. Marsh & D. Hocevar (1985)--Does the structure of the self-concept change across different grade lovolo?

D. Rindskopf & H. Everson (1984)--assessing racial discrimination in medical school admissions.

J. C. Loehlin (1985)--fitting heredity-environment models to data from a personality inventory in two twin samples and an adoption sample.

R. P. Bagozzi & M. F. Van Loo (1988)--wives who work and family sizes.

J. Kuusinen & E. Leskinen (1988)--abilities at ages 5 to 7 and school grades at 14 to16.

E. M. Skaalvik & K. A. Hagtvet (1990)--development of self-esteem and academic achievement among Norwegian school children.

C. J. Holahan & R. H. Moos (1991)--life stress, resources, and depression over a 4-year period in adulthood.

Models with loops. Heise (1975) provides a good introduction to this topic, including the modifications of path rules required to deal with looped models.

Simplexes. Guttman (1954) originally proposed the simplex model for the case of a series of tests successively increasing in complexity, such that each required the skills of all the preceding tests, plus some new ones--an example would be addition, multiplication, long division. But simplex correlation patterns may occur in many other situations, such as the growth process considered in the chapter. Werts, Linn, and Jöreskog's example was slightly simplified for purposes of illustration by omitting data from one grade, the ninth. Jöreskog (Jöreskog & Sörbom, 1979, Chapter 3) discusses model-fitting involving a number of variants of the simplex. For a different approach to modeling growth, see the paper by McArdle cited below.

Genetic assumptions. The value of .5 for the genetic correlation between dizygotic twins (numerical-ability example) assumes that assortative mating (the tendency for like to marry like), genetic dominance, and epistasis (nonadditive effects of the genes on the trait), are all negligible in the case of numerical ability, or at least that to the extent they occur they offset one another. The first process would tend to raise the genetic correlation for fraternal twins, and the latter two would tend to lower it. Assortative mating tends to be substantial for general intelligence and verbal abilities but is usually modest for more specialized abilities, such as numerical and spatial skills (DeFries et al., 1979). In the sociability example, a path allowing for nonadditive genetic effects is included in the model.

McArdle (1986) discusses behavior genetic models of development and change. His models include means as well as covariances.

Another use of multiple-group analysis. Multiple-group latent variable modeling can also be used as a convenient method of data summary. This may sometimes have advantages over meta-analysis or similar techniques. If the same model is fit in a number of data samples, it represents an economical way of describing their areas of agreement, and of testing for differences among them. (For numerous examples, see Loehlin, in press.)

Chapter 4 Exercises

1. Repeat the test of the basic Duncan-Haller-Portes model of Fig. 4.1 (use the version with equality constraints--line 2 of Table 4-2). Then test to determine if each of the paths z_1 and z_2 makes a separate significant contribution to the goodness of fit of the model.

2. In the text, a question was raised about testing the assumption that a boy's aspiration for himself and his estimate of his parents' aspiration for him might be subject to correlated errors. How (in general) might this be tested? What problem would be presented if you were to attempt to test it using LISREL? How might you deal with this?

3. Fit the Tesser and Paulhus correlations (Table 4-4) as a confirmatory factor analysis involving five uncorrelated factors: a general attraction factor on which all eight measurements are loaded, and four specific factors, one for each test. Assume equal loadings across the two occasions for the general

and the specific factors and the residuals.

4. For the model in problem 3, relax the requirement that the loadings on the general factor are equal on the two occasions. Does this significantly improve the goodness of fit?

5. Test the hypothesis for the Judd-Milburn data that the measurement model is the same across groups, although the structural model may differ. (Note that covariances are analyzed, not correlations.)

6. Set up and solve the path problem for the genetics of numerical ability as in the text (sexes equal), for the correlations of Table 4-13. Still using correlations, test the additional hypothesis that the three subscales are parallel tests of numerical ability (i.e., have a single common parameter in each of the five sets in Table 4-14).

Chapter Five:
Exploratory Factor Analysis--I. Extracting the Factors

So far, we have been discussing cases in which a specific hypothesized model is fit to the data. Suppose we have a path diagram consisting of arrows from X and Y pointing to Z. The theory, represented in the path diagram, indicates that X and Y are independent causes, and the sole causes, of Z. The qualitative features of the situation are thus spelled out in advance, and the question we ask is, Does this model remain plausible, once we look at the data? And if so, what are the quantitative features of the situation? What is our best estimate of the relative strengths of the two causal effects?

In this chapter we turn to another class of latent variable problems, the class that has been widely familiar to psychologists and other social and biological scientists under the name *factor analysis*, but which we are calling *exploratory factor analysis* to distinguish it from confirmatory factor analysis, which we have treated as an example of the kind of model fitting described in the preceding paragraph.

In exploratory factor analysis we do not begin with a specific model, only with rather general specifications about what kind of a model we are looking for. We must then find the model as well as estimate the values of its paths and correlations.

One can do a certain amount of exploration with general model-fitting methods, via trial-and-error modification of an existing model to improve its fit to data. The methods we cover in this chapter and the next are different. They start out, *de novo*, to seek a model of a particular kind to fit to a set of data.

One thing that makes this feasible is that the class of acceptable models in the usual exploratory factor analysis is highly restricted: models with no causal links among the latent variables and with only a single layer of causal paths between latent and observed variables. (This implies, among other things, that these models have no looped or reciprocal paths.) Such models are, in the terminology of earlier chapters, mostly measurement model, with the structural model reduced to simple intercorrelations among the latent variables.

Indeed, in the perspective of earlier chapters, one way to think of exploratory factor analysis is as a process of discovering and defining latent variables and a measurement model that can then provide the basis for a causal analysis of relations among the latent variables.

The latent variables in factor analysis models are traditionally called *factors*. Most often, in practice, both observed and latent variables are kept in standardized form; that is to say, correlations rather than covariances are analyzed, and the latent variables--the factors--are scaled to unit standard deviations. We mostly follow this procedure in this chapter. However, it is important to be aware that this is *not* a neccessary feature of factor analysis-- that one can, and in certain circumstances should, keep data in its rawscore units and analyze covariances rather than correlations, and that some factor analytic methods scale factors to other metrics than standard deviations of 1.0.

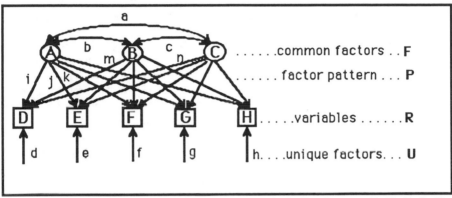

Fig. 5.1 Example of a factor analysis model. A, B, C = factors; D, E, F, G, H = observed variables; *a, b, c* = factor intercorrelations; *d, e, f,* etc. = specifics; *i, j, k,* etc. = factor pattern coefficients.

Figure 5.1 shows an example of a factor analysis model that reintroduces some of the factor analysis terminology that was presented in Chapter 1 and adds a few new matrix symbols. A, B, and C are three *common factors.* Their intercorrelations are represented by the curved arrows *a, b,* and *c,* which collectively form the *factor intercorrelation matrix,* which we designate **F**. D, E, F, G, and H are the *observed variables,* the tests or measures or other observations whose *intercorrelation matrix,* **R**, we are analyzing. The arrows *i, j, k,* etc. represent paths from latent to observed variables, the *factor pattern coefficients.* Collectively, these paths are known as the *factor pattern,* in matrix form **P**. Finally, paths *d, e, f,* etc. represent residual or *unique factors,* also called *specific factors.* They are expressed in matrix form as a diagonal matrix **U**, or as variances, **U**^{2}.

In the example, the dimensions of matrix **F** would be 3 x 3, matrices **R** and **U** would be 5 x 5 (although only the five nonzero diagonal values of **U** would be of interest), and **P** would be 5 x 3; conventionally, **P** is arranged so that the rows represent the observed variables and the columns the factors. Another matrix mentioned earlier, the *factor structure* matrix of correlations between factors and observed variables, is symbolized by **S**, its dimensions are also variables by factors, or 5 x 3 in the example. Recall that the elements of this matrix are a complex function of the paths and interfactor correlations--for example, the correlation between A and D is $i + bm + an$.

For a factor model, one can obtain the correlations implied by the model either by tracing the appropriate paths in the diagram according to Wright's rules, or, more compactly, by the matrix operations $_{imp}R = \mathbf{PFP'} + \mathbf{U}^2$, where the imp before **R** indicates that these are implied or predicted, rather than observed, values of the correlations. (**PFP'** by itself yields implied communalities in the diagonal instead of total variances--a so-called *reduced* correlation matrix that we symbolize by $\mathbf{R}_r$.) The reader may wish to satisfy him- or herself, by working through an example or two, that path tracing and matrix calculation indeed give identical results.

Now it is in general the case that there are an infinite number of possible path models that can reproduce any given set of intercorrelations, and this is true even if we restrict ourself to the class of factor models. To give our search any point we must redefine it more narrowly. Let us invoke parsimony, then, and say that we are looking for the *simplest* factor model that will do a *reasonable* job of explaining the observed intercorrelations.

How does one determine whether a particular model does a reasonable job of explaining observed correlations? This is by now a familiar problem with a familiar solution: One generates the set of correlations implied by the model and then uses a formal or informal criterion of goodness of fit to assess their discrepancy from the observed correlations. Smallest absolute differences, least squares, and maximum likelihood have all been used for this purpose.

What is meant by a *simple* model? Factor analysts typically use a two-step definition: (1) a model that requires the *smallest number of latent variables* (factors); (2) given this number of factors, the model with the *smallest number of nonzero paths* in its pattern matrix. Additional criteria are sometimes invoked, such as (3) uncorrelated factors, or (4) equal distribution of paths across variables or factors, but we focus on the first two, which are common to nearly all methods of exploratory factor analysis.

Applications of the first two criteria of simplicity correspond to the two main divisions of an exploratory factor analysis, *factor extraction* and *rotation.*

In the first step, factor extraction, methods are employed to yield models having the smallest number of factors that will do a reasonable job of explaining the correlations, although such methods typically produce models that are highly unsatisfactory according to the second criterion. Then in the second step, rotation, these models are transformed to retain the same small number of factors, but to improve them with respect to the second criterion of nonzero paths.

We consider methods of factor extraction in this chapter, and methods of rotation in the next.

Methods of Factor Extraction

One straightforward procedure goes as follows, beginning with the reduced correlation matrix R_r (which has estimated communalities replacing the 1s in the diagonal).

Step1. Solve for a general factor of R_r, using the centroid method described in Chapter 1, or other methods we discuss shortly.

Step 2. Obtain the matrix $_{imp}R_r$ implied by the obtained general factor and subtract it from the matrix used in Step 1, leaving a residual matrix that we designate $_{res}R$.

Step 3. Test the residual matrix $_{res}R$. Are you willing to regard it as trivial? If so, stop. If not, put $_{res}R$ in place of R_r in Step 1, and repeat.

This account glosses over a few details, but it gives the essentials of a procedure that will produce a series of factors of decreasing magnitude, each of which is uncorrelated with all the others. This facilitates reaching the first goal of simplicity, the smallest number of factors necessary to fit the data reasonably well, because if factors are solved for in order of size, when one cuts off the process in Step 3, one knows that no potential factor remains unconsidered whose contribution toward explaining R would exceed that of the least important factor examined so far. And because the factors are independent, each obtained factor will make a unique and nonoverlapping contribution to the explanation of R.

The factors resulting from the process described, being general factors, will tend to have many nonzero paths and thus not be simple according to the second of our two criteria; but we deal with this problem later when we discuss the second stage of exploratory factor analysis known as rotation.

Extracting a general factor

One method historically used for extracting a general factor, as we have noted, is the centroid method. Although it has largely been supplanted by the computer-based principal factor and maximum likelihood methods described shortly, the calculations of the centroid method are simple enough to be carried out readily by hand, so it is useful for illustrative purposes. An example is shown in Table 5-1. On the left is an intercorrelation matrix, with communalities (in parentheses) replacing the 1s in the diagonal; thus, it is a reduced correlation matrix R_r . For purposes of the example, we have inserted exact communalities in the diagonal--ordinarily, of course, one would not know these, and would have to begin with estimates of them (we mentioned one possible method of communality estimation in Chapter 1 and discuss others later in this chapter).

Table 5-1 Extraction of an initial general factor by three methods (hypothetical correlations with exact communalities)

R_r							First general factor		
	D	E	F	G	H		Centroid factor	Principal factor	Canonical factor
D	(.16)	.20	.24	.00	.00	D	.205	.170	.065
E	.20	(.74)	.58	.56	.21	E	.783	.782	.685
F	.24	.58	(.55)	.41	.21	F	.680	.649	.525
G	.00	.56	.41	(.91)	.51	G	.817	.857	.939
H	.00	.21	.21	.51	(.36)	H	.441	.450	.507
	.60	2.29	1.99	2.39	1.29				
			sum	=	8.56				
		$\sqrt{sum}$	=	2.9257					

The centroid calculations are carried through to arrive at the general factor shown in the first column on the right: i.e., the column sums of R_r are obtained, and summed, and divided by the square root of their sum, to yield the factor loadings given.

Also shown in Table 5-1 are general factors extracted from the same correlation matrix by two other methods. The column labeled *Principal factor* contains values obtained by an iterative search for a set of path coefficients that would yield the best fit of implied to observed correlations, according to a least squares criterion. The column labeled *Canonical factor* contains values obtained by a similar search using a maximum likelihood criterion instead. (The searches were carried out via LISREL, specifying one latent K variable, **LX** free, **PH** standardized, and **TD** fixed to U^2.)

Note that although each method leads to slightly different estimates of the paths from the factor to the variables, the solutions are generally similar, in that G is largest, D is smallest, with E then F and H falling between.

As we see later, there are other methods for obtaining principal and canonical factor loadings via the matrix attributes known as eigenvalues and eigenvectors, but those methods yield results equivalent to these.

Table 5-2 carries the process through to a second and third factor. The principal factor method is employed--either of the other two methods of obtaining general factors could be used in the same way. (If you try it with the centroid method, remember about the preliminary reflection of variables that is required when correlations are negative.)

In the first row of Table 5-2 are shown the correlation matrix, as in Table 5-1, with communalities in the diagonal. On the right, in the columns of factor pattern matrix **P**, the loadings of the three factors are entered as they are

Table 5-2 Extraction of three successive general factors by the principal factor method (data of Table 5-1)

R_r						P				
	D	E	F	G	H		I	II	III	h^2
D	(.16)	.20	.24	.00	.00	D	.170	.325	.161	.160
E	.20	(.74)	.58	.56	.21	E	.782	.302	-.193	.740
F	.24	.58	(.55)	.41	.21	F	.649	.330	.142	.550
G	.00	.56	.41	(.91)	.51	G	.857	-.413	-.071	.910
H	.00	.21	.21	.51	(.36)	H	.450	-.337	.208	.360

resR$_1$					impR$_1$				
(.131)	.067	.130	-.146	-.076	(.029)	.133	.110	.146	.076
.067	(.128)	.072	-.111	-.142	.133	(.612)	.508	.671	.352
.130	.072	(.129)	-.146	-.082	.110	.508	(.421)	.556	.292
-.146	-.111	-.146	(.175)	.124	.146	.671	.556	(.735)	.386
-.076	-.142	-.082	.124	(.157)	.076	.352	.292	.386	(.203)

resR$_2$					impR$_2$				
(.025)	-.031	.023	-.012	.034	(.106)	.098	.107	-.134	-.110
-.031	(.037)	-.028	.013	-.040	.098	(.091)	.100	-.124	-.102
.023	-.028	(.020)	-.010	.029	.107	.100	(.109)	-.136	-.111
-.012	.013	-.010	(.005)	-.015	-.134	-.124	-.136	(.170)	.139
.034	-.040	.029	-.015	(.043)	-.110	-.102	-.111	.139	(.114)

resR$_3$					impR$_3$				
(-.001)	.000	.000	-.001	.001	(.026)	-.031	.023	-.011	.033
.000	(.000)	-.001	-.001	.000	-.031	(.037)	-.027	.014	-.040
.000	-.100	(.000)	.000	-.001	.023	-.027	(.020)	-.010	.030
-.001	-.001	.000	(.000)	.000	-.011	.014	-.010	(.005)	-.015
.001	.000	-.001	.000	(.000)	.033	-.040	.030	-.015	(.043)

calculated. The first column, labeled I, is the first principal factor from Table 5-1, the single factor that by a least squares criterion comes closest to reproducing R_r. In the second row of matrices, on the right, are shown the correlations (and communalities) implied by the first general factor (obtained via **pp´**; e.g., $.170^2$ = .029; .170 x .782 = .133; etc.). On the left is what is left unexplained--the residual matrix resR, obtained by subtracting impR from R_r (e.g., .16 - .029 = .131; .20 - .133 = .067; etc.)

The basic principal factor procedure is then applied to this residual matrix, to find the single general factor best capable of explaining these remaining correlations: The result is the second principal factor, labeled II in the matrix **P**. (This was again obtained by LISREL, with **TD** now fixed at 1 - .131, etc.)

In the third row of matrices, these various steps are repeated. The matrix implied by factor II is $_{imp}R_2$, and the still unexplained correlations, $_{res}R_2$, are obtained by subtracting $_{imp}R_2$ from $_{res}R_1$. Clearly, not very much is left unexplained--the largest numbers in $_{res}R_2$ are on the order of .03 or .04. In many practical situations we might well decide that the small values left in $_{res}R_2$ are attributable to sampling or measurement error, less than perfect estimation of the communalities, or the like, and stop at this point. But in our hypothetical exact example we continue to a third factor, III, which, as shown in the bottom row, explains (except for minor rounding errors) everything that is left.

Note that the contributions of the three factors, that is, $_{imp}R_1 + {}_{imp}R_2 + {}_{imp}R_3$, plus the final residual matrix $_{res}R_3$, will always add up to the starting matrix R_r. This is a consequence of these being independent factors: Each explains a unique and nonoverlapping portion of the covariation in R_r. Note also that the sizes of the pattern coefficients tend on the whole to decrease as we move from I to II to III: Successive factors are less important; $_{imp}R_1$ explains more of R_r than does $_{imp}R_2$, and $_{imp}R_2$ more than $_{imp}R_3$.

Notice further that the total explained correlation R_r can be obtained either by $_{imp}R_1 + {}_{imp}R_2 + {}_{imp}R_3$ or by **PP′**. This equivalence is not surprising if one traces the steps of matrix multiplication, because exactly the same products are involved in both instances, and only the order of adding them up differs.

Finally, notice the column at the top right of Table 5-2 labeled h^2, the communalities implied by the solution. They are obtained as the diagonal of **PP′**, or, equivalently, as the sums of the squared elements of the rows of **P** (to see this equivalence, go mentally through the steps of the matrix multiplication **PP′**). In this case, because true communalities were used to begin with, and the solution is complete, the implied communalities agree with the diagonal of R_r.

Figure 5.2 compares the preceding solution, expressed in path diagram form, with the causal model that in fact was used to generate the correlation matrix analyzed in Table 5-2.

First, by the appropriate path tracing, either diagram yields the same correlations among variables and the same communalities. The communality of G in the top diagram is the sum of the squares of the paths to B and C, plus twice the product of these paths and the correlation r_{BC}; i.e., $.5^2 + .6^2 + 2 \times .5 \times .5 \times .6 = .91$. The communality of G in the bottom diagram is just the sum of the squared paths to I, II, and III, because the latter are all uncorrelated; i.e., $.86^2 + (-.41)^2 + (-.07)^2 = .91$. The correlation between D and E in the top

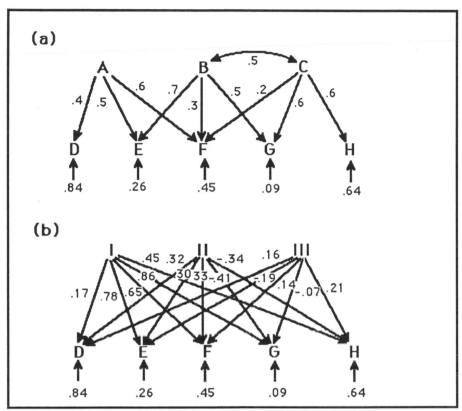

Fig. 5.2 Path models for Table 5-1. (a) Model used to generate correlations. (b) Model representing initial principal factor solution.

diagram is .4 x .5 = .20. That between D and E in the bottom diagram is .17 x .78 + .32 x .30 + .16 x (-.19), which also equals .20.

Both these three-factor models, then, explain the data equally well: They imply the same correlations and communalities (and hence the same specific variances). The one explains the data with a smaller number of paths (9) and has two of its factors correlated. The other explains the data with three uncorrelated general factors of decreasing magnitude, involving a total of 15 paths, one from every factor to every variable.

Most factor analysts believe that the action of causes in the real world is better represented by models like (a) than by models like (b). Causes typically have a limited range of effects--not every cause influences everything. And real-life causal influences may often be correlated in their actions. Nevertheless, a model like (b) has two great merits: (1) It can be arrived at by straightforward procedures from data, and (2) it establishes how many factors are necessary to explain the data to any desired degree of precision.

Furthermore, as was noted earlier, methods exist for transforming models like (b) into models more like (a), so that a model like (b) can be used as a first step in an exploratory analysis.

Direct calculation of principal factors

We have considered one way of arriving at an initial factor solution: by the successive extraction of independent general factors from a correlation matrix with communalities in the diagonal. In practice, however, a direct calculation can be used to obtain loadings for all the principal factors simultaneously. The availability of this calculation has contributed to making the principal factor method the most popular approach to exploratory factor analysis.

By this method, the principal factor pattern is obtained via the eigenvalues and eigenvectors of the reduced correlation matrix; i.e, the matrix $\mathbf{R_r}$. (Readers unfamiliar with the concepts of eigenvalues and eigenvectors should consult Appendix A or a matrix algebra text.) If we arrange the eigenvectors in the columns of a matrix $\mathbf{V}$ and the square roots of the eigenvalues from large to small in a diagonal matrix $\mathbf{L}$, we can obtain the principal factors by the matrix multiplication $\mathbf{P} = \mathbf{VL}$. Put another way, the principal factor pattern is a rescaling of the eigenvectors by the square roots of the eigenvalues. Postmultiplying a matrix by a diagonal matrix rescales its columns by the values in the diagonal matrix.

Given the eigenvalues and eigenvectors, then, the principal axis solution is simple. This just sweeps the computational effort under the rug, of course, by pushing it back into the chore of computing the eigenvalues and vectors. This is a very substantial computation, if carried out by hand for a large correlation matrix--think in terms of days or weeks, not minutes or hours. But fast and efficient computer routines exist for calculating the eigenvalues and vectors of symmetric matrices. Such routines are widely available, and access to one is assumed henceforward in this book; if for any reason you wish to solve for eigenvalues and vectors by hand, which is feasible for small examples, standard textbooks (e.g., Morrison, 1976) will show you how.

The eigenvalues corresponding to the principal factors are of interest in their own right--they represent the variance of observed variables explained by the successive factors. If we sum the squares of the factor loadings $\mathbf{P}$ in Table 5-2 by columns rather than rows, we will obtain the eigenvalues. They are, respectively, 2.00, .59, and .13. Their sum, 2.72, is the same as the sum of the communalities; it is the total explained variance. The first factor accounts for a substantial part of the total communality (2.00/2.72 of it, or about 74%). The second factor accounts for about 22%, and the third for 5%. Another way of looking at the three eigenvalues is as the sums of the diagonal elements (traces) of the three implied matrices in Table 5.2. (Can you see that these are algebraically equivalent?) Again, the eigenvalues reflect the relative contributions of the three factors.

Rescalings--Alpha and Canonical factors

We saw earlier that general factors may be obtained using a maximum
likelihood rather than a least squares criterion, and we called these Canonical
factors. It turns out that Canonical factors (Rao, 1955; Harris, 1962), and yet
another variety, Alpha factors (Kaiser & Caffrey, 1965) can be obtained via the
same basic eigenvalue-eigenvector procedure as principal factors, by rescaling
the starting correlation or covariance matrix before carrying out the calculation.
    The two methods use different preliminary scalings: Alpha analysis
rescales variables so that they have equal communalities of 1.0, whereas the
Canonical factor approach rescales variables so that they have equal
uniquenesses of 1.0.
    A numerical example of Alpha and Canonical factor analysis, based on
the correlation matrix of Table 5-1, is given in Appendix D. The results are
shown in Table 5-3. A general similarity to the centroid and principal factor
solutions of Table 5-2 is evident, although there are differences in the sizes of
coefficients. Those for the principal factor method tend to lie between the
values derived from the two rescalings.

Table 5-3 Alpha and Canonical factor pattern matrices (correlation matrix of
Table 5-1, exact communalities)

Alpha factors (rescaled)			Canonical factors (rescaled)		
I	II	III	I	II	III
.23	.31	.10	.06	.35	.18
.79	.15	-.31	.69	.51	-.12
.70	.23	.03	.53	.48	.20
.77	-.55	-.11	.94	-.17	-.01
.42	-.38	.20	.51	-.22	.24

    Rao arrived at his formulation of Canonical factor analysis via an attempt
to define factors that would have maximum generalizability to other samples of
subjects. Kaiser and Caffrey arrived at their formulation of Alpha factor analysis
via an attempt to define factors that would have maximum generalizability to
other measures of the underlying variables. Although it is not necessarily the
case that transformed versions of these solutions would retain these properties
for individual factors, one might perhaps still choose one of these two
approaches if one's primary concern lay with the one or the other kind of
generalization.
    Both the Alpha and Canonical factor methods can be said to be "scale
free," in the sense that they yield the same factors when starting from differently
scaled variables: for example, from a covariance matrix of variables in their

143

original raw units, or from a correlation matrix, where the variables are implicitly standardized. The principal factor approach will give different factor solutions in these two cases. The Alpha and Canonical approaches, because of their preliminary rescaling of both the correlation and covariance matrices to the same standard form, will not, arriving at the same solution in each case. These factors--as in Table 5-3--are often scaled back to an ordinary standard-score metric at the end for interpretability. However, the basic properties of the solutions--maximum accounting for communality by each factor, and so on-- apply, of course, to the scaling in which the eigenvalue solution is actually carried out.

From a more general perspective, we may speak of various possible alternative scalings of variables for a factor analysis: (1) Leave the variables in their original rawscore metrics, i.e, do a principal factor analysis of the covariance matrix C (actually, of the reduced covariance matrix C_r, with common variances in the diagonal); (2) scale the variables by the square roots of their variances (their standard deviations), by factoring R_r; (3) scale the variables by the square roots of the common portions of their variances, i.e., do an Alpha analysis; or, (4) scale the variables by the square roots of the unique portions of their variances, i.e., do a Canonical analysis.

Alternative (2), the factor analysis of ordinary correlations, is by far the most widely used in practice. It might perhaps be regarded as a compromise between (3) and (4) when one is concerned, as one usually is, with generalizing across both subjects and variables. Alternative (1), the factoring of covariances, may suffer excessively from arbitrariness of scale: A variable, e.g., annual income, can have a quite different effect on the factor analysis if it is expressed in dollars or in thousands of dollars, because of the huge difference in the size of the variance and covariances in the two cases. However, when differing sizes of variances are at the heart of the issue, as may be the case in comparing factor analyses across different groups (e.g., different cultures, different ages, or the like), one would not want to lose the differences among the groups by restandardizing for each, and hence would prefer to work with the covariance matrices directly. As we have noted earlier, a possible way to eat one's cake and have it too is to standardize all one's variables over the combined groups, to deal with the problem of noncomparable units of the different variables, and then to factor analyze covariance matrices for the separate groups using this common metric.

We need now to return to two matters that we have so far finessed in our examples: namely, (1) estimating the communalities, and (2) deciding at what point the residuals become negligible. In real-life data analyses we do not usually have advance knowledge of how much of a variable's variance is shared with other variables and how much is specific. And in real life, we will usually have many trivial influences on our variables in addition to the main causes we hope to isolate, so that after the factors representing the latter are extracted we still expect to find a certain amount of residual covariance. At what point do we conclude that all the major factors have been accounted for, and what is left in the residual matrix is just miscellaneous debris? We consider these topics in turn.

Estimating Communalities

As we have seen, an exploratory factor analysis begins by removing unique variance from the diagonal of the correlation or covariance matrix among the variables. Because one rarely knows in advance what proportion of the variance is unique and what is shared with other variables in the matrix (if one did, one would probably not need to be doing an exploratory analysis), some sort of estimate must be used. How does one arrive at such an estimate? How important is it that the estimate be an accurate one?

The answer to the second question is easy: The larger the number of variables being analyzed, the less important it is to have accurate estimates of the communalities. Why? Because the larger the matrix, the less of it lies in the diagonal. In a 2 x 2 matrix, half the elements are diagonal elements. In a 10 x 10 matrix, only one-tenth are (10 diagonal cells out of a total of 100). In a 100 x 100 matrix, 1% of the matrix is in the diagonal, and 99% consists of off-diagonal cells. In a 2 x 2 matrix, an error in a communality would be an error in one of two cells making up a row or column total. In a 100 x 100 matrix, it would be an error in one of a hundred numbers entering into the total, and its effect would be greatly attenuated. In factoring a correlation matrix of more than, say, 40 variables, it hardly matters what numbers one puts into the principal diagonal, even 1's or 0's--although since it is very easy to arrive at better estimates than these, one might as well do so. Many different methods have been proposed. One was mentioned earlier (the method of triads--see Chapter 1). We discuss two more in this chapter, plus a strategy for improving any initial estimate via iteration.

Highest correlation of a variable

A very simpleminded but serviceable approach is to use as the communality estimate for a given variable the highest absolute value of its correlation with any other variable in the matrix; that is, the largest off-diagonal number in each row in the matrix is put into the diagonal with positive sign.

The highest correlation of a variable with another variable in the matrix *isn't* its communality, of course, but it will in a general way resemble it: Variables that share much variance with other variables in the matrix will have high correlations with those variables and hence get high communality estimates, as they should, whereas variables that don't have much in common with any other variables in the matrix will have low correlations and hence get low communality estimates, again correctly. Some cases won't work out quite so well--e.g., a variable that has moderate correlations with each of several quite different variables might have a high true communality but would receive only a moderate estimate by this method. Nevertheless, in reasonably large matrices, or as a starting point for an iterative solution, this quick and easy method is often quite adequate.

Squared multiple correlations

A more sophisticated method, but one requiring considerably more computation, is to estimate the communality of a given variable by the squared multiple correlation of that variable with all the remaining variables in the matrix. In practice, this is usually done by obtaining R^{-1}, the inverse of the (unreduced) correlation matrix R. The reciprocals of the diagonal elements of R^{-1}, subtracted from 1, yield the desired squared multiple correlations (often called SMCs for short); that is, for the i th variable:

$$SMC_i = 1 - 1/k_{ii},$$

where k_{ii} is the i th element of the main diagonal of R^{-1}.

Table 5-4 illustrates the calculation of SMCs for the example of Table 5-1.

Table 5-4 Calculation of squared multiple correlations of each variable with all others (data of Table 5-1)

R					
	1.00	.20	.24	.00	.00
	.20	1.00	.58	.56	.21
	.24	.58	1.00	.41	.21
	.00	.56	.41	1.00	.51
	.00	.21	.21	.51	1.00

R^{-1}					
	1.096	-.204	-.230	.219	-.021
	-.204	1.921	-.751	-.869	.197
	-.230	-.751	1.585	-.189	-.079
	.219	-.869	-.189	1.961	-.778
	-.021	.197	-.079	-.778	1.372

	diagonal	1/diag.	SMC
D	1.096	.912	.088
E	1.921	.521	.479
F	1.585	.631	.369
G	1.961	.510	.490
H	1.372	.729	.271

R is the correlation matrix; $\mathbf{R}^{-1}$ is its inverse, calculated by a standard computer routine. The bottom part of the table shows the steps in obtaining the SMCs.

SMCs are not communalities either; in fact, they are systematically lower than (at most equal to) the true communalities. Nevertheless, they are related to the communalities in a general way, in that if a variable is highly predictable from other variables in the matrix, it will tend to have a good deal of variance in common with them, and if it is unpredictable from the other variables, it means that it has little common variance. In large matrices, the SMCs are often only slightly below the theoretical true communalities.

Iterative improvement of the estimate

The basic idea, mentioned briefly in Chapter 1, is that one makes an initial communality estimate somehow, obtains a factor pattern matrix **P**, and then uses that to obtain the set of communalities implied by the factor solution. In the usual case of uncorrelated initial factors, these are just the sums of the squares of the elements in the rows of **P**; more generally, they may be obtained as the diagonal of **PFP′**, where **F** is the matrix of factor intercorrelations.

One can then take these implied communalities, which should represent a better estimate than the initial ones, put them in place of the original estimates in $\mathbf{R}_r$, and repeat the process. The **P** from this should yield still better estimates of the communalities, which can be reinserted in $\mathbf{R}_r$, and the process repeated until successive repetitions no longer lead to material changes in the estimates. Such a process involves a good deal of calculation, but it is easily programmed for a computer, and most factor analysis programs provide iterative improvement of initial communality estimates as an option.

Table 5-5 shows several different communality estimates based on the artificial example of Table 5-1. The first estimate, highest correlation in the row,

Table 5-5 Comparison of some communality estimates for the correlation matrix of Table 5-1

Variable	h^2	1	2	3	4
		\multicolumn{4}{c}{h^2 estimate}			
C	.16	.24	.09	.19	.13
D	.74	.58	.48	.73	.69
E	.55	.58	.37	.52	.61
F	.91	.56	.49	.81	.96
G	.36	.51	.27	.46	.34
	2.72	2.47	1.70	2.71	2.73

Note: h^2 = communality from model which generated r's. Estimates: (1) highest r in row; (2) SMC; (3) SMC with iteration (3 principal factors); (4) SMC with iteration (3 Alpha factors).

shows a not-atypical pattern for this method of overestimating low communalities and underestimating high ones. The second, SMCs, shows, as expected, all estimates on the low side. Columns 3 and 4 show the outcome of iterative solutions starting with SMCs: Column 3 shows a solution based on a principal factor analysis, and column 4 shows a solution based on an Alpha factor analysis. No solution recovers the exact set of communalities of the model generating the correlations, but the iterative solutions come much closer than either of the direct estimates, and the total estimated communality is also fairly close to that of the theoretical factors.

One disadvantage of iterative solutions for the communalities is that they will sometimes lead to a "Heywood case": A communality will converge on a value greater than 1.0. This is embarrassing; a hypothetical variable that shares more than all of its variance with other variables is not too meaningful. Some factor analysis computer programs will stop the iterative process automatically when an offending communality reaches 1.0, but this really isn't much better, because a variable with no unique variance is usually not plausible either. A possible alternative strategy in such a case might be to show, e.g., by means of a χ^2 test, that the fit of the model with the communality reduced to a sensible value is not significantly worse than it is with the Heywood case communality. If this proves *not* to be the case, the model is unsatisfactory and something else must be considered--extracting a different number of factors, rescaling variables to linearize relationships, eliminating the offending variable or one of its correlates, or the like.

If you are a very alert reader, it may have occurred to you that there is another potential fly in the ointment in using iterative approaches. In order to use such an approach to improving communality estimates, one must first know how many factors to extract--because using a different number of columns in **P** will result in different implied communalities. In the case of our hypothetical example, we used the three factors known to account for the data as the basis of our iterative improvement, but in real life one must first decide how many factors to use if one wishes to iteratively improve communality estimates. To this problem of determining the number of factors we now turn.

Determining the Number of Factors

In practice, deciding on the number of factors is a much stickier problem than communality estimation. As mentioned in the last section, with reasonably large correlation matrices even quite gross errors in estimating the communalities of individual variables will usually have only minor effects on the outcome of a factor analysis. Not so with extracting too many or too few factors. This will not make too much difference in the initial step of factor extraction, other than adding or subtracting a few columns of relatively small factors from the factor pattern matrix **P**, but it will often make a material difference when the next, transformation, stage is reached. Admitting an additional latent variable or two often leads to a substantial rearrangement of paths from existing latent variables; trying to fit the data with one or two fewer latent variables can also lead to a substantial reshuffling of paths. Such rearrangements can lead to quite different interpretations of the causal structure underlying the observed correlations.

So the problem is not a trivial one. What is its solution? As a matter of fact, several possible solutions have been proposed. We describe four: the Kaiser-Guttman rule, the scree test, a chi-square test for further significance of the residuals, and a cross-validation procedure due to Cudeck and Browne.

The Kaiser-Guttman rule

This is easily stated: (1) Obtain the eigenvalues of the correlation matrix R (*not* the reduced matrix R_r); (2) ascertain how many eigenvalues are greater than 1.0. That number is the number of nontrivial factors that there will be in the factor analysis.

Although various rationales have been offered for the choice of the particular value 1.0, none is entirely compelling, and it is perhaps best thought of as an empirical rule that often works quite well. Because it is easy to apply and has been incorporated into various popular computer programs for factor analysis, it has undoubtedly been the method most often used to answer the question "How many factors?" in factor analyses conducted over the last decade or two.

It is not, however, infallible. If you apply it, for example, to a set of eigenvalues obtained by factoring the intercorrelations of random data, the Kaiser-Guttman rule will not tell you that there are no interpretable factors to be found. On the contrary, there will typically be a sizeable number of factors from such data with eigenvalues greater than 1.0, so the rule will tell you to extract that many factors. (To see that there must be eigenvalues greater than 1.0, consider that their sum must be *m* for an *m*-variable matrix. When you extract them in order of size, there will be some larger than 1.0 at the beginning of the list and some smaller than 1.0 at the end.)

Table 5-6 provides an example, in which eigenvalues from the correlations of random scores and real psychological test data are compared. If one were to apply the Kaiser-Guttman rule to the random data, it would suggest the presence of 11 meaningful factors; there are, of course, actually none. For the real psychological data, the rule would suggest 5 factors, which is not unreasonable--factor analysts, using various criteria, have usually argued for either 4 or 5 factors in these particular data. (Note that the fifth eigenvalue is only just slightly above 1.0, which suggests another difficulty with a Kaiser-Guttman type of rule: Chance fluctuations in correlations might easily shift a borderline eigenvalue from, say, .999 to 1.001, leading to a different decision for the number of factors, but would one really want to take such a small difference seriously?)

Table 5-6. Eigenvalues from random and real data

Rank in size	Random data	Real data	Rank in size	Random data	Real data
1	1.737	8.135	13	.902	.533
2	1.670	2.096	14	.850	.509
3	1.621	1.693	15	.806	.477
4	1.522	1.502	16	.730	.390
5	1.450	1.025	17	.717	.382
6	1.393	.943	18	.707	.340
7	1.293	.901	19	.672	.334
8	1.156	.816	20	.614	.316
9	1.138	.790	21	.581	.297
10	1.063	.707	22	.545	.268
11	1.014	.639	23	.445	.190
12	.964	.543	24	.412	.172

Note: Random data = correlation matrix of random scores on 24 variables for 145 cases. Real data = Holzinger-Swineford data on 24 ability tests for 145 7th- and 8th-grade children, from Harman (1976, p. 161).

Presumably, one does not often factor correlations based on random data intentionally, but one may occasionally want to factor analyze something similar--say, intercorrelations of measures of quite low reliability, such as individual questionnaire items, which could be substantially influenced by random measurement errors. In such cases one could be led badly astray by blind reliance on the Kaiser-Guttman rule.

The scree test

This procedure also employs eigenvalues. However, instead of using a 1.0 cutoff, the user plots successive eigenvalues on a graph and arrives at a decision based on the point at which the curve of decreasing eigenvalues changes from a rapid, decelerating decline to a flat gradual slope.

The nature of this change can be best illustrated by an example. The eigenvalues for the real data from Table 5-6 are plotted in Fig. 5.3. Notice how the first few eigenvalues drop precipitously, and then after the fourth, how a gradual linear decline sets in. This decline is seldom absolutely linear out to the last eigenvalue--often, as here, it may shift to a more gradual slope somewhere en route. This linear or near-linear slope of gradually declining eigenvalues was called the *scree* by R.B. Cattell (1966b), who proposed this test. He arrived at this name from the geological term for the rubble of boulders and debris extending out from the base of a steep mountain slope. The idea is that when you come up to the top of the scree, you have reached the real mountain slope--or the real factors. Below that, you have a rubble of trivial or

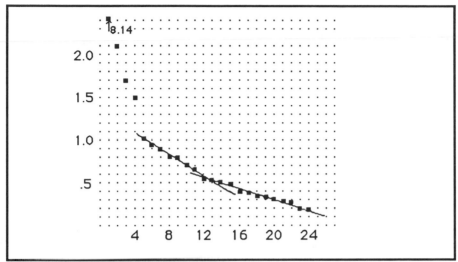

Fig. 5.3 Scree test for Holzinger-Swineford data of Table 5-6. Horizontal axis: eigenvalue number; vertical axis: eigenvalue size.

error factors. The scree test would suggest four factors in this example, for the four eigenvalues rising above the scree.

Figure 5.4 shows the scree test applied to the eigenvalues from random data. In this case, there are no true factors arising above the rubble of the scree, which begins with the first eigenvalue. Again, the scree has an initial, approximately linear segment, and then further out another section of slightly

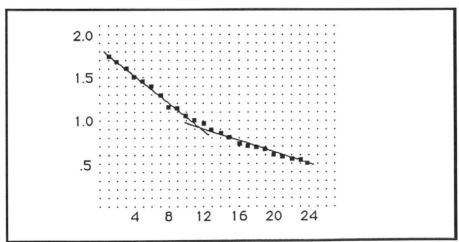

Fig. 5.4 Scree test for random data of Table 5-6. Horizontal axis: eigenvalue number; vertical axis: eigenvalue size.

lesser slope. In this example, the scree test would provide much better guidance to the number of factors than would the Kaiser-Guttman rule-- although either approach would work fairly well for the data of Fig. 5.3.

Figure 5.5 applies the scree test to the artificial example of Table 5-1. This illustrates a difficulty of applying the scree test in small problems: There is not enough excess of variables over factors to yield sufficient rubble for a

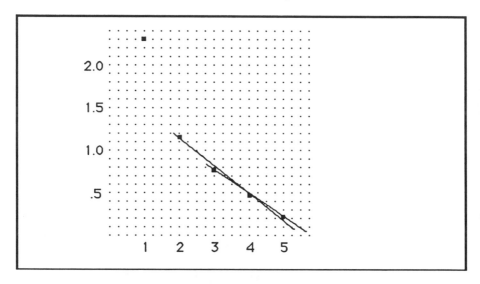

Fig. 5.5 Scree test for data of sample problem of Table 5-1. Horizontal axis: eigenvalue number; vertical axis: eigenvalue size.

well-defined scree. The Kaiser-Guttman rule would suggest 2 factors in this case. A scree test would indicate the presence of at least one real factor and would not be very compelling after that--one could make a case for 1, 2, 3, or more factors. The graph is *consistent* with the presence of 3 factors, but one's confidence in the true linearity of a slope defined with just two points cannot be very high!

Most users of the scree test inspect visual plots of the eigenvalues in the manner we have described. However, a computer-based version also exists (Gorsuch,1983, p.168).

Chi-square test of residuals

As noted earlier in this chapter, the Canonical factors are maximum likelihood factors; that is, each factor represents the best possible fit to the residual correlations, according to a maximum likelihood criterion. This presents the possibility of a χ^2 test after the addition of each factor, as to whether the correlations implied by the factors extracted so far constitute an adequate account of the original correlations. Such a test may be thought of either as a test of the goodness of fit of the model to the data, or as a test for the insignificance of the residuals left when the correlations implied by the model are subtracted from the observed correlations.

Table 5-7 Chi square test of residuals after each factor (sample problem of Table 5-1, with communalities assumed known), N = 100

	Factor pattern		
	I	II	III
D	.06	.35	.18
E	.68	.51	-.12
F	.52	.48	.20
G	.94	-.17	-.01
H	.51	-.22	.24
χ^2	94.67	3.15	0.00
df	10	6	3
p	<.001	>.50	--

Note: Maximum likelihood factors extracted successively from residual matrices via LISREL. Chi-square test is for the significance of residuals after the extraction of the given factor (= test of goodness of fit of R_r to impR_r based on all factors so far); df given by Table 5-8 formula + n, since the n communalities are not solved for.

The calculations for the example problem of Table 5-1 are shown in Table 5-7. The maximum likelihood factors were obtained by successive extractions of a single factor from residual matrices using LISREL; as can be seen, they are essentially identical to the rescaled canonical factors calculated via eigenvalues and vectors in Table 5-3. Chi squares were obtained on the assumption that the correlations were based on 100 subjects. As can be seen, a statistical test at a conventional significance level would have concluded that two factors, plus sampling error, provide a plausible explanation of the data-- agreeing, in this case, with the Kaiser-Guttman rule. Only if the expected sampling error were considerably decreased, e.g., if a sample size of upward of 400 were assumed, would a χ^2 test suggest the extraction of a third factor from this particular matrix of correlations. (Note that such "what if" questions are easily answered in such cases because the χ^2s go up proportionally to N - 1.)

Maximum likelihood factors are often obtained in conjunction with an iterative solution for the communalities, as illustrated in Table 5-8. In this approach one solves iteratively, using a maximum likelihood criterion, for

Table 5-8 Maximum likelihood solution with iterated communalities (sample problem of Table 5-1), N = 100

	Factor pattern		
	I	II	h^2
D	.00	.37	.14
E	.56	.56	.63
F	.41	.63	.56
G	1.00	.00	1.00
H	.51	-.06	.26
χ^2	25.90	1.19	
df	5	1	
p	<.001	>.20	

Note: df = 1/2 [$(n\text{-}m)^2$ - n - m], where n = number of variables and m = number of factors (Harman, 1976, p. 205).

the pattern coefficients and communalities for 1, 2, . . . , k factors, stopping when a model is reached that is not rejected by the χ^2 test at the prechosen level of significance.

Such a solution for the example problem of Table 5-1 is given in Table 5-8. The initial communality estimates were squared multiple correlations. A Heywood case was encountered for variable G on the second iteration; its communality was fixed at 1.00 and the iteration allowed to proceed to completion. Again, the χ^2 test after the extraction of the second factor is no longer significant. In this case the next factor would have negative degrees of freedom for a χ^2 test. The dfs for successive factors are fewer in this analysis than in that of the preceding table because the communalities are solved for in addition to the pattern coefficients.

Cross-validation

The ultimate test of any method of choosing the number of factors to extract is that it selects factors that will be found again in new samples of subjects and new sets of tests covering the same domain. If the ultimate criterion is cross-validation, why not use it as the immediate criterion? Indeed, several such procedures have been suggested. One such method, which cross-validates across subject samples, has been proposed by Cudeck and Browne (1983).

The method goes as follows:

1. Split the subjects randomly into two equal subsamples, call them A and B.
2. Take one subsample, say A, and factor with increasing numbers of factors, 1, 2, 3, . . . , *k*.
3. After each factor is extracted, apply a goodness-of-fit test, such as maximum likelihood, to the discrepancy between the correlations implied by the factors extracted in A and the observed correlations in the *other* subsample, B.
4. Repeat, factoring in B and testing against A.
5. Take as the optimum number of factors the one that yields the best cross-validation indices of fit. Ideally, this number will turn out to be the same for both directions of cross-validation. If it is not, one could argue either for taking the smaller of the two, or an intermediate number. In Cudeck and Browne's examples (discussed shortly), if the number was not the same in both directions it was usually close.

The fit of the model to the correlations in the original subsample necessarily improves as the number of factors increases. But the fit to the correlations in the opposite subsample typically improves and then deteriorates, suggesting that after awhile the factoring in the first subsample is merely fitting idiosyncracies of sampling error, making the fit in the second sample get worse instead of better.

Table 5-9 provides some examples from Cudeck and Browne. The data are subsamples drawn from a large study in which six ability tests were given on three occasions to a large group of high school students. There were thus 18 measures intercorrelated for each subsample, from which 9 factors were extracted using a maximum likelihood procedure. After each factor, the maximum likelihood criterion was calculated for the fit to the opposite subsample correlations; these numbers are presented in the table. As you can see, for the smallest subsample size (75 subjects apiece), the best cross-validation in each direction was for a 3-factor solution. For the 200-subject subsamples, 4 or 5 factors represented the best cross-validation, and for 800-subject subsamples, 8 or 9 factors were optimum.

The authors also reported the number of factors that would have been chosen in each case based on a χ^2 test in the original sample. These χ^2s are not shown in the table, but a § symbol marks the smallest number of factors that yielded an acceptable solution (p > .05). For the smaller samples, the number of factors cross-validating tended to be less than than the number that were statistically significant in the original sample (3 factors versus 5 factors for N = 75). For large samples, the two criteria tended to yield comparable numbers of factors. Cudeck and Browne studied other sample sizes as well as those shown; they also demonstrated that their procedure can be used with other structural models besides factor models.

155

Table 5-9 Using a cross-validation criterion in choosing the number of factors, for three sample sizes (data from Cudeck & Browne, 1983)

Number of factors	N = 75		N = 200		N = 800	
	A	B	A	B	A	B
1	5.02	4.99	2.56	2.52	1.75	1.82
2	4.94	5.14	2.05	2.13	1.31	1.34
3	4.91*	4.71*	1.85	1.87	.92	.97
4	5.30¶	5.05	1.83*	1.90	.81	.81
5	5.55§	5.20§¶	1.90	1.66*	.72	.73
6	5.72	5.37	1.83§¶	1.77§	.69	.68
7	5.97	5.61	1.86	1.74¶	.61	.68
8	5.88	5.79	1.88	1.79	.56*	.64§
9	--	5.70	1.91	1.75	.58¶§	.64*¶

* best cross-validation criterion.
§ smallest number of factors with p > .05.
¶ number of factors chosen by Akaike's criterion.

In addition, they report results for Akaike's information criterion (see Chapter 2) based on the χ^2 in the original sample. The number of factors yielding the most parsimonious solution based on this criterion is shown by the ¶ symbol in Table 5-9. In general, the parsimonious solution by Akaike's criterion corresponded quite well with the first solution acceptable at the .05 level of significance. Both methods slightly overfactored relative to the cross-validation criterion in smaller samples but tended to agree with it in large ones.

Factor Extraction Using Packaged Programs--SPSS, BMDP, SAS, MINITAB

Several widely used statistical program packages contain facilities for doing factor analysis. This section describes the handling of factor extraction by several such programs; their use in factor rotation is considered in Chapter 6. Additional information may be found in a paper by MacCallum (1983), which compares the SPSS, BMDP, and SAS factor analysis programs in some detail. Two cautions: Programs are not static entities--they get revised by their makers from time to time; and program packages are not monolithic--sometimes different subprograms within a package do things differently. There is no substitute for a direct test to determine what the version of program X currently on your local computer actually does in situation Y.

Here we consider the SPSS program called FACTOR (SPSS Inc., 1990), the SAS program PROC FACTOR (SAS Institute, 1990b), and the BMDP program called 4M (Dixon, 1988). These three programs are generally similar in what they do, but not identical. Furthermore, they contain some minor differences in the way they go about doing it that may trip up the unwary user who is familiar with one of them and tries to use another with only a superficial glance at the manual.

In ease of use, the overriding consideration is familiarity with the general system: Someone who knows other SAS or BMDP or SPSS programs should find the corresponding factor analysis program fairly easy to learn and use, whereas someone coming as a complete stranger to a system must acquire a considerable baggage of information about forms of data input, handling of missing values, managing of data and output files, conventions for program representation, etc., common to all the programs in that system. A user might in practice find it easier to accomplish a particular analysis in devious or arcane ways in the system he or she knows, than to learn from scratch another system in which the same analysis can be carried out in a simple and straightforward manner.

In the factor extraction step, all three programs can carry out a simple principal factor analysis of a correlation matrix, with user-supplied communalities. (If these are 1.0, this is a principal components analysis.) BMDP and SAS can also analyze covariance matrices; SPSS cannot. Appendix E shows examples of program setups in the three systems that will accomplish a principal factor analysis for the correlation matrix of Table 5-1, yielding the solution given in Table 5-2.

All three programs can carry out a principal factor analysis with iteration to improve communalities. SPSS starts this process from SMCs (unless the correlation matrix is singular, in which case it automatically switches to the highest r in the row as a starting point). BMDP and SAS allow the user more flexibility. Both allow SMCs or highest r in the row, as well as user-specified values, and SAS has a couple of other options as well (including setting communalities at random!).

.... All three programs allow control of the number of factors either by the user specifying a fixed number of factors, or by declaring a minimum eigenvalue beyond which factoring will not continue. There is, however, a difference in how this is done. SPSS gives priority to the number of factors declaration--i.e., it ignores the minimum eigenvalue specification if the FACTORS criterion is set. SAS and BMDP, however, will use whichever criterion is satisfied first. Thus to insure extracting a given number of factors, a low eigenvalue must be set; to insure a cutoff at a particular eigenvalue, a large number of factors should be specified. SAS uses "all" and "zero" as the default values for number of factors and minimum eigenvalue, respectively, which usually means that if the user specifies one and not the other, the specified parameter will govern, but BMDP uses 1.0 as the default value for the minimum eigenvalue, so the user who simply designates a given number of factors may well find fewer being extracted.

One further complication in using the minimum eigenvalue cutoff is that

SAS and BMDP typically apply this to the eigenvalues of the matrix being factored, which is not the appropriate eigenvalue for the Kaiser-Guttman rule--recall that this refers to eigenvalues of the original correlation matrix **R**, not **R**$_r$. In order to use the Kaiser-Guttman rule in these cases, one must first carry out a principal components analysis to ascertain the appropriate number of factors and then use this number to control the factor analysis. SPSS always bases its minimum eigenvalue cutoff on the eigenvalues of the original correlation matrix and uses 1.0 as the default value for the minimum eigenvalue, making it very easy to apply the Kaiser-Guttman rule.

To do a scree test with BMDP or SPSS, one must obtain the appropriate eigenvalues and plot them by hand or other program. SAS can produce a crude scree plot as an available option, although replotting is usually desirable.

SAS offers a considerable array of alternative procedures for factor extraction: alpha factor analysis, maximum likelihood factor analysis, and several other methods, including some we have not discussed, such as image analysis, least squares analysis, and Harris component analysis. SPSS FACTOR offers alpha analysis, image analysis, maximum likelihood, and ordinary and generalized least squares. BMDP offers the least extensive array of additional alternatives for factor extraction: maximum likelihood and image analysis--the latter only as a component of a package called *little jiffy*.

Finally, the programs differ in what they do if a Heywood case arises during the iteration of communalities. SPSS and BMDP stop, print out an error message, and print out no results from the factor extraction. SAS allows the user to select from several options for dealing with Heywood cases, including fixing the communality to 1.0, stopping, or permitting the Heywood solution to proceed.

All three of the programs allow the user to begin an analysis from raw data or from a correlation matrix entered by the user or produced by other programs in the series. All permit either proceeding directly from the factor extraction to the factor rotation step, or saving the results of the factor extraction for reentry into different rotation procedures.

Packaged factor analysis programs such as these are convenient for use in many practical situations, but there is another approach that allows one complete freedom to experiment with new methods and procedures, or to verify the analyses that existing programs actually carry out (which may sometimes be at variance with what they appear to be from descriptions in the manual, or with what other programs with similar names may do). This approach is to make use of a general-purpose program capable of doing matrix operations. One can then carry out any sequence of operations that can be stated in the language of matrix algebra, which is the primary language of documentation of factor analysis procedures in the technical literature.

Two strategies of this kind might be mentioned. One is the use of MINITAB (Ryan, Joiner, & Ryan, 1985). This is an easy-to-use, undergraduate-oriented language for simple statistical procedures, but it contains matrix facilities as well: It can read, copy, and transpose matrices, and execute the elementary matrix operations of addition, subtraction, multiplication, and inversion. It can also obtain the eigenvalues and vectors of a matrix, and so can carry out essentially all the basic operations involved in the factor extraction phase of factor analysis.

A second option is provided by the matrix facilities in SAS or SPSS. SAS contains an interactive matrix language called IML (SAS Institute, 1990a); SPSS contains a language called MATRIX (SPSS Inc., 1990). These are complex and flexible languages, which put considerably more extensive sets of matrix operations at the disposal of the user, and consequently may be somewhat more difficult for a beginner to use.

There are other possibilities as well: For example, the International Mathematical and Statistical Library of computer subroutines (IMSL, 1987) contains many matrix-oriented FORTRAN subroutines that the user can assemble into programs. Clearly, one's horizons need not be limited by the options that the standard factor analysis packages elect to provide.

Several methods have now been presented for arriving at an initial factor solution. In the next chapter we will consider ways in which this initial solution may be transformed so as to simplify its factor pattern.

Chapter 5 Notes

There are a number of excellent books on factor analysis in which you can pursue further the topics of this and the next chapter. Examples include:

Harman, H. H. (1976). *Modern factor analysis* (3rd ed.). Probably the best systematic treatment of the many variants of factor analysis. Extensive worked examples.

Mulaik, S. A. (1972). *The foundations of factor analysis.* A well-regarded general text.

Gorsuch, R. L. (1983). *Factor analysis* (2nd ed.). Broad and readable, with a practical research emphasis. Less formal than Harman or Mulaik.

Lawley, D. N., & Maxwell, A. E. (1971). *Factor analysis as a statistical method* (2nd ed.). An emphasis on statistical inference and the use of maximum likelihood methods.

Cattell, R. B. (1978). *The scientific use of factor analysis.* A rich but opinionated discussion by a creative contributor to the field.

McDonald, R. P. (1985). *Factor analysis and related methods.* Good on relationships between factor analysis and other latent variable modeling.

Communality estimation. Kaiser (1990) suggests the *square* of the highest correlation of a variable as a good starting point for iterative estimation.

Chapter 5 Exercises

Problems 1-3 involve the following correlation matrix **R**:

$$
\begin{array}{cccc}
1.00 & .28 & -.14 & .42 \\
.28 & 1.00 & -.08 & .24 \\
-.14 & -.08 & 1.00 & -.12 \\
.42 & .24 & -.12 & 1.00
\end{array}
$$

1. Obtain eigenvalues and eigenvectors of **R**, using any available computer program that yields normalized eigenvectors ($\mathbf{V'V = I}$). Rescale the eigenvectors to principal factor pattern coefficients, **P**, by **VL**, where **L** is a diagonal matrix of the square roots of the eigenvalues. Show that by using 1, 2, 3, and 4 factors (i.e, 1 to 4 columns of **P**) **PP′** gives increasingly accurate reconstructions of **R** (but comment).

2. If $\mathbf{U}^2$ is a diagonal matrix of uniquenesses with elements .51, .84, .96, and .64, obtain $\mathbf{R}_r$ as $\mathbf{R - U}^2$. Obtain the eigenvalues and eigenvectors of $\mathbf{R}_r$, and convert to **P** (set any small imaginary square roots to zero). Use the first column of **P** to reconstruct **R**. Comment.

3. Extract a single centroid factor from **R** using the highest *r* method of estimating the communality (don't forget to reflect). Compare to the first principal factors obtained in problems 1 and 2.

Problems 4 to 8 involve the following **R** matrix of five socioeconomic variables for a group of Los Angeles census tracts (Harman, 1976, p. 14).

Variable	1	2	3	4	5
1. Total population	1.00	.01	.97	.44	.02
2. Median school years		1.00	.15	.69	.86
3. Total employment			1.00	.51	.12
4. Professional services				1.00	.78
5. Median house value					1.00
Standard deviations	3440	1.8	1241	115	6368

4. Estimate the communalities of **R** by squared multiple correlations, using any available matrix inversion program.

5. How many factors would be indicated for **R** by the Kaiser-Guttman rule? By the scree test?

6. Using the communalities estimated in problem 4, obtain R_r. Convert this to a (reduced) covariance matrix C_r by SR_rS, where S is a diagonal matrix of the standard deviations of the variables. Obtain principal factor pattern matrices P for R_r and C_r via eigenvalues and vectors. Rescale the latter by $S^{-1}P$. Comment.

7. Assuming that the correlations of R were based on 25 census tracts, test the hypothesis using LISREL that a single common factor would fit these data. (Hint: Fix TD to U^2 and analyze R matrix.) Would you accept or reject the hypothesis of a single common factor?

8. Using any standard factor analysis computer program package, obtain--if available--(unrotated) principal factors, Alpha factors, and maximum likelihood factors. If your program package permits it (not all do), use SMCs without iteration as communality estimates. (If you use iterative estimation, watch out for Heywood cases.) In any event, compare your results to those obtained in problem 6.

Chapter Six:
Exploratory Factor Analysis--II. Transforming the Factors to Simpler Structure

In the last chapter we pursued one approach to simplicity: to account adequately for the data with the smallest number of latent variables, or factors. The strategy was to solve for a series of uncorrelated general factors of decreasing size, each accounting for as much as possible of the covariation left unaccounted for by the preceding factors.

As we noted earlier, the next step is to transform such solutions to simplify them in another way--to minimize the number of paths appearing in the path diagram. This process is what factor analysts have traditionally called *rotation*. It received this name because it is possible to visualize these transformations as rotations of coordinate axes in a multidimensional space. A serious student of factor analysis will certainly want to explore this way of viewing the problem, but we do not need to do so for our purposes here. References to the spatial approach crop up from time to time in our terminology--uncorrelated factors are called *orthogonal* (at right angles), and correlated factors are called *oblique*, because that is the way they looked when the early factor analysts plotted them on their graph paper. But for the most part we view the matter in terms of iterative searches for transformation matrices that will change initial factor solutions into final ones that account just as well for the original correlations but are simpler in other ways. Table 6-1 provides an example, based on a correlation matrix derived from Fig. 6.1 (by now you should be able to verify readily that the path diagram would indeed produce this correlation matrix and the communalities h^2 shown alongside it). The matrix P_0 represents principal factors derived from the eigenvalues and vectors of R_r (using exact communalities), in the manner outlined in the last chapter. It is simple in the first sense we have considered: $P_0 P_0'$ reconstructs R_r exactly (within rounding error); i.e., the two factors account for all the common variance and covariance in the matrix, and the first accounts for as much as possible by itself. The factor pattern is not, however, simple in the second sense. Only one, or at most two,

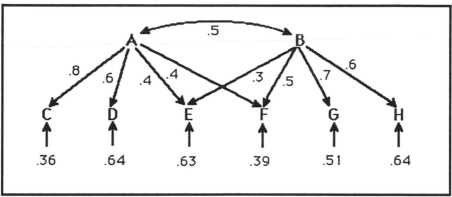

Fig. 6.1 Two factor example to illustrate rotation.

Table 6-1 Example of rotated two-factor solution (artificial data based on Fig. 6.1; exact communalities)

R

	C	D	E	F	G	H	h^2
C	1.00	.48	.44	.52	.28	.24	.64
D	.48	1.00	.33	.39	.21	.18	.36
E	.44	.33	1.00	.47	.35	.30	.37
F	.52	.39	.47	1.00	.49	.42	.61
G	.28	.21	.35	.49	1.00	.42	.49
H	.24	.18	.30	.42	.42	1.00	.36

P_0

	I	II
C	.704	-.379
D	.528	-.284
E	.607	-.032
F	.778	.073
G	.596	.368
H	.510	.315

T

	A	B
I	.607	.547
II	-.982	1.017

$$F = (T'T)^{-1}$$

	A	B
A	1.00	.50
B	.50	1.00

P

	A	B
C	.80	-.00
D	.60	-.00
E	.40	.30
F	.40	.50
G	.00	.70
H	.00	.60

Note: **R** = correlation matrix; **P_0** = initial principal factor pattern; **T** = transformation matrix; **P** = transformed factor pattern; **F** = factor intercorrelations.

paths (from the second factor to E and F) are small enough to plausibly be considered negligible.

Next to **P_0** in the table is a matrix **T**. For the moment we will not worry about how it was obtained--by magic, perhaps. But what it does is to produce by the matrix multiplication P_0T a new matrix P, one that has several zero paths (four, in fact), and whose remaining paths--to two decimal places--agree perfectly with those of the model that generated the data. As shown below T, one can also obtain as a function of T the intercorrelation matrix of the factors, F, again in agreement with the model of Fig. 6.1.

The factor pattern P is "just as good as" P_0 in the sense that both can reconstruct the original (reduced) correlation matrix R_r with two factors-- although because the factors represented by P are correlated, we must take this into account. For P_0, we can use P_0P_0' to yield the matrix R_r. With P, we use PFP', where F is the factor intercorrelation matrix. This is the more general formulation and includes P_0P_0' as a special case: because the initial factors are uncorrelated, their intercorrelation matrix is an identity matrix and can be dropped from the expression.

If we know T, then, we can transform P_0 to the simpler pattern P that we seek (assuming that such a simpler pattern exists). How can we find T? In some cases it can be obtained by direct calculation, but in general it is pursued by a process of iterative trial and error, and nowadays a computer usually carries out the search.

A variety of different procedures exist for this purpose, going by such exotic names as Varimax, Quartimax, Oblimin, Orthoblique, and Promax, to name just a few of the more popular ones. (Gorsuch, 1983, gives a table listing 19 such procedures and describes it as a "sample.") We will say something in a moment about the differences among the methods, but for the moment let us consider them as all doing the same thing: modifying some initial arbitrary T (such as an identity matrix) by some form of systematic trial and error so that it yields a P which, while retaining its capacity to reconstruct R_r, gets progressively simpler and simpler in the second sense of containing an increasing number of zero or near-zero paths.

Why are there 19-plus methods extant? Several reasons might be mentioned. First, some procedures incorporate particular constraints. For example, some seek the best solution with uncorrelated factors, others allow factors to become correlated. Some procedures allow a general factor to emerge, others avoid one. Second, the different procedures differ in such practical characteristics as how widely they are available, how expensive they are to run, how robust they are in the face of various adversities, and so on. And finally, none of them works best on all problems. On a particular correlation matrix, method A finds a simple P that method B does not; on another matrix, method B goes to an elegant solution like a hot knife through butter, whereas method A bogs down hopelessly. Of course, on many problems with fairly simple and clear-cut structure, any of a variety of procedures will locate that structure and yield basically similar results, as we shall see in the case of the simple example problem that we have just considered.

Orthogonal Transformations--Quartimax and Varimax

We begin by considering two orthogonal procedures, Quartimax (Neuhaus & Wrigley, 1954) and Varimax (Kaiser, 1958). These two procedures seek a **T** that will produce factors that are uncorrelated with one another; that is, after the transformation the factors remain independent, but they are simpler in the sense of having more zero or near-zero paths.

Both methods use a criterion of simplicity of **P** that is based on the sum of the fourth powers of the pattern coefficients, and both modify **T** in an iterative fashion until a **P** is reached for which the criterion cannot be improved. In both, the changes in **T** are introduced in such a way that $(\mathbf{T'T})^{-1}$, the factor intercorrelation matrix **F**, always remains an identity matrix. The criteria used, and hence the properties of the solutions, are, however, a little different.

Quartimax uses as a criterion just the sum of the fourth powers of the elements of **P**: in symbols,

$$\Sigma\Sigma p^4,$$

where p represents a pattern coefficient, and the $\Sigma\Sigma$ means to sum over both rows and columns.

Varimax subtracts from this sum a function of the sum of squared coefficents within columns of **P**. The Varimax criterion may be given as

$$\Sigma\Sigma p^4 - {}^1\!/_k \, \Sigma_f(\Sigma_v p^2)^2,$$

where Σ_f and Σ_v indicate summing across factors and variables, respectively, and k is the number of variables.

The sums of fourth powers of the coefficients in a **P** matrix will tend to be greater when some coefficients are high and some are low than when all are middling (given that in both cases the correlation matrix is equally well reconstructed, and the factors remain orthogonal). Thus, the iterative process will tend to move toward a **P** matrix with a few high values and many near-zero values, if such a matrix can be found that continues to meet the other requirements.

The Quartimax criterion is indifferent to where the high values are located within the **P** matrix--many of them could be on a single general factor, for example. The Varimax modification awards a bonus to solutions in which the variance is spread out more evenly across the factors in **P**, so Varimax tends to avoid solutions containing a general factor.

Either procedure may be, and Varimax usually is, applied to variables that have first been rescaled so their communality equals 1.0; that is, the scaling used in Alpha factor analysis is employed. This tends to prevent the transformation process from being dominated by a few variables of high communality. Varimax applied to variables rescaled in this way is usually referred to as "normal" or "normalized" Varimax--as opposed to "raw" Varimax, in which the criterion is calculated on coefficients in their ordinary scaling. The rescaling is easily accomplished by dividing every coefficient in a row of the factor pattern matrix by the h^2 of that variable before beginning the rotational process, and then scaling back by multiplying by h^2 at the end. This procedure is also sometimes referred to as "Kaiser normalization," after its inventor.

Both Quartimax and Varimax are relatively fast and robust procedures and are widely available in standard computer factor analysis packages. They can be used with confidence whenever conditions are suitable (i.e, where the causal factors underlying the observed correlations are expected to be independent of one another, or nearly so). The choice between them would depend on whether one wishes to encourage or discourage the appearance of a general factor. If in doubt, one can, of course, try it both ways. If they arrive at the same solution, well and good. If they do not, one knows that there is more than one plausible intepretation of the data.

Even when moderately correlated factors are expected, these methods are sometimes still used because of their other virtues. With correlated factors, they cannot be expected to provide very neat solutions, but they will often identify the main factors correctly. If an orthogonal procedure is used when factors are really correlated, the low correlations will only be relatively low, not near zero as they would be with an oblique factor solution, but the high and low correlations will often match fairly well in the two solutions.

Table 6-2 gives examples of Quartimax and Varimax solutions based on the sample problem of Table 6-1. An initial principal factor solution was transformed so as to maximize the Quartimax or Varimax criterion. The raw versions were used to keep the examples simple. Note that the **T**s for orthogonal rotations are symmetrical, apart from signs.

It will be observed that the Varimax **P** approximates the values of the original path model fairly well in its larger coefficients, but that the small ones are systematically overestimated. The Quartimax **P** assigns relatively more variance to the first factor, making it a fairly general factor.

From the values of the Quartimax and Varimax criteria given at the bottom of the table, you can see that each criterion is highest for its own solution (as it should be). The initial principal factor solution is not too bad by the Quartimax criterion because it does have some high and some low loadings, but it is unsatisfactory to Varimax because the principal factor solution maximizes the difference in variance between the two factors.

In this example, Varimax does better than Quartimax at approximating the paths of the original model, and either one does better than the initial principal factor solution. The advantage Varimax has here results from the fact that the model to be approximated has two roughly equal factors--that is, there is no general factor present.

Varimax and Quartimax can be considered special cases of a general class of orthogonal transformations called Orthomax, whose criterion can be written:

$$\Sigma\Sigma p^4 - w\,{}^1\!/_k \Sigma_f (\Sigma_v p^2)^2\,.$$

The weight w determines the particular criterion. If $w = 0$, the second part of the expression vanishes, and we have the Quartimax criterion. With $w = 1$, we have Varimax. Intermediate values of w would yield solutions with intermediate properties. A negative value of w would award a bonus to solutions with unequal factors, instead of a penalty, and so on.

Table 6-2 Factor pattern matrices, factor intercorrelations, and transformation matrices for Quartimax and Varimax transformations of an initial principal factor solution (example problem of Fig. 6-1)

P	Initial		Quartimax		Varimax		Paths	
	I	II	A	B	A	B	A	B
C	.70	-.38	.78	-.17	.78	.20	.80	.00
D	.53	-.28	.59	-.13	.58	.15	.60	.00
E	.61	-.03	.59	.13	.47	.39	.40	.30
F	.78	.07	.73	.28	.52	.58	.40	.50
G	.60	.37	.47	.52	.19	.67	.00	.70
H	.51	.32	.41	.44	.16	.58	.00	.60

F	I	II		A	B		A	B		A	B
I	1.00	.00	A	1.00	.00	A	1.00	.00	A	1.00	.50
II	.00	1.00	B	.00	1.00	B	.00	1.00	B	.50	1.00

T			A	B		A	B
I			.962	.273		.736	.677
II			-.273	.962		-.677	.736

Criteria:

Quartimax	1.082		1.092	1.060
Varimax	.107		.204	.389

Note: Communalities for initial solution iterated from SMCs. Raw Quartimax and Varimax transformations. Paths from path diagram.

Oblique Transformations

When operating in a situation where the true underlying factors are substantially correlated, the procedures of the last section cannot achieve ideal solutions. A number of methods have been proposed for locating good solutions when factors are correlated with one another ("oblique"). Because the factor intercorrelations represent additional free variables, there are more possibilities for strange things to happen in oblique than in orthogonal solutions. For example, two tentative factors may converge on the same destination during an iterative search, as evidenced by the correlation between them becoming high and eventually moving toward 1.00--this cannot happen if factors are kept orthogonal. Despite their real theoretical merits, oblique solutions tend to be more expensive to compute, more vulnerable to idiosyncracies in the data, and generally more likely to go extravagantly awry than orthogonal ones. There is no one oblique procedure that works well in all situations, hence the proliferation of methods. We discuss in detail only two of the many existing methods and mention a few others briefly. First, we consider Direct Oblimin, an approach that pursues a general iterative solution based on improving a criterion as in the Quartimax or Varimax solutions, except that the requirement that factors be uncorrelated is dropped. Then we discuss a procedure, Promax, which attempts to retain the general robustness of the orthogonal methods while arriving at an oblique factor solution.

Direct Oblimin

The criterion used in the Direct Oblimin procedure (Jennrich & Sampson, 1966) is as follows--the criterion is minimized rather than maximized:

$$\Sigma_{ij} \left(\Sigma_v p_i^2 p_j^2 - w \, {}^1\!/_k \, \Sigma_v p_i^2 \, \Sigma_v p_j^2 \right).$$

Σ_{ij} refers to the sum over all factor pairs ij ($i < j$), and the other symbols are as used for the Varimax criterion. The weight w (sometimes given as δ) specifies different variants of Oblimin that differ in the degree to which correlation among the factors is encouraged. If $w = 0$, only the first part of the expression, the products of the squared pattern coefficients on different factors, is operative. This variant is sometimes given a special name, Direct Quartimin. It tends to result in solutions with fairly substantial correlations among the factors. By making the weight w negative, high correlations among factors are penalized. Most often, zero weights or modest negative weights (e.g., $w = -.5$) will work best. Large negative weights (e.g., $w = -10$) will yield essentially orthogonal factors. Positive weights (e.g., $w = .5$) tend to produce overoblique and often problematic solutions.

    The term *direct* in the title of Direct Oblimin indicates that the criterion is applied directly to the factor pattern matrix **P**. (There also exists an Indirect

Oblimin, in which the criterion is applied to another matrix.) Again, as in the case of the orthogonal procedures, the scaling of Alpha factor analysis may be used, so that the transformation is carried out on a factor matrix rescaled so that all the communalities are equal to 1.0, with a return to the original metric at the end.

Table 6-3 presents a Direct Oblimin solution for the sample 2-factor problem. (The Quartimin version--$w = 0$--was used.) Observe that the pattern coefficients approximate the paths of the initial model quite well, except that the near-zero loadings are slightly negative. The correlation between factors is a little on the high side (.57 vs. .50), but on the whole the solution has recovered quite well the characteristics of the path diagram that generated the correlations.

Below the **F** in the table is the **T**, the transformation matrix that produces the Oblimin **P** from the **P₀** of the initial solution. It is this **T**, of course, that has resulted from iterative modifications by the computer program until the resulting **P** has as low a score as possible on the Oblimin criterion. In the bottom row of

Table 6-3. Factor pattern matrices, factor intercorrelations and transformation matrices for two oblique transformations of an initial principal factor solution (example problem of Fig. 6-1)

P	Initial I	Initial II		Oblimin A	Oblimin B		Promax A	Promax B		Paths A	Paths B
C	.70	-.38		.81	-.02		.86	-.10		.80	.00
D	.53	-.28		.61	-.01		.65	-.07		.60	.00
E	.61	-.03		.38	.30		.39	.27		.40	.30
F	.78	.07		.37	.51		.37	.49		.40	.50
G	.60	.37		-.05	.73		-.08	.75		.00	.70
H	.51	.32		-.04	.62		-.07	.64		.00	.60

F	I	II		A	B		A	B		A	B
I	1.00	.00	A	1.00	.57	A	1.00	.65	A	1.00	.50
II	.00	1.00	B	.57	1.00	B	.65	1.00	B	.50	1.00

T				A	B		A	B			
I				.575	.555		.587	.513			
II				-1.071	1.081		-1.178	1.212			

Criterion:
Oblimin   .172   .051   .059

Note: Same initial solution as Table 6-2. Oblimin is Direct Quartimin (*w*=0), not normalized. Both **T** matrices are for rotation from initial solution. Promax based on raw Varimax to 4th power.

the table are given values of the Oblimin criterion for the initial solution, for the Oblimin solution, and for another solution, Promax, discussed shortly. The Promax solution is reasonably good by the Oblimin criterion, although of course not quite as good as Oblimin; both are much better than the initial unrotated solution.

Promax

The Promax solution (Hendrickson & White, 1964) proceeds in two steps. First a Varimax solution is obtained. Then it is transformed to an oblique solution that has the same high and low loadings, but with the low loadings reduced (if possible) to near-zero values. The second step is done by direct calculation, not iteration, so that if an orthogonal solution can correctly identify the factors, Promax provides an efficient route to an oblique solution.

The second step of a Promax solution is a variant of a procedure called Procrustes (Hurley & Cattell, 1962), which forces a factor pattern matrix to a best least squares fit to a predesignated target matrix. It gets its name from the legendary Greek who forced travelers to fit his guest bed by stretching or lopping them as necessary.

In Promax, the target matrix is obtained by raising the elements of the Varimax-rotated pattern matrix to a higher power--usually the third or fourth--and restoring minus signs if the power is even. By raising the pattern coefficients to a higher power, the low values go essentially to zero, and the high values, although they are lowered, remain appreciable, so the contrast between high and low values is sharpened. For example, at the fourth power all loadings of .26 or less become zero to two decimal places, whereas loadings of .70 and .80 remain .24 and .41.

Call the target matrix P_t. Then an initial transformation matrix T_i is obtained by a least squares matrix solution of an overdetermined set of simultaneous equations:

$$T_i = (P_0'P_0)^{-1}P_0'P_t \, ,$$

where P_0 is the initial unrotated factor pattern matrix. This is the first part of the Procrustes solution. The second part is to rescale T_i to its final form T by postmultiplying it by a diagonal matrix D, chosen to make the factor intercorrelation matrix $(T'T)^{-1}$ have diagonal elements equal to 1.0. The necessary D may be obtained as the square roots of the diagonal elements of $(T_i'T_i)^{-1}$.

Table 6-4 illustrates these steps for the Promax solution of Table 6-3, based on the Varimax solution of Table 6-2. At the left of the table is P_t, obtained from the Varimax solution by raising its elements to the fourth power (because they were all initially positive, no restoration of minus signs is

170

Table 6-4 Calculation of a Promax solution via Procrustes, from the Varimax solution of Table 6-2

P_t		T_i		D		$P = P_0T$	
A	B	A	B	A	B	A	B
.37	.00	I .171	.115	A 3.253	.000	.84	-.06
.11	.00	II -.362	.247	B .000	4.779	.62	-.04
.05	.02					.37	.30
.07	.11	$(T_i'T_i)^{-1}$		$T = T_iD$		.35	.51
.00	.20	A	B	A	B	-.10	.77
.00	.11	A 10.583	9.947	I .556	.549	-.09	.66
		B 9.947	22.842	II -1.176	1.180		

Note: P_t is target factor pattern = Varimax solution of Table 6-2 with elements raised to 4th power. $T_i = (P_0'P_0)^{-1}P_0'P_t$ = transformation matrix before rescaling. D = square roots of diagonal elements of $(T_i'T_i)^{-1}$. T = rescaled transformation matrix. P_0 = unrotated factor pattern. P = rotated factor pattern.

required). In the center of the table, T_i, $(T_i'T_i)^{-1}$, D, and T are successively calculated. At the right, T is applied to the unrotated solution to yield a Promax solution. (The resulting solution is similar but not quite identical to the Promax solution in Table 6-3, which was obtained via a computer package program that calculates its target matrix in a slightly more complicated fashion.)

Other oblique rotation methods

As noted earlier, a large number of different methods for oblique factor rotation have been proposed. Some represent slight variations on those mentioned here; the reader can consult other sources (such as Gorsuch, 1983) for more details and citations to original articles. Two methods operating on rather different principles are worth mentioning briefly. One is the method called Orthoblique (Harris & Kaiser, 1964). This procedure, like Promax, reaches an oblique solution via an orthogonal rotation, but the strategy is a slightly different one. The first *k* eigenvectors of the correlation matrix (where *k* is the desired number of factors) are subjected to an orthogonal rotation (originally, raw Quartimax, although others can also be used). The transformation matrix developed in this step is then rescaled in its rows or columns or both by suitable diagonal matrices, to become the final transformation matrix T, the matrix that transforms an initial principal factor solution into the final rotated oblique solution.

The other principle to be considered is embodied in procedures such as Maxplane (Cattell & Muerle, 1960) and the KD transformation (Kaiser &

Madow,1974). These methods focus specifically on low pattern coefficients and work at transforming factors to get as many pattern coefficients close to zero as possible. Methods such as these strive directly for the second kind of simplicity in a pattern matrix--a large number of near-zero paths. They are most often used to apply final touches to an approximate solution arrived at by another procedure. As a case in point, the KD procedure applied following an Orthoblique rotation yielded a solution in the Table 6-3 rotation problem that was an almost exact reproduction of the underlying path model, differing from it by no more than .01 in any correlation or path coefficient.

Factor pattern and factor structure in oblique solutions

As mentioned previously, two matrices relating the observed variables to the latent variables are frequently reported. One is the factor pattern matrix **P** that we have already discussed. The other is the factor structure matrix **S**, which is a matrix giving the correlations between the factors and the variables. When factors are uncorrelated (orthogonal), there is just a single path from any factor to any variable, and hence the correlation between them is numerically equal to the path coefficient. In this case, therefore, **S** equals **P**, and only one need be reported. However, in an oblique solution, there will be additional compound paths between factors and variables via correlations with other factors, and **S** will in general not be equal to **P**. However, **S** may readily be calculated from **P** and the factor intercorrelations **F** by the equation:

$$\mathbf{S} = \mathbf{PF}.$$

Table 6-5 gives an example for the oblique solution of Table 6-1 (two-factor example with exact communalities). Note that the **S** matrix does not have the zero paths of the **P** matrix; because the factors are correlated, each is

Table 6-5 Factor structure, for example of Table 6-1

	Factor pattern **P**			Factor intercorrelations **F**			Factor structure **S**	
	A	B		A	B		A	B
C	.80	.00	A	1.00	.50	C	.80	.40
D	.60	.00	B	.50	1.00	D	.60	.30
E	.40	.30				E	.55	.50
F	.40	.50				F	.65	.70
G	.00	.70				G	.35	.70
H	.00	.60				H	.30	.60

correlated with variables on which it has no direct causal influence. (The reader should verify from Fig. 6.1 that the matrix multiplication that yields **S** is equivalent to determining the correlations from tracing the paths in the path diagram.)

The reference vector system

When factor analyses were done by hand on desk calculators, the minimization of computations took precedence over conceptual simplicity, and a clever scheme of Thurstone's (1947) that permitted carrying out the factor analysis calculations indirectly on a system of *reference vectors* was widely employed, because it required fewer matrix inversions during the analysis. Although this scheme is not much used nowadays (and if it is, it is likely to be concealed within the computer program), the student needs to be aware of its existence in reading the earlier literature, where results are often presented in this form.

When factors are orthogonal, the distinction between the two systems may be ignored because the factor pattern and structure not only coincide with each other, but also with the pattern and structure expressed in terms of the reference vectors.

When factors are correlated the two systems become distinct, but there is a simple relationship of proportionality between the reference vector structure-- the correlations of variables with the reference vectors--and the factor pattern **P**. Note that this is a relation of structure (correlations) in one system to pattern (path coefficients) in the other. Thurstone's famous criterion of "simple structure," which was the goal of his solutions in the reference vector system, corresponds to simplicity of the pattern matrix **P**, which is the goal of the factor transformation procedures we have described in this chapter.

For the details of calculating the diagonal matrices that will transform results back and forth between the two systems, the reader may consult Harman (1976) or other standard factor analysis texts.

Estimating Factor Scores

Given a factor solution, and the scores of individuals on the observed variables, can we assign to the individuals scores on the latent variables, the factors? This would be attractive to do, if we assume the latent variables to represent fundamental causal influences underlying the interrelations of the superficial measures we actually observe.

The answer is, in general, that we cannot, although we can provide *estimates* of such scores. These estimates may be quite good if the observed variables are strongly related to the latent variables, or quite poor if they are not.

A number of different methods have been proposed and are discussed in standard factor analysis texts such as Gorsuch (1983) or Harman (1976). One simple one is to add together, with equal weight, the scores on the observed variables that are most highly correlated with the factor--a robust approach that has a good deal to be said for it. However, the most widely used method is to recognize that we are dealing with a prediction situation, in which we want to predict the latent variable, the factor, from the set of observed variables. An accepted way of making predictions of a given variable from a set of related variables is by carrying out a multiple regression.

Recall that in multiple regression one solves for a set of weights (called *beta weights*), which can be applied to the observed variables to predict the unknown variable. To solve for such weights, one needs to know the correlations among the predictor variables, and the correlations of these with the variable being predicted. Then the vector of beta weights may be obtained by premultiplying the latter by the inverse of the former. The matrix of correlations among the predictors (the observed variables) is of course obtainable--it is just the correlation matrix **R**. The correlations of the observed variables with a factor is a column of the factor structure matrix **S**, let's call this **s**. So we can get the desired beta weights **b** for estimating a factor as follows:

$$\mathbf{b} = \mathbf{R}^{-1}\mathbf{s} .$$

These weights **b**, applied to the observed variables in standard-score form, will yield the best prediction, in the least squares sense, of this factor from these variables. The equation

$$\mathbf{B} = \mathbf{R}^{-1}\mathbf{S}$$

will give the beta weights, as columns of **B**, for the whole set of factors simultaneously.

One can work with raw instead of standard scores by rescaling the betas appropriately and supplying an additive constant, but we need not deal with such complications here. Any standard text on multiple regression will supply the details.

All the other paraphernalia of regression analysis apply. The vector multiplication **b´s** gives the square of the multiple correlation of the factor with the predictors and thus represents the proportion of variance of the factor that is predictable from the observed variables. This will give one some notion of how well the factor scores are estimated in the present set of data. To get an idea of how well these factor estimation weights will transfer to new samples, a cross-validity coefficient can be calculated (Rozeboom, 1978):

$$R_c^2 = 1 - (1 - R^2)(N + m)/(N - m) .$$

The R^2 inside the parentheses is the squared multiple correlation, N is the sample size, and m is the number of predictors (observed variables). The corrected value R_c^2 is an estimate of how well the beta weights calculated in the given sample will predict in the population (and hence, on the average, in new random samples from that population). If the measurement is good--that is, the obtained multiple correlation is high--and if the ratio of subjects to variables is large, one would not expect much falling off of prediction in a new sample. For instance, in a 6-variable problem based on 100 subjects in which the obtained multiple correlation is .90, the expected drop-off when using the factor estimation weights in a new sample is only to a correlation of .89: $R_c^2 = 1 - (1 - .81)\ 106/94 = .786;\ \sqrt{.786} = .89$. If one were to do a 17-variable factor analysis on 50 subjects and obtain a multiple correlation of .70, the expected drop would be all the way to zero (try it in the formula and see), and the factor score estimation would be completely worthless.

The factor scores estimated by regression using beta weights and standardized predictors will have a mean of zero and a variance equal to R^2. If it is desired to produce the factor scores in standard score form, which is customary, the beta weights can simply be multiplied by 1/R before applying them to the (standardized) predictors. (A moment's reflection should show why this is so: If it doesn't, ask yourself, What is the standard deviation of the initial set of estimated factor scores? and reread this paragraph.)

Table 6-6 (next page) illustrates the calculation of factor scores for our two-factor example. At the top of the table are **R**⁻¹, the inverse of the correlation matrix, and **S**, the factor structure matrix (the latter from Table 6-5). **R**⁻¹**S** yields the beta weights, **B**. **B′S** yields a matrix that has the squared multiple correlations from the regressions in its principal diagonal; the reciprocals of their square roots constitute the rescaling matrix **D**⁻¹ᐟ², which rescales **B** to **W**. **W** contains the coefficients that produce standardized estimates of the factor scores.

The final step is taken in the bottom row of the table. Hypothetical data for three subjects on the six variables are shown. Postmultiplied by **W**, these yield the estimates (in standard-score form) of scores for these three individuals on the two factors A and B.

The correlation among these factor estimates can be obtained, if desired, by pre- and postmultiplying **B′S** by **D**⁻¹ᐟ². The estimates for the two factors turn out to be correlated .67, somewhat higher than the correlation of .50 between the factors themselves. This is a typical result when estimating factor scores by this method.

Table 6-6 Estimating factor scores by regression (two-factor example of Tables 6-1 and 6-5)

R⁻¹		Inverse of correlation matrix					S	Factor structure	
	C	D	E	F	G	H		A	B
C	1.64	-.48	-.32	.52	.01	.00	C	.80	.40
D	-.48	1.36	-.14	-.22	.00	.00	D	.60	.30
E	-.32	-.14	1.43	-.31	-.18	-.12	E	.55	.50
F	-.52	-.22	-.31	1.88	-.48	-.33	F	.65	.70
G	.01	.00	-.18	-.48	1.44	-.35	G	.35	.70
H	.00	.00	-.12	-.33	-.35	1.32	H	.30	.60

B	Beta weights					W	Factor score weights	
	A	B	B′S				A	B
C	.51	-.01	.769	.502		C	.58	-.01
D	.22	-.00	.502	.725		D	.25	-.00
E	.15	.13				E	.17	.15
F	.23	.35	D⁻¹ᐟ²			F	.27	.41
G	-.00	.38	1.140	.000		G	-.00	.44
H	-.00	.26	.000	1.174		H	-.00	.30

Z	Data (standard scores)						Z_F	Factor scores	
	C	D	E	F	G	H		A	B
	1.2	.6	1.5	.8	.1	1.1		1.31	.92
	-1.0	-1.6	-.1	.0	.8	-1.4		-.99	-.07
	-.7	1.2	.9	-1.0	-1.3	.7		-.23	-.64
	.	.	.	.	.	.		.	.
	.	.	.	.	.	.		.	.

Note: $B = R^{-1}S$; $D = \text{diag } B'S$; $W = BD^{-1/2}$; $Z_F = ZW$.

Factor score indeterminacy

It is tempting to interpret the factor score estimation problem as though there were a "real" set of factor scores out there somewhere, and our difficulty is in not being able to estimate them accurately. But in a sense, the fundamental problem is not really one of estimation; it is that a given factor solution (**P, S,** and **F**) just doesn't define factors uniquely. For any given **P, S,** and **F** there is a range of potential factors that are equally compatible with the obtained results. If the communalities of the original variables are high, these potential factors will tend to be highly correlated, much like one another, and the choice among them may not be crucial. But if the communalities are low, some potential factors may actually have zero correlations with others (McDonald & Mulaik,

1979). In short, if we hope to score subjects accurately on latent variables, they should be latent variables with strong and preferably multiple links to data. If there are important aspects of our latent constructs that are not well-reflected in our measurements, and many aspects of our measures unrelated to the latent constructs, we should not be surprised if there is ambiguity in trying to assess the one from the other.

Extension analysis

Suppose we carry out an exploratory factor analysis on a set of variables, and have available the scores of additional variables for the same subjects. Can we extend the factor solution to these new variables? The answer is that we can, but subject to the same limitation as with calculating scores on the factors.

The simplest way, conceptually, is just to obtain the estimated scores on a factor and correlate these scores with the scores on the additional variables. This will provide the matrix **S** for the new variables, their correlations with the (estimated) factors. One can then obtain the factor pattern matrix **P** for the new variables by the relationship $P = SF^{-1}$, the inverse of the relationship $S = PF$ given earlier for getting the factor structure from the factor pattern matrix. Again, this is the factor pattern for the new variables with respect to the estimated factors, and the utility of an extension analysis thus is dependent, to a considerable degree, on the presence of conditions that minimize factor indeterminacy and lead to accurate estimation of factor scores.

In practice we do not actually have to go through the step of calculating factor scores for individuals--a matrix shortcut exists. To obtain the estimated correlations of a factor with the new variables, one may multiply the matrix of correlations of the new variables with the old ones, call it **Q**, times the vector of beta weights scaled to produce standardized factor scores, call it **w**; that is,

s = Qw.

If **W** is a matrix with rescaled beta weights as its columns, the equation becomes:

S = QW,

providing a convenient way of calculating **S**, and thence **P**.

Table 6-7 illustrates the extension of the example two-factor analysis to two new variables, I and J. Hypothetical correlations of the two new variables with the original six variables are shown as **Q**, as are the factor score coefficients **W** from the preceding table. The factor structure matrix **S** for the new variables is obtained by the matrix multiplication **QW**, and the factor pattern matrix **P** by SF^{-1}, where F^{-1} is the inverse of the factor intercorrelation matrix **F** from Table 6-1. The matrix **S** gives the estimated correlations of the new variables with the two factors A and B, and **P** gives estimates of the paths

Table 6-7 Extension of factor analysis of Table 6-1 to two new variables I and J

Q		Correlations of new variables with original variables						W	Factor score weights	
	C	D	E	F	G	H			A	B
I	.60	.40	.50	.60	.50	.40		C	.58	-.01
J	.20	.10	-.10	-.30	-.10	-.20		D	.25	-.00
								E	.17	.15
S	Factor structure			P	Factor pattern			F	.27	.41
								G	-.00	.44
	A	B			A	B		H	-.00	.30
I	.69	.66		I	.48	.42				
J	.05	-.24		J	.22	-.36				

Note: $S = QW$; $P = SF^{-1}$. Factor score weights from Table 6-6.

from the factors to the new variables.

There is a question that might have occurred to some readers: If one has scores on the additional variables for the same subjects, why weren't these variables just entered into the factor analysis in the first place, yielding correlations and path coefficients with the factors directly? There could be several reasons why one might not do this. The additional scores might only have become available after the factor analysis was carried out. Or the additional variables might have been excluded from the factor analysis to avoid distorting it or biasing it in some way; for example, some variables might have been excluded because of artifactually high correlations with included variables, or because they were external reference variables which were desired for help in interpreting the factors, but which one did not want influencing the factor analysis itself. Or one might have an extremely large number of variables available, only a subset of which could feasibly be used for a factor analysis, but all of whose relationships with the factors would be of interest. In any of these situations, an extension analysis could be the answer.

Factor Rotation Programs--SPSS, BMDP, and SAS

In the last chapter, the factor extraction procedures contained in a number of statistical program packages were considered. In this section we briefly examine the procedures for rotation that these packages offer.

All three packages provide the basic orthogonal rotation procedures Varimax and Quartimax, either raw or normalized; BMDP and SAS also provide the more general Orthomax procedure of which these two are special cases.

There is more variation among oblique rotation procedures. SPSS offers only one, Direct Oblimin, which BMDP also provides, although SAS does not. SAS, on the other hand, offers both Promax and Procrustes, which the others don't. SAS has Orthoblique as well; BMDP has it only as part of the separate "little jiffy" package, and SPSS does not have it at all.

The packages differ in their default philosophy--i.e., in what they do if no specification is made concerning rotation. SPSS and BMDP rotate automatically, using their default rotation procedure, which in both cases is Varimax. In order not to rotate, the user must specify a no-rotation option. In SAS the default is for no rotation, so if the user wishes to rotate he or she must specify a particular rotation procedure.

All the rotation methods described in this chapter, except Procrustes, are iterative in character and so would be quite tedious to carry out by simple matrix calculations, as in MINITAB. MATRIX and IML permit more extensive programming, and so would allow iterative procedures. In any event, one can go a long way with one basic iterative orthogonal routine, say Varimax, and a matrix package. Such oblique procedures as Promax and Orthoblique do their basic iterative rotation orthogonally and then transform to an oblique solution at the end.

An Example: Thurstone's Box Problem

In this section, we carry through an exploratory factor analysis from raw scores to factor scores. We use as an example a demonstration problem originally devised by Thurstone (1947) and later modified by Kaiser and Horst (1975). The intent is to illustrate exploratory factor analysis in a situation in which the true underlying latent variables are known, so we can check our results.

Thurstone began with a hypothetical population of 20 rectangular boxes; the first three are illustrated at the top of Table 6-8. For each box, a number of "scores" were derived, as mathematical functions of one or more of its three dimensions: length (= X), width (= Y), and height (= Z). Thus, the first box, which was 3 units long by 2 wide by 1 high, had a score on the first variable (X^2) of 9, on the second (Y^2) of 4, and so on. The 4th, 5th, and 6th variables are products of two dimensions each, the 7th through 9th are natural logarithms, and the 10th is the triple product XYZ. (Thurstone actually created 20 variables, but we are using only 10 of them to keep the example more manageable.)

Kaiser and Horst added 5% random error to Thurstone's scores, in the interest of greater realism, and doubled the number of boxes from 20 to 40 by using each twice (with different random errors). The resulting scores for the first three boxes, rounded to one decimal place, are shown in the columns labeled *Observed* in Table 6-8. The complete data matrix is given in Appendix F. The matrix of score intercorrelations is given in Table 6-9, and the eigenvalues and

Table 6-8 Scores on 10 variables for first three boxes, Thurstone's box problem (data from Kaiser & Horst, 1975)

Variable	Box 1		Box 2		Box 3	
	True	Observed	True	Observed	True	Observed
1. X^2	9.0	8.9	9.0	9.4	9.0	6.9
2. Y^2	4.0	5.0	4.0	4.5	9.0	10.2
3. Z^2	1.0	2.7	4.0	3.8	1.0	.7
4. XY	6.0	5.6	6.0	5.4	9.0	10.3
5. XZ	3.0	3.4	6.0	8.1	3.0	4.2
6. YZ	2.0	2.1	4.0	3.4	3.0	3.2
7. ln X	1.1	1.1	1.1	1.1	1.1	1.1
8. ln Y	.7	.8	.7	.6	1.1	1.1
9. ln Z	0	.3	.7	.4	0	.0
10. XYZ	6.0	2.3	12.0	9.8	9.0	9.9

Table 6-9 Correlation matrix, Thurstone box problem

	V1	V2	V3	V4	V5	V6	V7	V8	V9	V10
V1	1.00	.23	.08	.64	.42	.15	.92	.10	.10	.46
V2		1.00	.17	.84	.21	.57	.37	.93	.13	.53
V3			1.00	.14	.85	.84	.16	.27	.91	.77
V4				1.00	.34	.50	.73	.76	.12	.65
V5					1.00	.78	.50	.22	.87	.87
V6						1.00	.30	.64	.81	.91
V7							1.00	.28	.18	.59
V8								1.00	.21	.58
V9									1.00	.76
V10										1.00

a scree test in Table 6-10 and Fig. 6.2. Clearly, by either the Kaiser-Guttman rule or the scree test, a three-factor solution is indicated. Table 6-11 shows three principal factors based on the (unrounded) correlation matrix, using iterated communality estimates starting from SMCs. As you can see, the communality estimates are all quite high, in the range .90 to .97, consistent with the fact that the variables contain about 5% random error.

Table 6-10 Eigenvalues, Thurstone box problem

1.	5.621	6.	.079
2.	2.348	7.	.072
3.	1.602	8.	.049
4.	.100	9.	.025
5.	.088	10.	.015

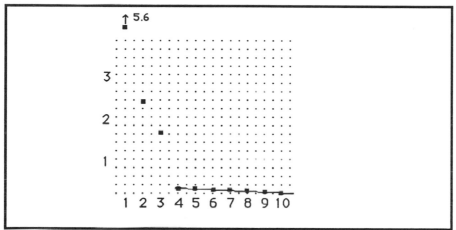

Fig. 6.2 Scree test for Thurstone box problem.

Table 6-11 Unrotated principal factors, Thurstone box problem

Variables	F1	F2	F3	h²
V1	.503	.468	.683	.938
V2	.649	.506	-.499	.925
V3	.732	-.615	-.020	.914
V4	.736	.647	-.056	.963
V5	.834	-.400	.282	.934
V6	.904	-.280	-.252	.959
V7	.633	.470	.558	.933
V8	.664	.382	-.604	.951
V9	.717	-.627	.045	.909
V10	.971	-.108	.047	.956

Table 6-12 shows two transformed solutions and a direct confirmatory maximum likelihood solution. The first solution is an orthogonal rotation using Varimax. For most practical purposes, this would be quite adequate: It correctly identifies the three factors as respectively reflecting the latent dimensions Z, Y, and X that underlie the manifest measurements, as one may verify by comparing the rotated factor pattern to the path diagram of Fig. 6.3.

Table 6-12 Final factor solutions, Thurstone box problem

	Varimax			Direct Oblimin			Confirmatory		
	F1	F2	F3	F1	F2	F3	F1	F2	F3
V1	.08	.06	.96	-.00	-.08	.99	.00	.00	.96
V2	.11	.94	.16	-.03	.96	.03	.00	.96	.00
V3	.95	.08	-.02	.98	-.04	-.11	.95	.00	.00
V4	.10	.77	.60	-.05	.72	.51	.00	.70	.53
V5	.90	.05	.36	.90	-.12	.29	.85	.00	.36
V6	.84	.50	.05	.80	.41	-.09	.79	.48	.00
V7	.17	.22	.93	.07	.08	.92	.00	.00	.95
V8	.20	.95	.02	.08	.98	-.12	.00	.95	.00
V9	.95	.02	.02	.99	-.10	-.07	.95	.00	.00
V10	.79	.43	.39	.73	.30	.28	.71	.36	.36
F1	1.00	.00	.00	1.00	.28	.22	1.00	.15	.11
F2		1.00	.00		1.00	.29		1.00	.25
F3			1.00			1.00			1.00

Note: Kaiser normalization used for Varimax and Oblimin solutions.

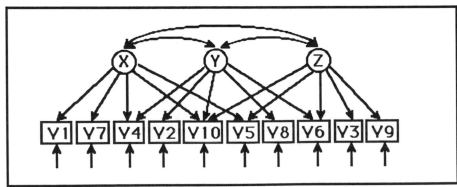

Fig. 6.3 Path diagram of Thurstone box problem.

Nevertheless, because nearly all the minor loadings in the Varimax solution are positive, there is an indication that the underlying dimensions X, Y, and Z are slightly correlated with one another; i.e., that there is a general size factor in the population of boxes. Therefore, an oblique solution (Direct Oblimin; $w = 0$) was carried out; it is also shown in Table 6-12. This yields a slightly cleaner solution; whereas the Varimax factor pattern had several of its minor loadings in the .15 to .25 range, the oblique solution has all its near-zero loadings .12 or less in absolute value. The correlations among the factors are modest--in the .20s. There is, however, a suggestion that this solution may be a little too oblique: 11 of the 15 near-zero loadings are negative.

On the far right in Table 6-12 is a confirmatory maximum likelihood analysis of the correlation matrix via LISREL, based on the path diagram of Fig. 6.3: the zero values shown were fixed, and the nonzero values solved for. Note that this solution is a trifle less oblique than the Oblimin solution but agrees with it in finding the three dimensions to be slightly correlated in these data, suggesting the presence of a (modest) general size factor. We can compare the factor intercorrelations with the true correlations among the length, width, and height dimensions, calculated for Thurstone's original population of boxes: $r_{XY} = .25$, $r_{YZ} = .25$, $r_{XZ} = .10$. The two oblique factor solutions have come reasonably close--the Oblimin, as suspected, has slightly overestimated the correlations.

Finally, Table 6-13 shows factor scores for the first three boxes, from the Oblimin solution. Comparison to standardized values of the true scores suggests that, with these high communalities, the factor scores do a reasonable (although not a perfect) job of estimating the true-score values.

Table 6-13 Theoretical true standard scores compared to factor scores, first three boxes (Oblimin solution)

	Original			Standardized			Factor scores		
	X	Y	Z	X	Y	Z	F3	F2	F1
Box 1	3	2	1	-1.43	-1.29	-1.17	-1.47	-1.05	-.93
Box 2	3	2	2	-1.43	-1.29	.13	-1.26	-1.40	-.26
Box 3	3	3	1	-1.43	.00	-1.17	-1.42	.13	-1.05

Note: Means for original scores over population of 40 boxes: 4.1, 3.0, 1.9; SDs: .768, .775, .768; factors reordered for ease of comparison.

Thus, a factor analysis *can* correctly recover information about known latent variables, even in the face of a certain amount of random error and nonlinearities of relationship between the latent and manifest variables. However, a caution: It is not always this easy. This is, after all, an example in which three and only three major latent dimensions are present. In most real-life data sets confronting social and behavioral scientists, there are likely to be numerous lesser causal factors in addition to the few major factors the analyst is interested in. The smaller of these extraneous factors can usually be safely lumped together under the heading of random error--this means, incidentally, that the communalities are likely to be rather lower than the .95s of the box example. But in addition there are likely to be some appreciable nuisance factors present, not quite large enough to isolate successfully, yet sufficiently large to distort the picture presented by the main variables. The investigator may be deemed fortunate who encounters a situation as clear-cut as Thurstone's boxes.

Chapter 6 Notes

Many references to the research literature using exploratory factor analysis can be found in the texts listed at the end of Chapter 5. Harman (1976, pp. 7-8), for example, cites studies in fields as diverse as economics, medicine, geology, meteorology, political science, sociology, biological taxonomy, anthropology, architecture, human engineering, communication, and the study of lightplane accidents. If you want to get really serious, Hinman and Bolton (1979) give short descriptions of approximately 1,000 factor analytic studies published in the areas of experimental, animal, developmental, social, personality, clinical, educational, and industrial psychology during the period 1971 to 1975!

Other model data sets. Other sets of data with known underlying properties that can be used to try out exploratory factor analysis methods include populations of real measured boxes (Thurstone, 1947, p. 369; Gorsuch, 1983, p. 11), chicken eggs (Coan, 1959), and cups of coffee (Cattell & Sullivan, 1962). An elaborate artificial data set is provided by Cattell and Jaspers (1967).

Rotation criteria. Some computer packages calculate these criteria in forms that are slightly different from but equivalent to those given here. For example, in orthogonal rotations BMDP minimizes a squared cross-products criterion rather than maximizing the sum of fourth powers, but these lead to the same end result.

Factor scores. For a discussion of some alternative approaches, see Saris, de Pijper, and Mulder (1978) and ten Berge and Knol (1985).

Chapter 6 Exercises

Given the initial pattern matrix P_0 below, for two tests of verbal ability and two tests of mechanical aptitude, and the transformation matrix T:

P_0	I	II		T	A	B
V1	.8	.2		I	.75	.36
V2	.8	.3		II	.96	-1.16
M1	.6	-.4				
M2	.4	-.4				

1. Calculate the rotated factor pattern P. Obtain the factor intercorrelations F, and the factor structure S.

2. Draw the path diagrams for the rotated and unrotated factors, omitting any paths less than .10 in absolute value.

3. Calculate the communalities from the path diagram for the rotated factors, and as the sum of the squares of the rows of P_0. Comment.

4. If your factor analysis program will let you enter P_0 directly, carry out a Varimax and either a Direct Oblimin ($w = 0$) or Orthoblique rotation of P_0. Use Kaiser normalization. Compare the orthogonal and oblique solutions to each other and to the problem 1 solution.

5. Verify by direct matrix calculation (PFP') that both rotated solutions imply the same R_r, and that this is the same as that implied by the unrotated matrix P_0.

6. Using the Varimax solution of problem 4 raised to the 4th power as a target matrix, carry out the Procrustes matrix calculations. Obtain P and F for this Promax solution and compare to the oblique solution of problem 4.

7.   If your factor analysis program will let you do so, rotate the following initial factor pattern matrix to oblique solutions, with (normalized) Direct Oblimin, and *w* values of -1.0, 0, and .5. Discuss the results.

P			
	.511	-.104	.252
	.426	-.082	.252
	.853	-.311	-.031
	.587	.479	-.041
	.666	-.300	-.275
	.542	.501	-.043

8.   Extend the analysis of Table 6-7 to incorporate a third new variable whose correlations with variables C through H are .00, -.20, .00, .80, .50, and .00, respectively.

9.   Repeat the analysis of Thurstone's box problem, using a different method of factor extraction and a different oblique rotation procedure. Compare your results with those given in the chapter.

Chapter Seven:
Elaborations and Extensions of Latent Variable Analysis

In this chapter we expand our horizons with regard to latent variable analysis. We begin with a discussion of exploratory model modification, and we end with a couple of critiques of the causal modeling enterprise. In between, we consider several examples of how latent variable analysis can be extended in various ways to handle additional kinds of problems. Some of these developments are still recent, and how useful they will prove to be in the long run is therefore not yet clear. Others are well established. All of them, however, represent directions in which latent variable analysis can move beyond the topics and methods we have so far discussed in this book. The sections of this chapter are largely independent. Many readers may elect to browse among them according to their interests. However, most should read the first four sections, on exploratory model modification, alternative representations, power, and models involving means, and none should omit the last section on critiques of causal modeling.

Exploratory Modification of a Model

A model is applied to some data. It fits badly. What next?

A sensible strategy in many cases is to try to find out why the model doesn't fit, and change it so that it fits better. One needs to be a bit careful here, because presumably one is not just interested in fitting this particular data set better, but in fitting other data sets well in the future--data sets that involve these same measures in new samples of subjects, or other measures presumed to be relevant to the same underlying constructs, or other situations in which these constructs are involved. In other words, one wants genuine improvement in measurement or theory, not just a procedure for decreasing chi-square in the present sample.

Remember that the chi-square after model modifications based on information from the present data set no longer has the same statistical meaning as chi-square from the initial test of a model, because of possible capitalization on chance features of the data in making the changes. The smaller the sample, the greater this risk, because in a small sample, chance will have more effect on the correlations or covariances, and so there is a greater likelihood that some model changes will be made to accomodate features of this particular data set that will simply not be there in the next one.

Keeping in mind, then, that we will need to discount the apparent merits of a revised model--the more so, the smaller the sample and the more extensive the data-influenced revisions--how do we go about accomplishing these modifications in the first place? There is no one prescription that will fit every case, but there are strategies that may be helpful.

Divide and conquer

A first step that is nearly always worth considering is to ascertain to what extent the lack of fit resides in the measurement and in the structural parts of the model. This is straightforward to do. One simply fits to the data a confirmatory factor analysis model in which the latent variables are allowed to be completely intercorrelated, and the paths from them to the observed variables are as specified in the measurement part of the original model. To the extent that this model fits badly, we know that the misfit is in the measurement part of the original model, because in allowing all possible correlations among the latent variables, we have a structural submodel that is guaranteed to fit perfectly.

It is also instructive to compare the χ^2 from this confirmatory factor analysis with the χ^2 from the original model fitting. If they do not differ significantly, we know that the structural part of the original model is not creating a substantial additional misfit to that produced by the measurement part.

In this event, should we congratulate ourselves that our structural theory, which is probably what mainly interests us, is correct, even though our measurement is rotten? No. On the face of it, what we have shown is that a theory of the form we propose could account for the relationships among the latent variables, but until we have a satisfactory measurement model, we don't know that the latent variables are, in fact, the constructs specified by our theory.

Had it turned out in the confirmatory factor analysis that the measurement part of the model fit well, and significantly better than the whole model, we would have localized the problem to the structural model, and we could proceed to tackle that directly. However, if, as usually happens, the initial tests suggest problems in the measurement model or in both, it will normally be desirable to start work with the measurement model, as there is little point in having a theory that works, but not for the variables intended.

Improving a measurement model

Suppose, then, that there are problems in the measurement model. Inspecting the results of the confirmatory factor analysis solution should give clues to their nature.

There are two main sources of difficulty in measurement models. First, some indicators may fail to reflect the constructs they are supposed to measure. For example, they may have low factor loadings, or factor loadings of the wrong sign. (If they appear to have *large* loadings of the wrong sign, one should check the possibility that something has been inadvertently reversed in scoring.) One way of dealing with a variable that loads poorly is simply to drop it. However, one should always consider the consequences before doing this. Are the remaining measures conceptually adequate for defining the latent variable? Suppose there are, say, three indicators reflecting one aspect of the latent variable, and two indicators that reflect some other, essential aspect. Even though the fit of the measurement model would be improved by dropping the latter two, you shouldn't do it if it will produce a shift in the meaning of the latent variable that makes it unsuitable for testing the original theory.

If you have a latent variable that has only two indicators, and there appear to be measurement problems with it--again, think before acting. If one measure is conceptually superior to the other, you might be better off using just it, fixing its path to an estimate of the square root of its reliability. If both measures seem conceptually valid, you might try setting their paths equal. Adding this constraint will increase chi-square, but often by very little, and to the extent that it produces a more sensible measurement model, there should be better results in cross-validation. Later in this chapter we will discuss circumstances in which one might wish to consider reversing the direction of the arrows between latent and observed variables to deal with measurement model problems.

The second main source of measurement model misfit is that indicators may to some extent reflect constructs other than the one they are intended to measure. If an indicator in fact reflects two constructs, but it is taken as a measure of one and given a zero path from the other, there will be a misfit. The model is now discrepant with reality, because the correlations of this measure with others are reflecting both aspects of it, but the model assumes that only one aspect is present. Again, the choice of whether to omit such an ambiguous measure or to allow paths to it from both latent variables will depend on such considerations as whether one has adequate measures of both without it (drop it) or not (probably keep it, although it may distort relations between the two constructs by bringing in a correlation due to the specific aspects of the measure).

Model-fitting programs such as EQS or LISREL provide diagnostic indicators that can be helpful in deciding which additional paths from latent variables to indicators might improve the fit of the model. These are called Modification Indices in LISREL and Lagrange Multiplier Tests in EQS. What they do for you is tell you roughly how much the χ^2 for the model will be improved by freeing each fixed path present in the model. In the case of a typical confirmatory factor analysis model, the fixed paths are the zero paths between each factor and the variables that are *not* supposed to load on it. If a few of these have large modification indices, they should be examined as possible cases of measures loading on multiple factors, and suitable remedies considered. As both the LISREL and the EQS manuals emphasize, one should not just free paths blindly. This will reduce χ^2s, but it can also produce nonsensical models. Furthermore, freeing certain paths can have major effects on the modification indices of others, so that one should be cautious about introducing wholesale changes at a given step. EQS has a multivariate version of the Lagrange test that can help here.

There are other possibilities that may be considered in tackling an ailing measurement model. (1) Consider the introduction of one or more method variables, to account for covariation among measures that is due to shared methods rather than the latent variables of the theory--see the discussion of multitrait-multimethod matrices in Chapter 3. The contribution of method variance to the correlations among measures in the social and behavioral sciences is often considerable. One recent review estimated that method variance accounts for about 25% and trait variance about 40% of the total for personality and aptitude measures, with the remainder error variance. For attitude measures, method variance played an even larger role--about 40% method variance and 30% content variance. (2) Allow correlated residuals between pairs of measures that share some specific basis of covariation over and above their participation in common factors. Modification indices can give clues to possible candidates for this treatment, as can large isolated entries in the residual matrix (the difference between the observed and implied correlation matrices). Correlated residuals can be introduced between the indicants of a given latent variable or across latent variables. Again, if they have a rational basis, their chances of standing up in cross-validation are much better.

The choice between (1) and (2) above depends largely on how many variables are involved. If a method artifact or shared specific variance affects just two variables, introducing a correlated residual is the simplest way to handle it. If several variables are involved, introducing an additional factor is more efficient, and conceptually more powerful. In between are cases that can be handled either way.

A final possible strategy is to decide that the measurement model is "good enough," despite a significant χ^2, and go directly on to the structural model. For example, one may determine from the confirmatory factor analysis that each latent variable is well measured by its proposed indicators, and that the only problem is that there are a number of lesser secondary loadings, correlated residuals, and the like, that are clearly nonzero, hence the χ^2, but are small in comparison with the defining loadings. One would then use the χ^2 from the confirmatory factor analysis as a reference from which to examine the effects of changes in the structural part of the model. This strategy may be particularly attractive when working with very large samples, where quite small departures from ideal measurement can lead to large χ^2s. If one is in an exploratory mode anyway, there is clearly no mandate that *all* measurement problems must be resolved completely before *any* structural problems can be addressed.

A variant of this last strategy is to form a composite variable from the indicators of each factor and use that as a single indicator of the latent variable, with its path fixed to the square root of the internal consistency reliability (for a standardized variable) and its residual fixed to the error variance. The merit of this strategy is that the investigation of the structural model is quicker, cheaper, and cleaner, because of the smaller matrix and the elimination of distractions from the measurement model. A possible disadvantage is that the measurement part of the model is frozen, and changes in it can no longer develop in response to changes in the structural part of the model.

Improving the fit of a structural model

Changing a structural model is changing one's theory, and should always be done with that in mind. No simple rules will always apply. One can use the information provided by the fitting program to see whether existing paths are significantly different from zero. If not, one might consider dropping some of them from the model. Or one can look at modification indices to get an idea what the effects on the fit would be if one were to add particular paths, free up variances, allow covariances, or the like. Or one can inspect residuals to see what aspects of the data are not well accounted for by the model as it stands. Probably one should consider all of these sources of information to get ideas about possible changes, but modifications should not be made without careful consideration of their implications for the substantive theory that the model is intended to reflect.

Such a caution is emphasized by a study by MacCallum (1986), who investigated the merits of a simple automatic model-improvement strategy: If a model does not fit, make the single change that most improves its fit. Repeat as necessary until a nonsignificant χ^2 is achieved. Then test for and delete any unnecessary paths.

MacCallum took known models, imposed simple specification errors (e.g., a path might be omitted or an extra one added), and fit the models to random samples of data from populations in which the true models held. All models had a correctly specified measurement portion--the errors occurred only in the structural model. The model-improvement strategy described above was applied in each case.

The results were moderately complex, but the following examples should

191

give a feel for them. For a sample size of 300 cases and just a single omitted path, only 10 of 20 attempts were successful in reaching the true model. With the same sample size and a more poorly specified model (two paths omitted, one added), the true model was never achieved in 20 tries, although sometimes one or two correct steps toward it were taken. With the latter model and N = 100 there were many problems, such as improper solutions or a failure to reject the initial incorrect model. Only 8 of 20 tries even got as far as making one legitimate change, and in 7 of the 8 it was a wrong one.

In short, such an automatic procedure of structural model modification cannot generally be recommended--and if one tries it with small samples, one must be very brave indeed. In a subsequent study (Silvia & MacCallum, 1988), it was shown that with large samples (N = 500) and with the incorporation of some relevant prior theoretical knowledge, such searches were more often successful in arriving at a known true model, although by no means always so.

In any case, the outcome of any structural model modification is a new theory. It should hardly be necessary to point out that one needs to *test* that new theory on fresh data before proclaiming its merits to the world--i.e., cross-validation is essential when exploratory modification of a structural model is undertaken. And it is prudent even when changes are confined to the measurement model, particularly when the changes are extensive or the samples are small.

Alternative Models

There is always more than one way to account for a particular set of interrelationships among variables, and the path modeler should be aware of this fact. In this section we consider two examples, one involving the direction of the causal arrows between latent and manifest variables, and one involving more general issues of equivalence among models.

Are observed variables causes or effects of latent variables?

It is traditional in structural equation modeling--as evidenced in most of the path diagrams in this book--to have the arrows in the measurement model go from the latent variable to the observed indicator of it. But as Cohen et al. (1990) point out, this may not always be sensible.

Consider the path model in Fig. 7.1, from a hypothetical study of life satisfaction in an elderly population, drawn as a traditional structural modeler would do it. On the left side we have two latent variables, Health, indexed by several particular classes of medical problems, and Financial Resources, indexed by Current Earnings and Retirement Income; these are seen as contributing to Life Satisfaction on the right, indexed by ratings by Self, Spouse, and Friend. Let's worry a little about the direction of the causal arrows for the latent variables on the left side of the diagram. The way the diagram is

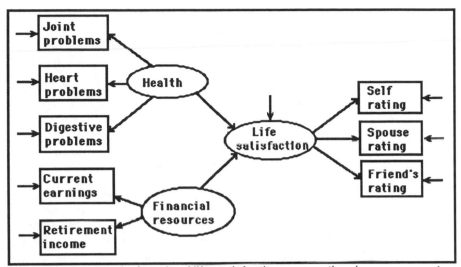

Fig. 7.1 A hypothetical study of life satisfaction: conventional measurement model.

drawn, health is a general condition of the individual, which is reflected in the pathology of various body systems. But one could look at it differently, as in Fig. 7.2, which holds that health is just a summary construct reflecting the degree to which a person has things wrong with various bodily systems.

An important difference is that looking at it as in Fig. 7.1 implies that there

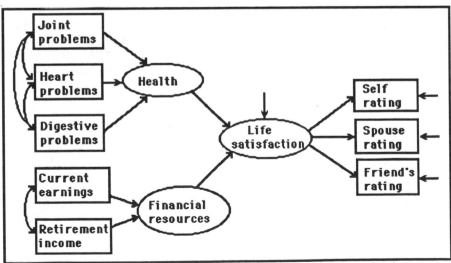

Fig. 7.2 A hypothetical study of life satisfaction: indicators causing latent variables.

will be positive correlations among the indicators, and looking at it as in Fig. 7.2 does not. That is, Fig. 7.1 says that because heart problems and joint problems are both indicators of a general condition called health, their correlation will be the product of the individual paths from that construct; thus if both are good measures of health they will by that fact be substantially correlated. Figure 7.2 makes no such claim. The conditions could be correlated, but they could be independent. In any case, their correlation would not depend on their status as measures of health. Without arguing the merits of either approach in this particular case, it is clear that the approaches are different, and that in constructing a path model, one might want to consider both as possibilities.

A more striking instance is presented by the Financial Resources latent variable, because here one would clearly want to have current earnings and retirement income act as contributors (Fig. 7.2) rather than as indicants (Fig. 7.1). Fig. 7.1 implies that current earnings will be positively correlated with retirement income, but in a real-life elderly population the correlation might well be negative, if individuals who have inadequate retirement incomes must depend on income from working. In an ordinary measurement model, two negatively correlated indicators, each with positive paths to the construct (Fig. 7.1) will create problems, but there is no inherent difficulty with having alternative sources of something called Financial Resources (Fig. 7.2), which is in turn an important contributor to something called Life Satisfaction. (The measurement of the latter, by the way, is quite satisfactorily handled by the traditional paradigm in this example: One can think of Life Satisfaction as a condition of the individual that affects the ratings given by the three informants, and one would expect their ratings of it--if valid--to be postively correlated.) In short, sometimes one will want to do it one way, sometimes the other, but both possibilities should be kept in mind.

Constructing models in which causal arrows run from observed to latent variables can be done directly in some programs (e.g., EQS), but may require a little legerdemain in others (e.g., LISREL). In the latter, one can link the observed variables by fixed 1.0 paths to latent variables. Then paths can be run from these variables to others in the model.

Equivalent structural models

Arrows that might run in either direction are not just a feature of measurement models. As you deal with structural models, you should be aware that often one can make quite radical changes in a model--for example, by reversing the direction of one or more of its causal arrows--and still have a model that fits the data exactly as well as before, but with quite different values for its paths. (Stelzl, 1986, discusses the conditions under which this will happen.) Let us consider the example shown in Table 7-1 and Fig. 7.3.

The six variables D through I represent two measures for each of three latent variables: a mother's verbal aptitude, her child's verbal aptitude, and the amount of reading aloud to the child that the mother has done.

Table 7-1 Correlations among six hypothetical variables (for example of Fig. 7.3), N = 100

	D	E	F	G	H	I
D	1.00	.56	.38	.34	.50	.50
E		1.00	.43	.38	.58	.58
F			1.00	.72	.43	.43
G				1.00	.38	.38
H					1.00	.64
I						1.00

Fig. 7.3 Three alternative models of relations among MV, mother's verbal aptitude, CV, child's verbal aptitude, and MR, mother's reading to child. (Same measurement model throughout.)

On the left in the figure, model (a), is a model whose structural portion assumes that a mother's reading aloud to her child has a causal effect on the development of the child's verbal aptitude. The model also assumes that a mother's verbal aptitude may affect how much she is inclined to read to the child, as well as possibly having a direct effect on the child's verbal aptitude, an effect that might, for example, occur via the genes. If we solve this model for the correlations in Table 7-1, we obtain a very good fit indeed, the χ^2 is .02, based on 7 df. The value of the path from mother's verbal aptitude to her reading to the child (path *a*) is .60, the direct path from her own verbal aptitude to her child's verbal aptitude (path *b*) is .09, and the effect of mother's reading on child's verbal aptitude (path *c*) is .85. Obviously, mother's reading aloud is a key variable in explaining the child's verbal aptitude.

But suppose that we were to entertain a quite different hypothesis, namely, that a mother's reading to her child has no effect whatever on the verbal aptitude of the child; but, on the other hand, that the amount of reading a mother does to her child over the years is affected by how much the child enjoys it, which is in part a function of the child's verbal aptitude. We now have the structural model shown as (b). If we fit that model to the data, we obtain exactly the same good fit, and the same low χ^2. But the values of the paths, and the interpretation of the model, are now quite different. There is a substantial direct determination of child's verbal aptitude by mother's verbal aptitude (*b* = .60). Mother's verbal aptitude has only a very minor effect on how much she reads to the child (*a* = .10). Path *c* remains strong (.84), although now, of course, it represents an entirely different causal effect. A developmental psychologist with hereditarian theoretical preferences might like this second model better, with its direct mother-child transmission, and a psychologist of environmentalist inclinations might fancy the first. The point, however, is that both models are exactly equivalent in their fit to the data. And so, for that matter, are others--including such unlikely models as (c)--which both psychologists might be pained to find has an identical χ^2 of .02, for *a* = .32, *b* = .30, and *c* = .90.

The practical moral: Think about each causal arrow in your path diagram. If there is reasonable doubt about which direction it goes, it might make sense to replace the directed path by a simple correlation or a reversed path and see how much difference this makes for other paths in the model. Sometimes the effects of such a change will be quite localized. If so, the interpretation of other paths may still be secure. If not , . . . well, surely you would want at least to be aware of this fact when discussing your results.

The Power to Reject an Incorrect Model

When fitting models according to a chi-square criterion, large samples are desirable for statistical accuracy. Perhaps an even more important reason for using large samples is statistical power--to have a good chance of rejecting a model if it is wrong. If the acceptance of a model is to have any real meaning, there must have been a reasonable chance of rejecting it if it were false. The sample size one needs in order to reject an incorrect model depends on several things, including the nature of the misspecification involved and how confident one wants to be of detecting it.

Generally speaking, the power of a test of a hypothesis is the probability that one will reject it if it is false. To determine the power of a test in model-fitting requires four things:

1. A model.
2. A specific alternative to the model that one would want to be able to discriminate from it.
3. The desired level of sigificance.
4. The sample size, N.

For example, let us consider the simple factor analysis model shown in Fig. 7.4. What is our power to reject the basic model in favor of one with an added path indicated by the dashed line, assuming a .05 significance level and a sample size N = 500?

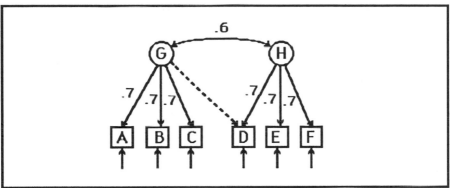

Fig 7.4 Simple factor analysis model for power example. Dashed arrow-- additional path to be detected.

To begin with, we need to assume a specific value for the added path--its detection will be relatively easy if it is large, because then it will have a substantial effect on the correlations, and difficult if it is small, because then it will not. We can estimate the power for any specified value of the path. Let us use .30 as an example. Now the procedure requires three steps (Satorra & Saris, 1985):

1. Obtain the implied covariance or correlation matrix *under the alternative hypothesis*, i.e., with the extra path included. This matrix is shown below the diagonal in Table 7-2. It can be obtained either directly from Fig. 7.4 via the path rules, or by specifying the model to the model-fitting program with all paths fixed to the desired values.

2. Use this obtained matrix as input to a model-fitting run *using the original model*, i.e., without the added path, and obtain the value of chi-square. This will be an approximation to what is called a "noncentral chi-square." In the example, the chi-square comes out to be 14.93, with 8 degrees of freedom.

3. Consult a table of noncentral chi-square to obtain the desired estimate of power. A condensed version of such a table is given as Appendix H. Looking across the row for df = 8 for a value close to 14.93, we find that the power is approximately .80. That is, there is about an 80% chance that if the

Table 7-2. Implied correlations under alternative models in power example

	A	B	C	D	E	F
A	1.000	.490	.490	.364	.294	.294
B	.490	1.000	.490	.364	.294	.294
C	.490	.490	1.000	.364	.294	.294
D	.504	.504	.504	1.000	.532	.532
E	.294	.294	.294	.616	1.000	.490
F	.294	.294	.294	.616	.490	1.000

Note: The implied correlations for the model of Fig. 7-4 with extra path of .30 are shown below the diagonal; with path of .10, above the diagonal.

true model contains the dotted path with a value of .30, we would reject the originally proposed model.

Suppose we had wished to detect a smaller departure from the original model, say an added path of .10 instead of .30. The implied matrix for this case is shown above the diagonal in Table 7-2. Step 2 now yields a chi-square of 1.95, still with 8 df, and consultation of the noncentral chi-square table shows that the power is well below .50--that is, the odds would be against our being able to detect a misspecification of this magnitude, using an N of 500. How large a sample would be needed to raise our power to .80, a level that has been suggested as a desirable minimum (Cohen, 1977)? Recall that chi-square increases roughly proportionately with N. Dividing the chi-square of 15.03 required for a power of .80 by the obtained 1.95 yields a factor of 7.7-- that is, we would need a sample size of about 7.7 x 500 or 3850 to do the job.

Power calculations with latent variable models, as in other research designs, are often sobering. Nevertheless, as with other research designs, the estimation of power should be a routine part of the planning of a study. Power calculations may also be useful in evaluating the claims of existing studies in the literature. If a given study had very little chance of rejecting substantively important departures from the accepted model, this should be taken into account in assessing the author's conclusions.

How does one obtain values for the paths to include in the original and alternative models? In planning a study, one simply chooses plausible values based on one's knowledge of prior research in the area--if in doubt, several possibilities may be tried. In evaluating an existing study, the path values from the original study can be used, along with an additional path or paths, to obtain the implied matrix.

Models Involving Means

In the discussion so far, models have been fitted to correlations and to variances and covariances, but they may be fitted to means as well (e.g., Sörbom, 1974).

This is often done when a model is being fitted in several subpopulations, as was discussed in Chapter 4. If the mean of a latent variable in a particular subpopulation is, say, x units above the grand mean for the total population, the regression coefficients in the model predict by what fraction of x units the means of the observed variables in this subpopulation will be above or below average. Thus, subpopulation differences among the means of observed variables may allow us to make inferences about latent variable means and path coefficients.

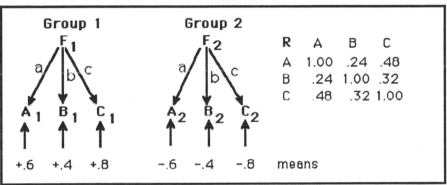

Fig. 7.5 Inferring latent variable means.

Figure 7.5 provides a simple example. Assume we have observed the correlations shown on the right, and that they are the same in the two subpopulations, designated Groups 1 and 2. Suppose that we have also observed the means shown below the path diagrams (given in standard scores based on the combined groups). By the method of triads we can infer from the correlations the path coefficients $a = .6$, $b = .4$ and $c = .8$, in both groups. Then from the path coefficients and the observed means, because $aF_1 = A_1$, etc., we can infer the mean of F_1 to be 1.0 and the mean of F_2 to be -1.0. (There is an arbitrariness of sign here--we could alternatively assume a, b, and c to be negative and the signs of F_1 and F_2 to be reversed. This amounts merely to reversing the direction of scoring the latent variable.)

In this example, the means are perfectly consistent with the correlations (mean F_1 is the same whether inferred from mean A_1, B_1, or C_1), and the correlations are identical in the two groups. But, of course, this need not always be the case. As usual, what we can do then is to carry out a least squares or maximum likelihood model fitting to the whole data set, means and covariances in both groups, to get simultaneous best estimates of both the path coefficients and the latent variable means. Any particular assumed values of the unknown latent variable means and path coefficients imply values for the observed means and covariances, and the fitting program iteratively adjusts the unknowns until the discrepancies between the implied and the observed values are minimized.

The fitting process can be carried out by writing equations for the observed values in terms of the unknown parameters, and solving them by a general-purpose fitting program, such as IPSOL. The solution can also be carried out via EQS or LISREL by extending the model to include a unit constant (see the respective manuals for details).

Table 7-3 provides an example, based on the path model of Fig. 7.6. The variables differ in variance in the two groups; they are scaled to unit variance in the first group.

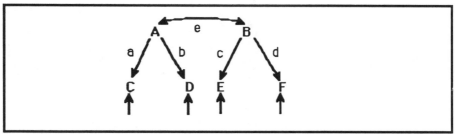

Fig. 7.6 Path diagram of a model to be fit in each of two groups.

Table 7-3 Data for example involving means in two groups

Observed covariances and means

	Group 1 (N = 100)					Group 2 (N = 120)				
	C	D	E	F	Mean	C	D	E	F	Mean
C	1.00	.50	.20	-.20	5.0	6.00	4.50	1.00	-1.50	14.0
D		1.00	.10	-.20	5.5		4.00	.50	-1.00	12.0
E			1.00	-.20	7.5			1.50	-1.00	4.5
F				1.00	5.5				2.00	10.0

Table 7-4 Solutions for means and variances in two groups, and common paths (based on Fig. 7.6 and data of Table 7-3)

Paths			Means			Variances			Residual variances		
	LS	ML		LS	ML		LS	ML		LS	ML
a	.88	.88	A_1	-5.6	-5.6	A_1	1.00	1.00	C	.14	.18
b	.65	.64	A_2	4.0	4.6	A_2	7.73	7.58	D	.64	.60
c	.40	-.39	B_1	4.6	-4.2	B_1	1.00	1.00	E	.86	.83
d	-.61	.58	B_2	-3.4	3.5	B_2	3.88	4.13	F	.59	.62
e_1	.44	-.44									
e_2	.48	-.51									

Note: LS = least squares solution, fit by general-purpose program; ML = maximum likelihood solution, by LISREL. Subscripts 1 and 2 designate groups.

Table 7-4 gives a solution based on the assumption of equal path coefficients and error variances in the two groups (one could, of course, make other assumptions). The table shows the results yielded by an iterative solution of the path equations by a general-purpose program using a least squares criterion, and by LISREL with a maximum likelihood criterion. Aside from reversals of sign, the two solutions are essentially similar. The sign reversals indicate that the programs have found two different but equivalent solutions, in which the difference on B between the groups is reversed, as are the signs of the paths from B to the other variables. In effect, the two solutions are assuming latent variable B to be scored in opposite directions, and the various relationships are simply reversed to reflect this.

The same principles can obviously be extended to situations involving more than two groups. Examples may be found in Sörbom (1974) and Jöreskog and Sörbom (1989). One can also use similar strategies to study changes in means over time. McArdle and Epstein (1987) provide an example.

Phantom Variables

A phantom variable (Rindskopf, 1984b) is an unmeasured latent variable with no residual. Phantom variables can be used to trick model-fitting programs into imposing constraints that are not normally within their repertoire.

Fig. 7.7 Phantom variables example: x^2

Fig. 7.8 Phantom variables example: $3x$

Fig. 7.9 Phantom variables example: xy

Fig. 7.10 Phantom variables example: $x + y$

For example, if one wishes to specify that the path from A to C in Fig. 7.7 (a) is equal to the square of the path from A to B, one can do it by inserting the phantom variable P in the lower path, as shown in (b), and setting the three paths labeled *x* to be equal. Or if one wishes the path AC to be three times the value of path AB, in Fig. 7.8 (a), one can proceed as in (b), fixing the path from A to P to the value 3 and equating *x*s.

If one wants AD to equal the product of paths AB and AC (Fig. 7.9 (a)), one can proceed as in (b), equating *x*s and *y*s. Or if one wants AD to equal the sum of AB and AC (Fig. 7.10 (a)), two phantom variables, as shown in (b), will do the trick. A weighted sum of *x* and *y* can be obtained by fixing appropriate values on the paths from A. Many other variations may be achieved, remembering that products are represented by serial paths, and sums by paths in parallel.

Fig. 7.11 Phantom variables examples: keeping a residual variance positive and Imposing an inequality constraint

If one wants to require a residual variance to remain positive, the arrangement shown in Fig. 7.11 (a) will do it. The variance of the phantom variable is fixed to 1.0, and its contribution to the variance of A is equal to the square of the path coefficient *x*, and thus must be positive (or zero). Finally, Fig. 7.11 (b) illustrates the imposition of an inequality constraint using phantom variables. It is desired to make the path from A to B greater than or equal to 2.0. The addition of the phantom variable P and its associated paths will do the trick, since the value of x^2 cannot be negative. If one wishes the path to be *less* than or equal to 2.0, insert a second phantom variable into one of the *x* paths, with -1.0 on one side and *x* on the other.

The topic of phantom variables is perhaps not likely to be of lasting importance in the field of path modeling--one may anticipate increasing facilities in model-fitting programs for imposing such constraints in more direct and convenient ways (for example, the Fig. 7.11 constraints are provided directly in EQS). In the meantime, phantom variables are fun, and can provide ways of escaping the nominal restrictions of a particular model-fitting program.

Multivariate Path Models

All path models are multivariate, of course, in the sense that several variables are involved, but in the present section the term refers to path models in which instead of a single variable at each point, there are several.

Consider Fig. 7.12: On the left is a simple path model in which, for some trait, mothers and fathers are correlated, and both influence their children (shown here as a son and a daughter, for concreteness). This will, of course, lead to a correlation between sons and daughters for that trait. By the usual path rules (taking the general, unstandardized case), the covariance between sons and daughters is:

$$C_{SD} = aV_Mb + cV_Fd + aC_{MF}d + cC_{FM}b,$$

where the Cs and Vs refer to covariances and variances, and the other symbols are as identified in the figure.

Fig. 7.12 Univariate and bivariate path diagrams. (M, F, S, D = Mother, Father, Son, Daughter; 1, 2 = two traits.)

Suppose, however, that each individual was measured on two traits, rather than one. Now the path diagram, shown on the right in Fig. 7.12, becomes considerably more complicated. The four between-generation paths *a* through *d* on the left become the thicket of 16 paths *a* through *p* on the right, and there are 6 mother-father covariances to contend with at the top of the diagram instead of just one. With more than two traits, of course, things get considerably worse. With three traits there would be 36 straight and 15 curved arrows, and with four traits, 64 and 28.

Writing the corresponding path equations gets to be a bit of a nightmare. As a sample, consider just one of the four son-daughter covariances in the two-variable case, C_{S1D1} (the others are C_{S1D2}, C_{S2D1} and C_{S2D2}). From the path diagram:

$$C_{S1D1} = aV_{M1}c + eV_{M2}g + iV_{F1}k + mV_{F2}o$$
$$+ aC_{M1M2}g + eC_{M2M1}c + aC_{M1F1}k + iC_{F1M1}c + aC_{M1F2}o$$
$$+ mC_{F2M1}c + eC_{M2F1}k + iC_{F1M2}g + eC_{M2F2}o + mC_{F2M2}g$$
$$+ iC_{F1F2}o + mC_{F2F1}k .$$

The other three equations are comparable. As one might suspect, things get much worse as the number of variables increases--for the three-variable case there are 9 equations, each more than twice the length of the one above. The four-variable case has 16 equations, with 64 terms apiece. You may not even want to think about the five-variable case--upward of 2,000 compound paths are involved in the equations.

As Vogler (1985a,b) has pointed out, one need not go to all this trouble-- one can get by with just the simple path diagram on the left of Fig. 7.12, if one replaces the single variables by matrices. Instead of our original equation:

$$C_{SD} = aV_Mb + cV_Fd + aC_{MF}d + cC_{FM}b ,$$

we have:

$$C_{SD} = A'C_MB + C'C_FD + A'C_{MF}D + C'C_{MF}'B .$$

The paths a, b, etc. have simply been replaced by the matrices **A**, **B**, etc., and the single variances and covariances by covariance matrices. Going backward along an arrow is represented by the transpose of the matrix for going forward (note that this applies to curved arrows as well).

You may wish to carry out algebraically the first matrix multiplication on the right-hand side of the preceding expression to convince yourself that it is yielding as its upper left-hand element terms from the lengthy expression for C_{S1D1}. Use:

$$\mathbf{A} = \begin{array}{cc} a & b \\ e & f \end{array} \qquad \mathbf{B} = \begin{array}{cc} c & d \\ g & h \end{array} \quad \text{and} \quad \mathbf{C_M} = \begin{array}{cc} V_{M1} & C_{M1M2} \\ C_{M2M1} & V_{M2} \end{array}$$

(i.e., the single path a from mother to son on the left in Fig. 7.12 becomes the matrix **A** of four paths a, b, e, and f between mother and son in the two-trait diagram on the right.)

It is important to realize that expressing the paths as matrices does not really decrease the number of calculations or the number of parameters involved, it merely simplifies the writing of the equations that generate the expected values from the trial values of the parameters. This is, of course, not a trivial simplification: It is the difference between doing it and not doing it, if one is dealing with more than a couple of variables in a moderately complex path model. And the chances of error in writing the path equations are also vastly decreased if much of the complexity is tucked away into the inner workings of standard matrix multiplication routines.

Further simplifications may be possible. In some cases it may be plausible to assume **A**, **B**, **C**, and **D** to be diagonal: That is, a given parental trait is assumed to influence only the corresponding trait in the child. This considerably reduces the number of free parameters (unknown paths that must be solved for) and thus improves the chances of arriving at robust solutions with reasonable amounts of data. One can still further simplify if, for example, one assumes that fathers and mothers are alike in their influences on their children, or that such influences are the same for both sons and daughters. Naturally, the plausibility of such simplifications will depend on the particular variables involved. In general, it should be possible to test the acceptability of the assumptions by comparing goodness-of-fit χ^2s with and without them.

Rice, Fulker, and DeFries (1986) have applied this method to data from adopted and control families from the Colorado Adoption Project. Their path diagrams for the single-variable case involved three observed variables (measures on mother, father, and child) in the control families, and four or five in the adoptive families (child, two adoptive parents, and either one or both birth parents). There were twice those numbers of latent variables (a genotype and environment for each person). With four manifest variables for each individual-- composite measures of verbal ability, spatial ability, memory, and perceptual speed--it would have been a truly daunting undertaking to write out the individual path equations for solution by their general-purpose model-fitting program. But the substitution of matrices for individual variables made it quite practicable to carry out the analysis.

It is perhaps worth noting that we have encountered examples of this general multivariate principle earlier in this book. Take a simple case from factor analysis. Consider the path diagram of Fig. 7.13, in which X is a

Fig. 7.13 A single-variable, single-factor factor analysis model.

variable, F is a factor, and *p* is a factor pattern coefficient (a path coefficient). The communality of X, i.e., the variance caused by F, may be obtained by path rules as p $s_F{}^2$ p. But suppose we had several Xs and several Fs? We just substitute matrices. The expression for the implied variance-covariance matrix of the Xs becomes the familiar **PFP**′. Given standardized latent and observed variables, **F** is the factor intercorrelation matrix, **P** is the factor pattern matrix, and the whole expression yields the implied intercorrelation matrix $\mathbf{R}_r$.

In this, and other such cases, the generalization from the single-variable to the multivariate situation is direct.

Nonlinear Effects of Latent Variables

The relationships expressed in path models are linear. Path models are, after all, a special application of linear regression. However, It Is well known that in linear regression one can express nonlinear and interactive relationships by the device of introducing squares, products, etc. of the original variables. Thus, to deal with a curvilinear prediction of Y from X we might use the prediction equation:

$$Y = aX + bX^2 + Z.$$

Or we could deal with an interactive effect of X and Z on Y with an equation such as:

$$Y = aX + bZ + cXZ + W.$$

These equations represent nonlinear relationships among observed variables by the use of linear regressions involving higher order or product terms. Can the same thing be done with *latent* variables? Kenny and Judd (1984) explore this question and conclude that the answer is "Yes." We follow their general strategy.

Suppose we wish to represent the first relationship in the preceding paragraph, but X is an unobserved, latent variable, indexed by two observed variables, call them A and B. In structural equation form:

$$A = aX + U$$
$$B = bX + V$$
$$Y = cX + dX^2 + Z.$$

The first two equations constitute the measurement model, the third the structural model. (For simplicity we are treating Y as an observed variable, but it could be a latent variable as well, with its own indexing measures.)

But how is X^2 to be linked to the data? Kenny and Judd point out that the preceding equations imply relationships of X^2 to A^2, B^2, and the product AB. For example, by squaring the equations for A and B we obtain the first two of the following equations, and by taking the product of the equations for A and B we obtain the third:

$$A^2 = a^2X^2 + 2aXU + U^2$$
$$B^2 = b^2X^2 + 2bXV + V^2$$
$$AB = abX^2 + aXV + bXU + UV.$$

Fig. 7.14 Path diagram for nonlinear effect of X on Z.

Figure 7.14 represents these various relationships in the form of a path diagram. Notice that X, X^2, XU, and XV are shown as uncorrelated. This will be the case if X, U, and V are normally distributed and expressed in deviation score form. Kenny and Judd also show that, given these assumptions, expressions can be derived for the variances of the square and product terms. Under these conditions the following relations hold:

$$V_{X^2} = 2V^2{}_X ; \quad V_{XU} = V_X V_U ,$$

and similarly for V_{U^2}, V_{UV}, etc.

This means that we can write equations for the observed variances and covariances of A, B, A^2, B^2, AB, and Y in terms of a moderate number of parameters. If we set to 1.0 one of the paths from X to an observed variable, say *a*, we have left as unknowns the paths *b*, *c*, *d*, the variance of X, and the variances of the residuals U, V, and Z. The remaining values can be obtained from these. The path equations are given in Table 7-5.

Kenny and Judd present illustrative variances and covariances for simulated data from a sample of 500 subjects. These are given in Table 7-6. We have 6x7/2 = 21 observed variances and covariances to fit using 7 parameters, so there are 14 degrees of freedom for the solution.

We cannot, however, do the fitting with LISREL. We wish to fix paths and variances in such relations as *b* and b^2, or *b* and 2*b*, and LISREL does not provide for other than EQUAL relationships. Incidentally, we would not want to use a maximum likelihood criterion either, for some of our variables are definitely not normally distributed. We have assumed, for example, that X is normal, but that means that X^2 will certainly not be.

Kenny and Judd fit their model with the program COSAN (McDonald, 1978) mentioned in Chapter 2 that allows the user to specify different relationships among paths. They used a generalized least squares fitting criterion that does not assume multivariate normality.

208

Table 7-5 Path equations based on path diagram of Fig. 7.14

	Path equations	
If:		
$V_X = x$	$V_A = x + u$	$V_{A^2} = 2x^2 + 4xu + 2u^2$
$V_U = u$	$C_{A,B} = bx$	$C_{A^2,B^2} = 2b^2x^2$
$V_V = v$	$C_{A,A^2} = 0$	$C_{A^2,AB} = 2bx^2 + 2bxu$
$V_Z = z$	$C_{A,B^2} = 0$	$C_{A^2,Y} = 2x^2d$
Then:	$C_{A,AB} = 0$	$V_{B^2} = 2b^4x^2 + 4b^2xv + 2v^2$
$V_{X^2} = 2x^2$	$C_{A,Y} = xc$	$C_{B^2,AB} = 2b^3x^2 + 2bxv$
$V_{U^2} = 2u^2$	$V_B = b^2x + v$	$C_{B^2,Y} = 2b^2x^2d$
$V_{V^2} = 2v^2$	$C_{B,A^2} = 0$	$V_{AB} = 2b^2x^2 + b^2xu + xv + uv$
$V_{XU} = xu$	$C_{B,B^2} = 0$	$C_{AB,Y} = 2bx^2d$
$V_{XV} = xv$	$C_{B,AB} = 0$	$V_Y = c^2x + 2d^2x^2 + z$
$V_{UV} = uv$	$C_{B,Y} = bxc$	

Note: C = covariance, V = variance; path *a* is set to 1.0.

Table 7-6 Covariance matrix of observed values (Kenny & Judd simulated data, N = 500)

	A	B	A^2	B^2	AB	Y
A	1.150					
B	.617	.981				
A^2	-.068	-.025	2.708			
B^2	.075	.159	.729	1.717		
AB	.063	.065	1.459	1.142	1.484	
Y	.256	.166	-1.017	-.340	-.610	.763

Their solution is shown in Table 7-7 (next page), along with the values used to generate the simulated data, and a solution of the path equations using IPSOL and ordinary least squares. (The program was the same as that given in Appendix B, except that a higher level of precision was used--the .001s in subroutine MINIM were changed to .0001-- and MAXFN was increased to 5000.) Both the COSAN and IPSOL solutions essentially recover the values used to generate the data.

Table 7-7 Solutions of path equations of Table 7-5 for data of Table 7-6

Parameter	Original	IPSOL	COSAN
b	.60	.61	.62
c	.25	.26	.25
d	-.50	-.49	-.50
x	1.00	1.01	.99
u	.15	.15	.16
v	.55	.56	.54
z	.20	.19	.20

Note: COSAN solution from Kenny & Judd (1984)

Kenny and Judd go on to carry out a similar analysis for the case of an interactive relationship between two variables, as represented in the second equation given at the beginning of this section. The general principles involved are the same. A path diagram for an example is shown in Fig. 7.15; as you can see, each of the latent variables X and Z is indexed by two observed variables, and there are a number of additional product and residual terms. The 9 observed variables provide 45 variances and covariances, and there are 13 parameters to be solved for (the variances of X and Z, their covariance *i*, the paths *g, h, c, d,* and *e,* and the residual variances S, T, U, V, and W).

Fig. 7.15 Path diagram for interactive effect of X and Z on Y. Unlabeled paths set to 1.0.

Again, Kenny and Judd were reasonably successful in recovering the values used to generate their simulated data.

Obviously, the possibility of constructing and solving path models of nonlinear and interactive relationships broadens considerably the range of latent variable problems that can be dealt with. It may be expected, however, that models involving nonlinear relationships will tend to be fairly demanding in the quantity and quality of data that are required in order to arrive at dependable solutions.

Nonlinear Factor Analysis

Ordinary factor analysis, like the other path models that have been discussed in the earlier chapters of this book, assumes linear relationships between the latent variables--the factors--and the observed, measured variables. What if the relationships in some real-world case are not linear?

If they are nonlinear but monotonic--i.e., the two change together in a constant direction, though not necessarily in equivalent amounts--an ordinary linear approach will often give a decent first approximation to a nonlinear but monotonic relationship. But suppose the relationship is nonmonotonic, say, an inverted-U function of the kind that may hold between motivation and complex performance, where increasing levels of motivation up to a point improve performance and therefter detract from it. What then?

The issue has been addressed by R. P. McDonald (1962,1967), who notes that in an ordinary factor analysis of the correlations among variables that are related to a latent variable by a curvilinear function of this type, one will tend to obtain two factors. But how can one distinguish the two factors obtained in this case from the two factors obtained when there are two latent variables and ordinary linear relationships?

McDonald's suggestion: Obtain scores for individual subjects on the two factors (actually, for technical reasons he prefers to use principal component rather than factor scores). Plot these scores on a scatter diagram. If the two sets of obtained component scores really reflect a single underlying variable curvilinearly related to the observed measurements, the plotted points should tend to fall along a curved line representing the relationship.

Let us consider an example. Suppose that we have several observed variables Y that are related to a latent variable X by equations of the general form:

$$Y = aX + bX^2 + c.$$

(Recognize the similarity to the case discussed earlier of nonlinear relationships among latent variables--there, however, the nonlinearities were in the structural model, and the measurement model was assumed to be linear; here we are considering a nonlinear measurement model.)

The preceding equation specifies a curvilinear relationship between X and Y. For example, suppose that $a = 1$, $b = -1$, $c = 15$, and X varies from -3 to +4 in integer steps. Fig. 7.16 shows the resulting curve. The linear correlation between X and Y is zero, but there is a perfect nonlinear relationship.

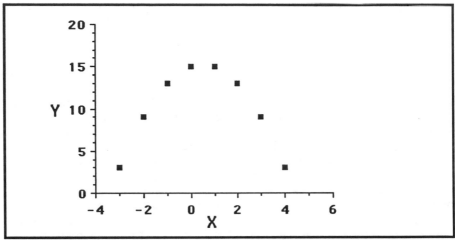

Fig. 7.16 Graph of curvilinear relationship ($a = 1$, $b = -1$, $c = 15$).

Table 7-8 shows a hypothetical example of five tests, Y1 to Y5, each of which is related to the underlying variable X by a quadratic equation of the type mentioned; the tests differ, however, in the relative strength and sign of the linear and quadratic components, and in the contribution of the unique component c.

Table 7-8 Equations to produce scores on tests Y1 to Y5 from given values of latent variable X and specific variables C1 to C5

$$Y1 = X + 2X^2 - C1$$

$$Y2 = 4X - X^2 + 2C2$$

$$Y3 = -X - 3X^2 + C3$$

$$Y4 = -2X + .5X^2 - 2C4$$

$$Y5 = -3X + X^2 + C5$$

Table 7-9 Principal components analysis of the intercorrelations of five hypothetical tests on 100 subjects

	Y1	Y2	Y3	Y4	Y5	C1	C2	h²
			Correlations				Factor Pattern	
Y1	1.00	-.20	-.98	.17	.47	.75	-.65	.99
Y2		1.00	.23	-.55	-.82	-.74	-.53	.83
Y3			1.00	-.19	-.50	-.77	.63	.99
Y4				1.00	.61	.64	.51	.68
Y5					1.00	.90	.28	.89

Eigenvalues: 2.92, 1.45, .49, .13, .02

For illustrative purposes, 100 simulated subjects were assigned scores on these five tests, by drawing for each subject six random integers in the range ±5, one representing X and one each of the 5 C's, and inserting them in the formulas for the five Y's. These scores were then intercorrelated and two factors extracted by a standard factor analysis program (SPSS FACTOR), using 1's in the diagonal to yield principal components. The correlation matrix, the pattern coefficients, and the eigenvalues are given in Table 7-9.

Notice that by the Kaiser-Guttman rule this is a very clear two-factor structure. Figure 7.17 shows a scatterplot of the scores on component 1 plotted against component 2. The curvilinear trend of the points is evident. The

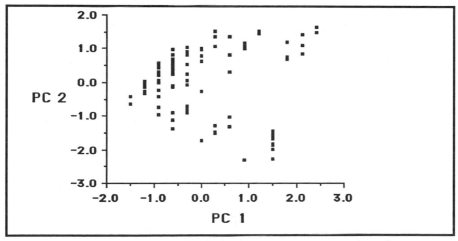

Fig. 7.17 Scatterplot of first two principal component scores from factor analysis of Table 7-9.

orientation of the parabolic curve on the graph is arbitrary, since it depends on just how the two factors emerge, and this will vary with the particular constitution of the tests. McDonald discusses methods of rotating the configuration to a standard orientation, and fitting a parabola to the data, but we need not pursue these matters here.

McDonald also discusses more complex possible cases. For example, a three-factor solution might reflect three ordinary linear latent variables, or one linear and one quadratic relationship, or two linear variables and their product, or first, second, and third powers of a single variable. Although such cases can in principle be handled by the present approach, in practice the discrimination among these alternatives would often place considerable demands on the quality and quantity of available data.

Fortunately for the simplicity of life, the variables that social and behavioral scientists measure are most often linearly or at least monotonically related to the underlying latent variables, so that linear methods will normally serve at least as a first approximation. But not always--so if you are working in a domain in which you suspect that nonmonotonic relationships might be present, it would probably not be a bad idea to calculate some principal component scores and do a little plotting. One caution: This method will work better with variables of fairly high communality. With variables of low communality, the amount of scatter of scores due to specificity and error is likely to make it difficult to distinguish any systematic trends in the data. If a latent variable is only very weakly related to observed variables, establishing the exact form of that relationship may not be easy.

Higher-Order Factors

One of the products of an analysis into oblique factors is the matrix **F** of correlations among the factors. This is an intercorrelation matrix, and intercorrelation matrices can be factored. Such a factor analysis of the intercorrelations among factors is called a *second-order* factor analysis.

If this factor analysis is also oblique, there will be a matrix of intercorrelations among the second-order factors, which can in turn be factored. This would be called a *third-order* factor analysis. If the third-order factor analysis is oblique . . . . And so on.

In principle, this process could go on indefinitely, provided one started with enough variables, but in practice second-order factor analyses are fairly uncommon, third-order factor analyses are decidedly rare, and fourth-order factor analyses are practically unheard of. However, the general idea of a hierarchical arrangement of factors is reasonably straightforward. One might, for example, imagine factoring a variety of arithmetic items to form scales for addition, multiplication, etc., with these in turn components of a numerical ability factor, and this as a subcomponent of general intelligence.

Because second- and third-order factor analyses are just factor analyses of correlation matrices, they can be carried out by the same methods used for first-order analyses, with the same issues involved: estimation of communalities, number of factors, orthogonal or oblique rotation, and so on. (A decision at any stage for orthogonal rotation terminates the sequence, of course.)

Factor methods involving statistical tests, such as maximum likelihood, should probably be avoided for higher order analyses, because the statistical rationales based on sample size are derived for the case of first-order correlations or covariances and would be of doubtful applicability to the factor intercorrelation matrices involved in higher order analyses. However, causal model-fitting methods, as described in earlier chapters, can be used to fit models involving first- and higher-order factors simultaneously to data in a confirmatory factor analysis.

Direct expression of higher-order factors

It may be useful in interpreting higher-order factors to express directly their relationship to the original variables (Cattell & White, see Cattell, 1978). The path diagram of Fig. 7.18 illustrates the situation. The pattern coefficients of

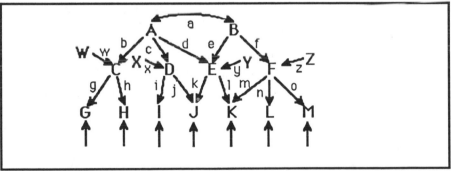

Fig. 7.18 Path diagram representing a higher-order factor analysis. C, D, E, F = 1st-order factors; A, B = 2nd-order factors; G, H, I, J, K, L, M = observed variables; W, X, Y, Z = residuals from 2nd order analysis.

second-order factor A would be *b, c,* and *d* for the first-order factors C, D, and E. For the original variables G, H, I, J, and K, they would be *bg, bh, ci, cj+dk,* and *dl,* respectively.

Table 7-10 (next page) shows the three pattern matrices involved.

Table 7-10 Factor patterns of Fig. 7.18: (a) variables related to first-order factors; (b) first-order factors related to second-order factors; (c) variables related directly to second-order factors

(a) P_{01}					(b) P_{12}			(c) P_{02}		
	C	D	E	F		A	B		A	B
G	g	-	-	-	C	b	-	G	bg	-
H	h	-	-	-	D	c	-	H	bh	-
I	-	i	-	-	E	d	e	I	ci	-
J	-	j	k	-	F	-	f	J	cj+dk	ek
K	-	-	l	m				K	dl	el+fm
L	-	-	-	n				L	-	fn
M	-	-	-	o				M	-	fo

Note: Dash indicates zero path. Subscripts 2, 1, 0 refer to 2nd-order factors, 1st-order factors, and variables.

P_{01} and P_{12} are the pattern matrices obtained in the first- and second-order factor analyses. As you should verify, the third matrix P_{02} can be obtained from these by the matrix multiplication $P_{01}P_{12}$. Thus, multiplication of the two factor pattern matrices will yield the factor pattern matrix directly relating second-order factors to the original variables. For a third-order analysis, $P_{01}P_{12}P_{23}$ would yield the factor pattern P_{03} relating the third-order factors to the original variables. The extension to still higher orders is straightforward.

Schmid-Leiman transformation

Another approach to relating higher-order factors directly to the observed variables is that due to Schmid and Leiman (1957). This representation is illustrated in Fig. 7.19 for the same case as that of Fig. 7.18.

The strategy followed is a hierarchical one: The higher order factors are allowed to account for as much of the correlation among the observed variables as they can, and the lower order factors are reduced to residual factors uncorrelated with each other and with the higher order factors. Although the relative amount of influence attributed to the lower order factors is decreased by this, they may gain in clarity of interpretation, for each now represents the independent contribution of the factor in question. If, say, A represented a broad influence in the personality domain such as extraversion, and C, D, and E represented such component traits as sociability, impulsivity, and risk-taking, this procedure would allow extraversion to account for as much as possible of the intercorrelation among observable extraverted

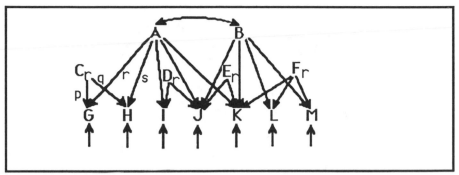

Fig. 7.19 Path diagram representing higher-order factor analysis with 1st-order factors residualized. A, B = 2nd-order factors of original analysis; C_r, D_r, E_r, F_r = residualized 1st-order factors of original analysis; G, H, I, J, K, L, M = variables.

behaviors (G, H, I, J, K), and the residualized C_r, D_r, and E_r would represent effects specific to impulsivity, risk-taking, and so on. One might well argue in particular cases whether this model better represents the underlying causal influences than does the original representation of Fig. 7.18, but when it does, the Schmid-Leiman transformation will be useful.

Basically, the procedure is as follows: The pattern matrix for the highest order (in this case the second) is obtained as for the Cattell-White transformation of the preceding section, by $P_{01}P_{12}$, based on the original first- and second-order analyses. Then, the next-lower order factors (here, the first-order factors) are residualized by scaling down their original pattern coefficients by the multiplication $P_{01}U_1$, where U_1 is a diagonal matrix of the square roots of the uniquenesses from the higher order analysis.

You may find this process easier to understand if it is looked at in path terms. The key step is to realize that the residualized factors C_r, D_r, etc. of Fig. 7.19 are the direct equivalents of the second-order residuals W, X, etc. in Fig. 7.18. The square roots of the uniquenesses, u, used in the rescaling are just the values of the paths w, x, etc. in Fig. 7.18, and the paths p, q, etc. in Fig. 7.19 are equivalent to the compound paths wg and wh in Fig. 7.18. In the Schmid-Leiman transformation we break the causation of, say, variable G into two independent paths (plus a residual). These two paths are labeled p and r in Fig. 7.19, and they correspond to wg and bg in Fig. 7.18. W is of course a causal source independent of A, by its definition as a residual.

Fig. 7.20 and Table 7-11 (next page) illustrate the procedure numerically with a simple example. (This particular example is too small actually to have yielded a determinate solution in an exploratory second-order analysis, but will suffice to illustrate the Schmid-Leiman procedure.) Fig. 7.20 (a) is the original two-level path model, whereas diagram (b) is the alternative

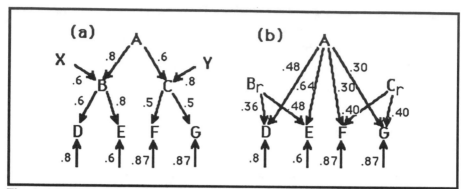

Fig. 7.20 (a) A simple two-level factor model, and (b) the same model after a Schmid-Leiman transformation. B_r and C_r are residualized versions of B and C.

Schmid-Leiman representation, after B and C have been transformed to uncorrelated residual factors. Diagrams (a) and (b) imply exactly the same correlation matrix and communalities: for example, r_{DE} is .6 x .8 = .48 on the left, and .36 x .48 + .48 x .64 = .48 on the right. The communality of D is $.6^2$ = .36 on the left, and $.36^2 + .48^2$ = .36 on the right.

Table 7-11 shows the correlation matrix **R** among the observed variables, the correlation matrix **F** among the first-order factors that is the basis of the second-order analysis, and (left, below) the pattern matrices P_{01} and P_{12} of the first- and second-order analyses (these matrices contain the paths at the first and second levels of Fig. 7.20 (a)). At the bottom center is the pattern matrix P_{02} relating the second-order factor A to the original variables (obtained via the Cattell-White formula), and to its right the pattern matrix P_{01} for the residualized factors B_r and C_r after the Schmid-Leiman transformation. These are proportional to the original P_{01} coefficients (bottom, left). The rescaling is by the square roots of the uniquenesses u of the original first-order factors (top right). Note that because C_r and B_r are independent of each other and of A, the communality for each variable can be obtained by summing the squares of the coefficients across rows of P_{02} and P_{01} (lower right in the table).

Note also that the reduced correlation matrix R_r (with communalities in the diagonal) can be obtained by adding together two independent components: $P_{02}P_{02}'$ and $P_{01}P_{01}'$, representing, respectively, the contribution of the general factor A and the group factors B_r and C_r.

218

Table 7-11 Matrices for Schmid-Leiman example of Fig. 7.20

R	D	E	F	G	h²		F	B	C	h²	u²	u
D	1.000	.480	.144	.144	.36		B	1.00	.48	.64	.36	.60
E		1.000	.192	.192	.64		C		1.00	.36	.64	.80
F			1.000	.250	.25							
G				1.000	.25							

P_{01}	B	C		P_{12}	A		P_{02}	A		P_{01}	B_r	C_r	h²
D	.60	.00		B	.80		D	.48		D	.36	.00	.36
E	.80	.00		C	.60		E	.64		E	.48	.00	.64
F	.00	.50					F	.30		F	.00	.40	.25
G	.00	.50					G	.30		G	.00	.40	.25

Note: P_{01} and P_{12} presumed to be obtained in a first- and second-order factor analysis of correlation matrix **R**, with the second-order analysis based on factor correlation matrix **F** from the first-order analysis. P_{02} obtained as $P_{01}P_{12}$, the Cattell-White formula. The P_{01} matrix on the right for the Schmid-Leiman residualized factors B_r and C_r is obtained as $P_{01}U_1$, where U_1 is a diagonal matrix of u, the square roots of the uniquenesses of B and C, based on the second-order analysis (upper right).

Finally, note the complete equivalence of the matrix results and the path results: that is, in this simple case the values in Fig. 7.20 (b) can be obtained virtually by inspection from Fig. 7.20 (a), as the products of the two levels of paths.

Hierarchical trait theories have long been popular, especially with British writers, since Spearman's successors first introduced a layer of group factors between *g* and the specifics. Higher-order factor analysis in general, and the Schmid-Leiman transformation in particular, represent convenient ways of formalizing theories of this character.

Modes of Latent Variable Analysis

In this section we look at a number of different modes in which data can be approached in factor analysis and other latent variable methods.

R, Q, P, O, T, and S techniques of factor analysis

Cattell (1952) has suggested that sets of data to be factor analyzed may be classified along three dimensions; by considering these in pairs he defines

Table 7-12 Relationships among R, Q, P, O, T, and S techniques

	What is factored	Correlation across	Example
One occasion			
R technique	measures	persons	basic personality traits
Q technique	persons	measures	personality typology
One person			
P technique	measures	occasions	individual personality structure
O technique	occasions	measures	individual psychological environment
One measure			
T technique	occasion⁻	persons	anxiety-arousing situations
S technique	persons	occasions	anxious person types

what he calls R, Q, P, O, T, and S techniques of factor analysis. The relationships among these are summarized in Table 7-12, which is based on a similar table in Gorsuch (1983, p. 312). The reader interested in more details than are given here, or further references to the literature on this topic, will find Gorsuch a useful source.

In this view, the three basic dimensions of data are tests or measures, persons or objects measured, and situations or occasions of measurement. In the most common form of factor analysis, one factors the relationships among tests or measures that are correlated for a sample of persons based on a single occasion of measurement. Cattell calls this *R technique.* A data matrix for typical R technique analysis is shown at the left in Table 7-13. Each of the seven tests has been given to a number of persons. A correlation coefficient is calculated for each pair of tests, i.e., between each pair of columns in Table 7-13 (a). The resulting 7 x 7 correlation matrix among tests is the basis for the factor analysis.

The data matrix on the right, Table 7-13 (b), is for the complement of R technique, *Q technique.* The form of data matrix is the transpose of that used in R technique--the rows are tests and the columns are people. The intercorrelations, still calculated among all possible pairs of columns and still for data gathered on a single occasion, are correlations among people rather than correlations among tests. They express how much Al is like Ben, or Ben is like Zach, on these tests. In the particular example in Table 7-13 (b), Al and Ben are negatively correlated. They are systematically unlike each

Table 7-13 Data matrices for R and Q techniques

	(a) R technique								(b) Q technique				
	T1	T2	T3	T4	T5	T6	T7		Al	Ben	Carl	...	Zach
Al	5	1	2	6	3	5	7	T1	5	2	7	...	1
Ben	2	6	7	1	8	5	2	T2	1	6	4	...	4
Carl	7	4	3	6	4	4	8	T3	2	7	3	...	5
⋮	⋮	⋮	⋮	⋮	⋮	⋮	⋮	⋮	⋮	⋮	⋮	⋮	⋮
Zach	1	4	5	2	5	6	4	T7	7	2	8	...	4

other--on those tests where Ben has relatively high scores Al scores low, and vice versa. Al and Carl, on the other hand, are positively correlated, agreeing on their high and low tests. Note that resemblances based on correlations ignore possible differences in means. Al and Carl's correlation reflects the fact that they show the same *pattern* of scores, even though Carl's scores tend to be systematically higher. The correlation between them would not change if we were to add two points to every one of Al's tests, although this would make Al and Carl's scores more alike in absolute terms. Nor would the correlation decrease if we were to add 10 points to each one of Carl's scores, although in some ways this would make Al and Carl very different. For these reasons one might prefer sometimes to use another measure of association than an ordinary Pearson correlation for Q technique--for example, some measure of distances between profiles (see Overall & Klett, 1972, Chapter 8, for a discussion).

One should also be aware that Q technique correlations can be quite sensitive to the scales of the tests over which they are computed. Merely changing the scoring of test 3 in Table 7-13, to give 10 points per item instead of one, although trivial in concept, will in fact drastically affect the correlations-- for example, it changes the correlation over the 7 tests between Al and Ben from -.81 to +.92. (Can you see why?) For this reason, it is often desirable to standardize the rows of the data matrix (i.e., express the test scores in standard score form) prior to doing the correlations for a Q-type factor analysis-- particularly if the test scores are in noncomparable units. (This is often referred to as *double-centering* the data matrix, because the correlation itself effectively standardizes by columns.)

R technique seeks the dimensions underlying groupings of tests or measures and might be used, for example, in a study of basic personality traits. Q technique seeks the dimensions underlying clusters of persons and might be used in a study of personality types. In practice, the two approaches might in fact lead to the same underlying latent variables: Either a study of personality scales or of person types might lead one to an introversion- extraversion dimension. Nevertheless, the routes taken and the intermediate products of the analyses would be quite different in the two cases.

Table 7-14 Data matrices for P and O techniques

(a) P technique					(b) O technique				
	T1	T2	T3	... Tm		Day1	Day2	Day3	... DayN
Day1	7	1	2	... 8	T1	7	4	2	... 1
Day2	4	2	3	... 5	T2	1	2	6	... 7
Day3	2	6	8	... 3	T3	2	3	8	... 6
:	:	:	:	:	:	:	:	:	:
DayN	1	7	6	... 2	Tm	8	5	3	... 2

The next two techniques, P and O, are also complementary to one another, but they both use just a single subject, tested on repeated occasions. In *P technique*, shown on the left in Table 7-14, one considers two measures similar if scores on them tend to vary together over occasions in the life of an individual. In the table, measures T1 and Tm appear to go together, as do T2 and T3, with the two sets tending to be negatively related. P technique is best suited for use with measures of states, such as moods or motive arousal, which can be expected to vary from day to day in the life of an individual. Its merit is that it can give a picture of the mood or motive structure of that particular person. Some personality psychologists, who have objected to the usual R-type factor analysis as only yielding a picture of a mythical "average person" (no example of which may actually exist!), should find a P technique approach more congenial.

An illustration of a study using P technique is that of Cattell and Cross (1952), in which multiple measures designed to assess the strengths of a number of motivational states (anxiety, self-confidence, sex drive, fatigue, and the like) were obtained twice daily for a particular individual--a 24-year-old drama student--over a period of 40 days. A factor analysis of the intercorrelations of these measures over the 80 occasions yielded some patterns much like those that had been found in previous R-type researches, but others that appeared to be idiosyncratic to this particular individual--or at any rate, to his life during this period.

O technique, the complement of P technique, has not apparently been used much, although it is an interesting idea. Its correlations (Table 7-14 (b)) are based on the similarity of occasions in one person's life, assessed across a multiplicity of measures. It asks which are the occasions that go together in terms of a person's reactions to them--which situations arouse anxiety, which are challenging, which depressing. One might think of this as a way of getting at the structure of a person's psychological environment, of the events to which he or she responds in characteristic ways. For the same reasons as in Q technique, preliminary standardization of scores on the measures used will often be desirable in O technique.

The final pair of complementary approaches, *T* and *S techniques*, seem also not to have been much explored. They restrict themselves to a single response measure but assess it across both persons and situations. In T technique one looks at resemblances among situations in their effect on the response measure, and in S technique at resemblances among persons. For example, in a study such as that of Endler, Hunt, and Rosenstein (1962), in which ratings of anxiety were obtained across both persons and situations, one could either factor the different types of situations to study the relationships among anxiety-arousing situations (T technique), or factor the persons to obtain a typology of persons based on the situations that arouse their anxiety (S technique). In either case one might infer latent dimensions such as physical versus social anxiety, or realistic versus imaginary fears.

Three-mode factor analysis

The six types of factor analysis described in the preceding section can be considered to represent different ways of collapsing a three-dimensional

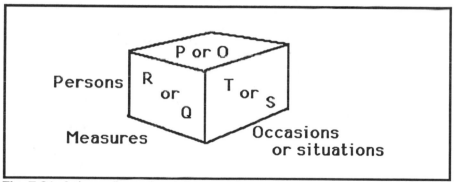

Fig. 7.21 A three-dimensional data matrix.

rectangular data matrix--see Fig. 7.21. The two horizontal dimensions of the cube are measures, and situations or occasions, the vertical dimension is persons. Any point within the cube represents the score of a particular person on a particular measure on a particular occasion.

If we take a slice off the left front face of the cube (or any slice parallel to it), we have data from a single occasion and hence an R or a Q technique study, depending on whether we choose to run our correlations vertically or horizontally. If we take a slice off the right face, or parallel to it, we have data from a single measure, and hence a T or S technique study. And if we take a slice off the top, or any horizontal slice, we have data from a single person, and P or O technique, depending on whether we calculate our correlations among the measures or the occasions.

But can we do a single, overall analysis of the whole data cube? Yes, we can. The procedure is known as three-mode factor analysis and was developed by Ledyard Tucker (1964). We do not attempt to describe the method at the level of calculational detail, but, roughly, it results in three sets of factors resulting from the analysis of correlations involving measures, persons, and situations, and a *core matrix* that relates the three separate sets of factors.

Tucker presents an analysis of the Endler et al. anxiety data. The measures were different reponses that might be associated with anxiety (e.g., "heart beats faster," "need to urinate frequently"); the situations were such potentially anxiety-arousing situations as making a speech or going on an initial date; and the persons were the student subjects doing the ratings. Factors were reported for each of the three modes separately: for example, "heart beats faster" and "get uneasy feeling" went together on a measures factor; "speak before large group" and "job interview" went together on a situations factor; and three person dimensions emerged among the subjects. The core matrix showed relationships involving all three modes: for example, one of the person types showed distress responses in interpersonal situations, while two other types tended to show exhilaration; the latter two types differed, however, in their responses to situations with inanimate or unknown dangers.

Three-mode analyses in structural equation modeling

Analogous approaches to data in three modes occur in structural equation analysis, although they have not been so formally systematized as in factor analysis. A multitrait-multimethod matrix is three-mode: traits, methods, and persons. And so may be a structural equation analysis of events over time: multiple measures on each of a sample of persons taken on each of several occasions. In each case the simultaneous analysis over the three modes is capable of providing information unattainable from any two modes considered separately.

Many opportunities have yet to be explored for extending such analyses to new kinds of problems. You might want to think about what it might mean to do, say, structural equation analyses of O or S types in your own substantive area of interest. Also, there is no law that says that three modes is the limit. For example, Cattell in one place discusses as many as 10 modes (1966a). Finally, there are many variations possible *within* any single design--for example, instead of achievement test scores on schoolchildren across grades, how about economic indicators on countries across decades? The risk of ever having to say "everything has been done" seems negligible.

Criticisms of Latent Variable Modeling

Any structural modeler who wants to find out what an intelligent and articulate critic can say against this enterprise should certainly read a trenchant critique by D. A. Freedman (1987a). This article, plus a number of responses by structural modelers and others and a reply by Freedman, constitute a whole issue of the *Journal of Educational Statistics.*

Freedman's critique

Freedman is not one to pull punches. In his second paragraph he says: "Indeed, path models are now widely used in the social sciences, to disentangle complex cause-and-effect relationships. Despite their popularity, I do not believe they have in fact created much new understanding of the phenomena they are intended to illuminate. On the whole, they may divert attention from the real issues, by purporting to do what cannot be done--given the limits on our knowledge of the underlying processes" (1987a, p. 101f). And later in his introduction: "At bottom, my critique is pretty simple-minded: Nobody pays much attention to the assumptions, and the technology tends to overwhelm common sense" (p. 102).

A key objection of Freedman's is that structural modelers tend to interpret the results of their model fitting *as if* they had done an experiment, when in fact they have not.

Suppose we fit a path model of the sort shown on the left in Figure 7.22, and obtain a value of .05 for the path coefficient. What do we conclude? That sending people to school for another year will increase their incomes by 5%? That, roughly, is what structural modelers *do* tend to conclude, if they conclude

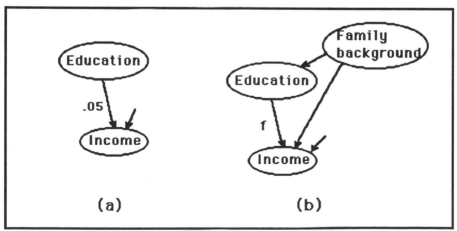

Fig. 7.22. Two models of the relationship between education and income.

anything at all, says Freedman, only they usually do it in situations sufficiently more complicated than this to obscure what is going on.

Now if we had actually done the experiment of sending a random sample of people to school for an extra year, fine. But as we have not, our conclusion is vulnerable to anything we have done wrong in our modeling, such as omitting important variables, and this is true *regardless of how well our model fits the data we have.* In the example, Freedman points out that there might be a third variable in this situation, family background, that affects both education and income, and whose inclusion would most likely change the value of the path *f* from education to income (righthand diagram). Very well, says the modeler, "now we've got it: *f* represents the impact of education on income, with family background controlled for."

"Unfortunately," Freedman continues, "it is not so easy. How do we know that it is right this time? How about age, sex, or ability, just for starters? How do we know when the equations will reliably predict the results of interventions-- without doing the experiment?" (p. 104).

Freedman distinguishes between *descriptive models,* which simply describe relationships, and *structural models,* which purport to give causal explanations. He believes that much of the latent variable modeling literature consists of the former masquerading as the latter. "In my opinion, the confusion between descriptive and structural models pervades the social-science scholarly literature of the past 20 years, and has distorted the research agenda of a generation. In the end, this confusion might easily destroy the idea of scientific right and wrong" (1987b, p. 221).

Freedman goes on: "The modelers I count among my friends are interesting and attractive personalities, and serious scholars. However, on behalf of the models themselves, the core of the enterprise, I can find only two points to make: They may have heuristic value for certain investigators; and some day, there may be a real one."

Freedman is right on the first point--latent variable models can be helpful in describing causal relationships involving measured and unmeasured variables, and that is why we have taken the time and effort to learn about them in this book. In one sense, he is wrong on the second, because there will *never* be a "real one." Causal models are inherently hypothetical; they have a big *If* up front. *If* we assume a model like this, then such and such consequences follow. This is a very useful thing to be able to do, because, as all causal modelers know, what follows from our model, at least on the first try, is usually quite discrepant from the real-world data that we are attempting to explain. However, Freedman is quite right to chide modelers who assume that when they eventually arrive at a model that does fit their data, the scientific enterprise is over. Of course not. What they then have is a theory that can explain these facts. *They do not know that this theory is true*, in the commonsense meaning of this term, until they (or others) have done the experiments or the cross-validitory and confirmatory observational studies necessary to test and support it.

As long as we want to try to describe complex real-life phenomena as they occur in their natural settings, it seems to me that our chief alternatives are the literary essay and the path model. Many as are the merits of literary essays, the path model has one immense advantage from a scientific standpoint. It is much, much easier to demonstrate that its conclusions are incorrect.

But having done this, and having found that our models have problems, then what? Should we retreat to simple models of simple situations, in the hope that eventually we will improve our understanding of the complex phenomenon with which we began? Or should we continue to work with our complex models to try to locate the wrong assumptions that are making them behave badly with respect to the data? Tastes will differ here, but as long as there are those who hold to the second view, there will be path modelers. Personally, I think that our best hope is that there continue to be both kinds of people; that they both vigorously continue to pursue their respective strategies; and that, at least from time to time, they talk to each other.

Cliff's caveats

In a somewhat friendlier article entitled "Some cautions concerning the application of causal modeling methods," Norman Cliff (1983) gives some gentle warnings and sensible advice to the users of programs such as LISREL: "Initially, these methods seemed to be a great boon to social science research, but there is some danger that they may instead become a disaster, a disaster because they seem to encourage one to suspend his normal critical faculties. Somehow the use of one of these computer procedures lends an air of unchallengeable sanctity to conclusions that would otherwise be subjected to the most intense scrutiny" (p. 116).

I hope that if you have got this far in this book you have enough sense of how these models work and do not work, and of some of the vicissitudes to which they are subject, that "unchallengeable sanctity" will not characterize your attitude toward conclusions drawn from their use. But it is worth reminding ourselves briefly of the four principles of elementary scientific inference that Cliff suggests are particularly likely to be violated in the initial flush of enthusiasm of causal modelers:

> The first principle is that the data do not confirm a model, they only fail to disconfirm it, together with the corollary that when the data do not disconfirm a model, there are many other models that are not disconfirmed either. The second principle is that *post hoc* does not imply *propter hoc.* That is, if *a* and *b* are related, and *a* followed *b* in time, it is not necessarily true that *b* caused *a.* The third principle is that just because we name something does not mean that we understand it, or even that we have named it correctly. And the fourth principle is that *ex post facto* explantions are untrustworthy. (pp. 116-117)

Let us look at each of these four principles in a little more detail.

The unanalyzed variable

Suppose that a particular model "fits"--i.e., is not rejected, given the data. That does not mean that other models would not fit equally well, or maybe even better. Suppose, for example, there is some variable V that we have overlooked that is related to the variables X, Y, and Z, which we have included in our model. We can run LISREL or EQS forward, backward, or upside down on a model of X, Y, and Z, but it will not tell us that a model with V in it would have fit better. We can only be reasonably sure that if there is such a V and it has causal effects on variables included in our model, our estimates of some of the paths in our model will be wrong. As Cliff puts it: "These programs are not magic. They cannot tell the user about what is not there" (p. 118).

Post hoc is not *propter hoc*

Cliff cites an incautious author who concluded, on the basis of a significant arrow in a path diagram, that "Father's Occupation caused [Child's] Intelligence." Cliff goes on, "It may be that it does, but somehow I doubt it. It seems unlikely that, if ever the causal variables involved in scores on modern 'intelligence' tests are sorted out, one's father's occupation will ever be one of them" (p. 120). Of course, there may be variables *correlated* with father's occupation that *do* play a causal role, but that takes us back to the preceding point.

To make things worse, time of measurement is not always a safe guide to the sequence of events. "Consider the possibility that we measure a child's intelligence in the fifth grade and her father's occupation when she is in the tenth" (p. 120). Should we then put in a causal arrow leading from the earlier to the later event?

The fact that we can name it does not mean we know what it is

Latent variables are only defined by way of their associations with manifest variables. Because we are always to some degree wrong about what our manifest variables mean (there is always some degree of invalidity and unreliability of measurement), Cliff says, ". . . we can only interpret our results very cautiously unless or until we have included enough indicators of a variable in our analysis, and have satisfied not only ourselves but skeptical colleagues and critics that we have done so" (p. 121). Even a "confirmatory" factor analysis does not escape these problems. It just tells us that we have *one* set of parameters that is consistent with the data. "There are typically an infinity of alternative sets of parameters which are equally consistent with the data, many of which would lead to entirely different conclusions concerning the nature of the latent variables" (pp. 122-123).

Chapter 7: Elaborations

Ex post facto explanations are untrustworthy

Once a model has been modified to make it fit better to a given data set, one can no longer take the probability values associated with subsequent goodness-of-fit tests at face value. If a model has been adjusted on the basis of its fit or lack of fit to a particular body of data, its statistical status is precarious until it can be tested on a new body of data that did not contribute to the adjustment.

One way to deal with this problem is cross-validation. Split the initial data set in half, play around with model-fitting on one half of the data until you get a model you are happy with, and *then* carry out the statistical test--once--on the unused half of the data. The χ^2 will then be legitimate. This procedure has its disadvantages--for one thing, it requires twice the sample size--but it has the preeminent advantage of not leaving the investigator and his readers with results that "they know are unstable to an unknown degree" (p. 124).

In conclusion

Neither Cliff nor I would wish to discourage you from the use of causal model-fitting methods, which in his view represent "perhaps the most important and influential statistical revolution to have occurred in the social sciences" (1983, p. 115). He concludes, and I can only echo: "programs such as LISREL and its relatives provide completely unprecedented opportunities . . . . With their aid, conclusions can be made which heretofore would have been impossible, but only provided the analysis is approached intelligently, tough-mindedly, and honestly" (p. 125).

Go do it.

Chapter 7 Notes

Improving measurement models. Anderson and Gerbing (1982, 1988) discuss the merits of doing a confirmatory factor analysis to start, and offer much other practical advice; other authors, e.g., Bentler and Bonett (1980), have also advocated localizing misfits to the structural or the measurement parts of the model. R. S. Burt (1981), under the label of "interpretational confounding," discusses the relative roles played by the covariance among the indicators of a given latent variable and covariances with the indicators of other latent variables in defining the construct. The smaller the number of indicators per latent variable, the greater tends to be the role of the latter kind of covariation, which may make latent variables hard to interpret. These various issues are further explored in an interchange between Kumar and Dillon (1987a,b) and Anderson, Gerbing, and Hunter (1987).

Modification indices, etc. A review of the status of Modification Indices/Lagrange Multiplier Tests and their opposite numbers, T-Values, z-tests, and Wald Tests, is provided by Satorra (1989).

Trait and method variance. The review mentioned in the text is by Cote and Buckley (1987); it covers some 70 multitrait-multimethod studies.

Improving structural models. Lance, Cornwell, and Mulaik (1988) use confirmatory factor analysis for dealing with the measurement model, but for the structural model suggest a different approach in which one examines the model one equation at a time (using ordinary multiple regression methods) rather than all at once. In a Monte Carlo study, they found this strategy to be relatively effective in detecting known misspecifications. Lehmann and Gupta (1989) propose a regression-based approach at both stages, first for the measurement model and then for the structural model. A more radically different approach is taken by Spirtes, Scheines, and Glymour (1990a). Their strategy, using a program named TETRAD (Glymour et al., 1988), emphasizes the systematic generation of many possible alternatives to a given model and rapid tests, rather than elaborate model-fitting with a few models. They report Monte Carlo studies in which TETRAD substantially outperformed EQS and LISREL in locating correct models. Not altogether surprisingly, Bentler and Chou (1990) and Jöreskog and Sörbom (1990) express some reservations; Spirtes et al. (1990b) reply.

Kaplan (1990) takes a more traditional approach to model modification, but advocates the use of an "expected parameter change" statistic in addition to the usual modification indices. His article is followed by a number of comments from experts in the field (MacCallum, Bentler, Steiger, Bollen, Tanaka, Hayduk), and a reply by Kaplan.

Equivalent structural models. Lee and Hershberger (1990) give an alternative formulation of Stelzl's rules for equivalence, and distinguish between "equivalence in principle" (models that are equivalent for any data set) and models that are equivalent for a particular data set under consideration, but may not be for others.

Experiments. Latent variable models need not be confined to correlational settings. They can be used in experimental designs to test for mean differences. See, for example, Bagozzi and Yi (1989), Kühnel (1988), and Muthén and Speckart (1985).

Multivariate path models. For examples of doing it the hard way see Neale and Fulker (1984) and Vogler and DeFries (1985)--both are bivariate cases handled by nonmatrix methods.

Nonlinear effects. See also Busemeyer and Jones (1983) on dealing with multiplicative effects.

Nonlinear factor analysis. A paper by Etezadi-Amoli and McDonald (1983) describes a "second generation" version. See Lingoes and Guttman (1967) for an approach to a "nonmetric factor analysis."

Higher-order factor analysis. Undheim and Gustafsson (1987) and Harlow and Newcomb (1990) provide examples. Rindskopf and Rose (1988) discuss a confirmatory factor analysis approach.

Modes of factor analysis. Cronbach (1984) discusses R, P, Q, etc. techniques. Kroonenberg (1983) provides an extensive annotated bibliography on three-mode factor analysis. See also a review by Snyder (1988). Three-mode longitudinal applications are discussed by Kroonenberg, Lammers, and Stoop (1985).

Critique and controversy. For other examples of criticisms of the causal modeling enterprise, varying widely along a friendliness/unfriendliness dimension, see Martin (1982), Baumrind (1983), Biddle and Marlin (1987), and Breckler (1990); Huba and Bentler (1982) reply to Martin. If you are planning to publish a study in this area you might find Steiger's (1988) advice and comments instructive.

Chapter 7 Exercises

1. For 100 married couples, two measures each of husband's happiness and wife's happiness are obtained, with the correlations shown below. Fit path models that assume (a) that husband's happiness affects wife's happiness, but not vice versa; (b) that wife's happiness affects husband's happiness, but not vice versa; (c) that husband's and wife's happiness affect each other equally; and (d) that husband's and wife's happiness are simply correlated. Comment on the results.

	HH1	HH2	WH1	WH2
Husband's Happiness 1	1.00	.65	.35	.30
Husband's Happiness 2		1.00	.30	.35
Wife's Happiness 1			1.00	.60
Wife's Happiness 2				1.00

2. You want to decide if G and H, in Fig. 7.23, are correlated. If N = 50, what would be your power to detect a correlation of .5 between G and H (as against a correlation of zero)? What N would give you 80% power to detect a correlation of .5?

Fig. 7.23 Path model for problem 2.

3. Table 7-15 shows means, standard deviations, and correlations on four hypothetical masculinity-femininity scales in samples of 200 men (below diagonal) and 208 women (above diagonal). Is it reasonable to conclude that there is a general masculinity-femininity latent variable that accounts both for the interrelationships among the measures and the differences in mean and variance between the samples? Are there differences between the sexes in how the tests measure this factor?

Table 7-15 Data for problem 3 (women above diagonal, men below)

Scale	A	B	C	D	Mean	SD
A	1.00	.48	.10	.28	5.2	.98
B	.50	1.00	.15	.40	7.0	1.00
C	.12	.16	1.00	.12	6.1	.99
D	.45	.70	.17	1.00	8.3	1.03
Mean	7.5	10.2	7.0	11.1	N	208
SD	1.08	1.15	1.01	1.18	200	

4. (a) Write from Fig. 7.12 the path equation C_{S1D2} for the covariance of sons on trait 1 with daughters on trait 2. (b) Obtain the numerical value for that covariance and for the one for C_{S1D1} given in the text, by substituting the appropriate values of paths and correlations from Table 7-16 below (assume standardized variables). (c) Set up the matrices required for the expression for C_{SD} given in the text and carry out the matrix calculation via MINITAB or some other program with matrix facilities; check for consistency with the results of part (b).

Table 7-16 Data for problem 4

	\multicolumn{4}{c}{Correlations}				\multicolumn{4}{c}{Paths}			
	F1	F2	M1	M2	S1	S2	D1	D2
F1	1.00	.50	.20	.10	.40	.10	.30	.20
F2		1.00	.10	.30	.10	.20	.20	.40
M1			1.00	.60	.50	.20	.50	.30
M2				1.00	.20	.40	.30	.50

5. Write the path equations for V_A, $C_{B,AC}$, $C_{AC,AD}$, and V_Y, from Fig. 7.15.

6. Apply a Varimax rotation to the factor pattern of Table 7-9. How would you interpret the resulting rotated factors in terms of the equations in Table 7-8?

7. Take the oblique Quartimin solution obtained in Chapter 6, problem 7. Carry out a second-order factor analysis; i.e., extract a single principal factor from the **F** obtained in that analysis. Report P_{12}.

8. Relate the second-order factor in the preceding problem directly to the original first-order variables.

9. Subject the analysis of problems 7 and 8 to a Schmid-Leiman transformation. Compare the final communalities to those from the original principal factors.

10. Carry out an exploratory Q-technique factor analysis of the data in Table 7-13, using the scores for the 4 persons on all 7 tests. Comment on your results.

11. Suggest an example of T technique that might be relevant to experimental psychology.

12. Is the study of Judd and Milburn (see Chapter 4) a four-mode structural analysis? (Give your reasoning.)

13. Think of an additional caveat that you might offer a beginner in causal modeling.

Appendix A: Simple Matrix Operations

This appendix reviews some basic aspects of matrix algebra, confining itself to those that are used in this book and proceeding largely by example rather than by formal definition and proof.

Matrices

A *matrix* is a rectangular array of numbers. Examples of three matrices, **A**, **B**, and **D**, are given in Fig. A.1. Matrix **A** has *dimensions* 4 x 3 (the number of *rows* precedes the number of *columns*). **B** and **D** are *square* 3 x 3 matrices; they can alternatively be described as being of *order* 3. Matrices **B** and **D** are also *symmetric* matrices: Each row of the matrix is identical with the corresponding column, so that the matrix is symmetrical around the *principal diagonal* that runs from its upper left to lower right. A symmetric matrix is necessarily square, but a square matrix is not necessarily symmetric: The first three rows of matrix **A** would constitute a square, nonsymmetric matrix.

```
     1  4  7      1.00  .32  .64      2   0   0
     6  2  5       .32 1.00  .27      0  -3   0
     3  3  0       .64  .27 1.00      0   0  -1
     4  6  1

        A              B                 D
```

Fig. A.1 Some examples of matrices.

Matrix **B** happens to be a familiar example of a symmetric matrix, a correlation matrix. A variance-covariance matrix would provide another example. Matrix **D** is a *diagonal* matrix: all zeroes except for the principal diagonal.   If the values in the diagonal of **D** were all 1s, it would have a special name: an *identity* matrix, symbolized **I**. A matrix of all zeroes is called a *null* matrix.

Matrices are ordinarily designated by bold-face capital letters.

The transpose of a matrix

The *transpose* of a matrix is obtained by interchanging each row with its corresponding column. Thus, the transpose of matrix **A** in Fig. A.1, conventionally designated **A′**, is:

```
     1  6  3  4
     4  2  3  6
     7  5  0  1
```

in which the first column of **A** becomes the first row of **A´**, and so on. In the case of a symmetric matrix, **A´ = A,** as you can see if you attempt to transpose matrix **B** or **D** in Fig. A.1.

Note that the transpose of a 4 x 3 matrix will have the dimensions 3 x 4 because rows and columns are interchanged. The transpose of a square matrix will be another square matrix of the same order, but it will not be the same matrix unless the original matrix was symmetric.

Vectors and scalars

A single row or column of numbers is called a *vector*. Examples of *column* and *row* vectors are shown in Fig. A.2. The two vectors are of *length* 4 and 3, respectively. Column vectors are designated by lower case bold-face letters-- e.g., vector **a**. Row vectors, as transposes of column vectors, are marked with a prime symbol--e.g., vector **b´**.

a:	1	**b´:**	.3 1.0 .5	
	2			
	4	**c:**	17.3	
	3			

Fig. A.2 Column and row vectors, and a scalar.

Single numbers, of the kind familiar in ordinary arithmetic, are referred to in matrix terminology as *scalars* and are usually designated by lower-case Roman letters--e.g., scalar c in Fig. A.2.

Addition and subtraction of matrices

Two matrices, which must be of the same dimensions, may be *added* together by adding algebraically the corresponding elements of the two matrices, as shown for the two 3 x 2 matrices **A** and **B** in Fig. A.3. A matrix may be *subtracted* from another by reversing the signs of its elements and then adding, as in ordinary algebra. Examples are shown at the right in Fig. A.3.

1 2	0 1	1 3	1 1	−1 −1
4 6	0 −1	4 5	4 7	−4 −7
5 −2	3 −1	8 −3	2 −1	−2 1
A	**B**	**A+B**	**A−B**	**B−A**

Fig. A.3 Matrix addition and subtraction.

Two column vectors of the same length, or two row vectors of the same length, may be added or subtracted in the same way. (As, of course, may two scalars.)

Multiplication of vectors and matrices

A row vector and a column vector of the same length may be multiplied by obtaining the sum of the products of their corresponding elements, as illustrated in Fig. A.4 for $a'b$. Note that this is a multiplication in the order *row* vector times *column* vector. In matrix arithmetic the order of matrices or vectors in a

$$a': 1 \quad 0 \quad 2 \quad 3 \qquad b: \begin{matrix} 1 \\ 2 \\ 4 \\ 3 \end{matrix} \qquad \begin{matrix} 1 \times 1 = 1 \\ 0 \times 2 = 0 \\ 2 \times 4 = 8 \\ 3 \times 3 = \underline{9} \\ a'b = 18 \end{matrix}$$

Fig. A.4 An example of the vector multiplication $a'b$.

multiplication is *not* the indifferent matter that it is in scalar arithmetic, where ab = ba. The product ba' is something entirely different from $a'b$ (as we see shortly). Two matrices may be multiplied by multiplying each of the row vectors of the first matrix in turn times each of the column vectors of the second matrix. Each of these vector multiplications yields a single number that constitutes an element of a row of the product matrix. A step-by-step example is given in Fig. A.5. Notice that the result matrix has as many *rows* as the *first* matrix, and as many *columns* as the *second*, and that for multiplication to be possible, the rows of the first matrix and the columns of the second must be equal in length. Two matrices are said to *conform* for multiplication when this last condition holds--an easy way of checking is to see that the second dimension of the first matrix agrees with the first dimension of the second: that is, a 3 x 5 matrix can be multiplied times a 5 x 2, or a 7 x 2 times a 2 x 3. The middle numbers in the sequence must match; the outer numbers give the dimensions of the result. In the first example, the 5's match and the result will be a 3 x 2 matrix; in the second example, the 2's match and the result will be 7 x 3. In Fig. A.5, the multiplication was of a 3 x 2 times a 2 x 2 matrix; the middle 2's match and the result was 3 x 2. Working through a sample case or two will make it evident to you why these rules hold.

These principles generalize to longer series of matrix multiplications: If **W, X, Y,** and **Z** are, respectively, of dimensions 4 x 2, 2 x 3, 3 x 7, and 7 x 5, the multiplication **WXYZ** can be carried out and the result will be of dimension 4 x 5. (You can see this by carrying out the steps successively: 4 x 2 times

```
1 3    4 5      1st row of A, 1st col of B      1 x 4 = 4
2 1    2 2                                      3 x 2 = 6
0 2                                                   10
A       B       1st row of A,  2nd col of B     1 x 5 = 5
                                                3 x 2 = 6
                                                     11

                2nd row of A,  1st col of B     2 x 4 = 8
                                                1 x 2 = 2
                                                     10

                2nd row of A,  2nd col of B     2 x 5 =10
                                                1 x 2 = 2
                                                     12

                3rd row of A,  1st col of B     0 x 4 = 0
                                                2 x 2 = 4
                                                      4

                3rd row of A,  2nd col of B     0 x 5 = 0
                                                2 x 2 = 4
result AB:  10  11                                    4
            10  12
             4   4
```

Fig. A.5 Step-by-step example of the matrix multiplication **A** times **B**.

2 x 3 is proper and will yield a 4 x 3 matrix; 4 x 3 times 3 x 7 will work and yield a 4 x 7 matrix; and so on.) The rules also hold for vectors, considered as 1 x n or n x 1 matrices. Thus, a 1 x 4 row vector times a 4 x 1 column vector yields a 1 x 1 single number result (as we have seen in Fig. A.4). A 4 x 1 column vector times a 1 x 4 row vector, on the other hand, would produce a 4 x 4 matrix as an answer, and that matrix would be obtained by applying the regular rules of matrix multiplication: taking each row (of length 1) of the column vector and multiplying it successively by each column of the row vector to yield the elements of the rows of the result vector. (You might want to verify that for the two vectors of Fig. A.4, the first two rows of the product **ab**′ would be 1 2 4 3 and 0 0 0 0, and the first two rows of **ba**′ would be 1 0 2 3 and 2 0 4 6.)

Because the order of matrix multiplication is important, the terms *pre-* and *postmultiplication* are often used to eliminate ambiguity. In the product **AB**, **B** is said to be premultiplied by **A**, or **A** to be postmultiplied by **B**. In the product **a**′**Ba**, the matrix is pre- and postmultiplied by the vector. (Incidentally, can you see that **B** must be a square matrix, that the result will be a scalar, and why one would seldom run across the alternative product **aBa**′?)

Some special cases of matrix multiplication

The basis of these rules will be self-evident if you work through an example or two.

(1) A matrix pre- or postmultiplied by a null matrix yields a null matrix. (The null matrix acts like a zero in scalar arithmetic.)

(2) A matrix pre- or postmultiplied by an identity matrix is unchanged. (The identity matrix acts like a 1 in scalar arithmetic.)

(3) Premultiplying a matrix by a diagonal matrix rescales the rows of the matrix by the corresponding elements of the diagonal matrix; postmultiplying by a diagonal matrix rescales the columns. (Try **AD** or **DB** in Fig. A.1, for example.)

(4) Pre- or postmultiplying a matrix by its transpose can always be done and yields a symmetric matrix.

Multiplying a vector or matrix by a scalar

Multiplying a matrix or vector by a scalar is done by multiplying every element in the matrix or vector by that scalar. In a series of matrix operations, the location of a scalar does not matter, and may be changed at will: **ka′BC = a′kBC = a′BkC = a′BC**k, where k is a scalar. (But of course **ka′BC** doesn't equal **kBa′C** or **ka′CB**--the vectors and matrices cannot in general be reordered.)

The inverse of a matrix

There is no operation of matrix division as such, but a matrix *inverse* is the matrix analogue of a reciprocal of a number in scalar arithmetic, so multiplying by an inverse is the matrix equivalent of dividing.

The inverse of a matrix **A**, symbolized by **A**$^{-1}$, is a matrix such that **AA**$^{-1}$ or **A**$^{-1}$**A** equals an identity matrix. (Just as k x 1/k = 1.) Only square matrices have inverses, and not all of them do--if a matrix has some rows or columns that are linearly predictable from others, it will have no inverse. A matrix that has no inverse is called *singular.* Matrix inversion is a basic step in solving matrix equations: If **BX = A** and **B** has an inverse, you can solve for **X** by premultiplying both sides of the equation by **B**$^{-1}$, i.e.:

$$BX = A$$
$$B^{-1}BX = B^{-1}A$$
$$IX = B^{-1}A$$
$$X = B^{-1}A$$

Obtaining the inverse of a matrix tends in general to be a large computational task. Let a computer do it. You can always check to see whether the result it has given you is correct by carrying out the multiplication

AA^{-1}, which should equal **I** within rounding error.
Some useful facts about inverses:
(1) The inverse of the transpose of a matrix is the transpose of its inverse: $(A')^{-1} = (A^{-1})'$.
(2) Taking the inverse of an inverse yields the original matrix: $(A^{-1})^{-1} = A$.
(3) The inverse of a symmetric matrix is also symmetric.

$$
\begin{array}{cccc}
\begin{array}{ccc} 1 & 0 & 0 \\ 0 & 1 & 0 \\ 0 & 0 & 1 \end{array} &
\begin{array}{ccc} 1 & 0 & 0 \\ 0 & 1 & 0 \\ 0 & 0 & 1 \end{array} &
\begin{array}{ccc} 2 & 0 & 0 \\ 0 & 3 & 0 \\ 0 & 0 & -4 \end{array} &
\begin{array}{ccc} 1/2 & 0 & 0 \\ 0 & 1/3 & 0 \\ 0 & 0 & -1/4 \end{array} \\[6pt]
\mathbf{I} & \mathbf{I}^{-1} & \mathbf{D} & \mathbf{D}^{-1}
\end{array}
$$

$$
\begin{array}{ccccc}
\begin{array}{cc} 4 & 2 \\ 5 & 3 \end{array} &
& \dfrac{1}{12-10}\begin{bmatrix} 3 & -2 \\ -5 & 4 \end{bmatrix} & = &
\begin{array}{cc} 1.5 & -1.0 \\ -2.5 & 2.0 \end{array} \\[6pt]
\mathbf{A} & & & & \mathbf{A}^{-1}
\end{array}
$$

Fig. A.6 Some special cases of matrix inversion.

A few special cases of matrix inversion that do not require extensive computation are illustrated in Fig. A.6. You might want to verify these by showing that $AA^{-1} = I$ in each case.
(1) The inverse of an identity matrix is itself.
(2) A diagonal matrix can be inverted by replacing each diagonal element by its reciprocal.
(3) The inverse of a 2 x 2 matrix, for example:

$$
\begin{array}{cc} a & b \\ c & d \end{array}
$$

may be obtained by interchanging the two diagonal elements *a* and *d*, changing the signs of the two off-diagonal elements *b* and *c*, and multiplying the result by the scalar *1/(ad - bc)*.

Inverse or transpose of a product

The *transpose* of a product of matrices is equal to the product of the transposes of the matrices, *taken in reverse order.* $(ABCD)' = D'C'B'A'$.
The *inverse* of a product of matrices is equal to the product of the inverses of the matrices, taken in reverse order:

$$(ABCD)^{-1} = D^{-1}C^{-1}B^{-1}A^{-1}$$

Of course, the latter case presupposes that the necessary inverses exist, i.e., that **A**, **B**, **C**, and **D** are square, nonsingular matrices (they must also all be of the same order for the multiplication to be possible).

Eigenvalues and eigenvectors of a correlation or covariance matrix

If **C** is an $m \times m$ variance-covariance or correlation matrix, it can be decomposed into a matrix product $\mathbf{VL^2V'}$, where **V** is a square $m \times m$ matrix whose columns are called the *eigenvectors* of matrix **C**, and $\mathbf{L^2}$ is a diagonal matrix of numbers, customarily arranged in descending order of size, called the *eigenvalues* of **C**. **V** and $\mathbf{L^2}$ are so chosen as to have the following additional properties:

$$\mathbf{V'V = I,}$$
$$\text{and} \quad \mathbf{Cv = l^2v,}$$

where l^2 is any one of the eigenvalues and **v** the corresponding eigenvector; that is, the eigenvectors are mutually *orthogonal* (= uncorrelated), and each has the property that when it postmultiplies the matrix **C** the result is a vector proportional to itself, the coefficient of proportionality being the eigenvalue.

Eigenvalues and eigenvectors are also sometimes known as *characteristic roots* and *characteristic vectors*, or *latent roots* and *latent vectors*.

The calculation of eigenvalues and eigenvectors, even more than the calculation of inverses, is a task for computers. Again, you can always verify that the results the computer gives you have the properties specified. Fig. A.7 gives an example of eigenvectors and eigenvalues for the correlation matrix of Fig. A.1.

1.00	.32	.64	1.846	0	0	−.641	.261	.721
.32	1.00	.27	0	.797	0	−.443	−.894	−.070
.64	.27	1.00	0	0	.358	−.627	.364	−.689
	C			$\mathbf{L^2}$			**V**	

$$\text{tr } \mathbf{L^2} = 3.00 \qquad |\mathbf{C}| = .526$$

Fig. A.7 Eigenvalues and eigenvectors of a correlation matrix.

A few useful additional properties of eigenvalues:

(1) The sum of the diagonals of **C** and $\mathbf{L^2}$ are the same; i.e., the sum of the eigenvalues of a matrix equals the trace of the matrix.

(2) The product of the eigenvalues of a matrix is called the *determinant* of the matrix. The determinant of matrix **C** is symbolized $|\mathbf{C}|$. A singular matrix, one that has one or more rows or columns linearly predictable from others, has one or more zero eigenvalues and thus a determinant of zero.

(3) The number of nonzero eigenvalues of a matrix is called the *rank* of the matrix, which is the number of nonredundant rows or columns it contains.

Appendix B: IPSOL

The simple program for iterative path solutions described in the text is given below. It is written in the FORTRAN computer language, which can be used on many computers. Lines beginning with an asterisk are comment lines, in ordinary English, not FORTRAN. If you are unfamiliar with FORTRAN, the comment lines should still give you a general sense of how the program is proceeding about its business.

```
        PROGRAM IPSOL
**A SIMPLE PROGRAM FOR ITERATIVE PATH SOLUTIONS.
**EXECUTIVE PROGRAM--READS INPUT, CALLS MINIMIZATION ROUTINE,
*   PRINTS OUTPUT.  DIMENSIONED FOR UP TO 200 OBSERVED VALUES
*   AND 20 UNKNOWN PARAMETERS TO BE SOLVED FOR.
**INPUT: (1) TITLE--ONE LINE OF UP TO 80 CHARACTERS.
*           (2) NOV=NO.OF OBSERVED VALUES; NU=NO.OF UNKNOWN
*               PARAMETERS;NSOL=NO.OF SOLUTIONS; ISTEP=INITIAL STEP
*               VALUE (IF LEFT BLANK, USES .1); INTEGERS, IN 3-DIGIT
*               FIELDS, RIGHT- JUSTIFIED, ON ONE LINE.
*           (3) OBSERVED VALUES, NOV OF THEM, IN 10 EIGHT-DIGIT FIELDS
*               PER LINE, AS MANY LINES AS NEEDED, DECIMAL POINTS
*               REQUIRED.
*           (4) ONE LINE PER DESIRED SOLUTION, WITH NU STARTING
*               VALUES OF UNKNOWN PARAMETERS, IN UP TO 20 THREE-
*               DIGIT FIELDS, DECIMAL POINTS REQUIRED.
        COMMON/ONE/OV(200),NOV
        DIMENSION X(20)
        CHARACTER*8 TITLE(10)
**READ INPUT, AND PRINT BACK OUT.
        READ 1,TITLE
   1    FORMAT(10A8)
        PRINT 13,TITLE
   13   FORMAT('1' 10A8)
        READ 2,NOV,NU,NSOL,ISTEP
   2    FORMAT(4I3)
        PRINT 14,NOV,NU,NSOL,ISTEP
   14   FORMAT(/' OBSERVED VALS=',I3,', UNKNOWNS=',I3,
       1', SOLUTIONS=',I3,', ISTEP=',I3)
        READ 3, (OV(I),I=1,NOV)
   3    FORMAT(10F8.3)
        PRINT 15,(OV(I),I=1,NOV)
   15   FORMAT(' OBS VALS: ',10F8.3)
**ONE PASS PER SOLUTION: SETS STARTING VALUES, CALLS
*   MINIMIZATION ROUTINE, PRINTS RESULTS.  MAXFN=MAXIMUM EFFORT
*   TO BE EXPENDED BEFORE QUITTING (NO.OF MAJOR CYCLES OF
```

```
*   MINIMIZATION ROUTINE).
    DO 30 K=1,NSOL
            READ 4, (X(I),I=1,NU)
    4       FORMAT(20F3.0)
            PRINT 5, (X(I),I=1,NU)
    5       FORMAT(/' START VALS= ',20F4.1)
            MAXFN=500
            MAX=MAXFN
            CALL MINIM(X,NU,MAXFN,ISTEP,FX,IER)
            NCYC=MAX-MAXFN
            IF(IER.NE.0)PRINT 8
    8       FORMAT(' EFFORT LIMIT EXCEEDED, QUIT AT ')
    30      PRINT 7, NCYC, FX, (X(I),I=1,NU)
    7       FORMAT(' NO. OF CYCLES=',I4/ ' MINIMUM FUNCTION VALUE=',
           1 F10.7/ ' SOLUTION: ',20F6.3)
            STOP
            END


            SUBROUTINE MINIM(X,NU,MAXFN,ISTEP,FX,IER)
**MINIMIZATION ROUTINE--CALLS SUBROUTINE FUNCT REPEATEDLY TO
*   EVALUATE EFFECTS OF TRIAL CHANGES IN PARAMETERS.  MAKES
*   MOST PROMISING CHANGE, AND REPEATS.  WHEN NO LONGER
*   IMPROVING, REDUCES STEP SIZE BY A FACTOR OF 10 AND TRIES
*   AGAIN. WHEN STEP SIZE LESS THAN .001, OR MAXIMUM EFFORT
*   EXCEEDED, QUITS AND RETURNS TO MAIN PROGRAM.
            DIMENSION X(20),XX(20),CHG(20)
            IER=0
            CALL FUNCT(NU,X,FX)
            STEP=ISTEP
            IF(ISTEP.LE.0)STEP=.1
    100     DO 80 I=1,NU
    80      CHG(I)=STEP
**BEGIN MAJOR CYCLE
    50      BEST=0.
            SBEST=0
            IB=0
**LOOK FOR MOST PROMISING CHANGE
            DO 30 J=1,NU
            DO 20 I=1,NU
    20      XX(I)=X(I)
            XX(J)=XX(J)+.001
            CALL FUNCT(NU,XX,FXX)
            DIF=ABS(FXX-FX)
            IF(DIF.LE.BEST) GO TO 30
            BEST=DIF
```

```
        IB=J
        SBEST=1
        IF(FXX.GT.FX)SBEST= -1.
   30   CONTINUE
**MAKE MOST PROMISING CHANGE, AND CHECK TO SEE THAT IT IS AN
*  IMPROVEMENT; IF NOT IMPROVING, GO TO DECREASE STEP SIZE.
        DO 40 I=1,NU
   40   XX(I)=X(I)
        XX(IB)=XX(IB)+CHG(IB)*SBEST
        CALL FUNCT(NU,XX,FXXX)
        IF((FX-FXXX).LT..00000001) GO TO 90
        FX=FXXX
        X(IB)=XX(IB)
        MAXFN=MAXFN-1
        IF(MAXFN.GE.0) GO TO 50
        IER=1
        RETURN
**DECREASE STEP SIZE;  IF TOO SMALL, QUIT.
   90   STEP=STEP*.1
        IF(STEP.LT..001)RETURN
        GO TO 100
        END


        SUBROUTINE FUNCT (NU,X,FX)
**CALCULATES FUNCTION FX FOR A GIVEN SET OF TRIAL VALUES.
        COMMON/ONE/OV(200),NOV
        DIMENSION X(20),CV(200)
**PATH EQUATIONS TO CALCULATE IMPLIED VALUES CV(I) FROM TRIAL
*  VALUES OF PARAMETERS X(I) BEGIN HERE.
        CV(1)=X(1)
        CV(2)=X(2)
        CV(3)=X(1)*X(2)
**PATH EQUATIONS END HERE.
**LEAST SQUARES FUNCTION TO BE MINIMIZED. (SUM OF SQUARED
*  DIFFERENCES BETWEEN OBSERVED VALUES OV AND CALCULATED
*  IMPLIED VALUES CV.)
        FX=0.
        DO 20 I=1,NOV
   20   FX=FX+(OV(I)-CV(I))**2
        RETURN
        END
```

Appendix B: IPSOL

Modifying IPSOL for a Generalized Least Squares Solution

An alternative version of the generalized least squares χ^2 criterion for correlations is given by $\mathbf{z'A^{-1}z}$, where $\mathbf{z}$ is a vector of differences between Fisher z transforms of the observed and implied correlations, and $\mathbf{A}$ is the variance-covariance matrix among the implied values (see Rao, Morton, Elston & Yee, 1977, or Steiger, 1980). $\mathbf{A}$ is obtained via the formulas for the correlations among correlations originally derived by Pearson and Filon (1898). If the correlations entering into $\mathbf{z}$ are based on independent groups, this computation takes a particularly simple form: $\mathbf{A}$ becomes diagonal, and its elements are N_i- 3, where N_i is the number of cases in the i th group. This is the inverse of the variance of a z transform, which is $1/(N-3)$, and is independent of the size of z, so that changes in the zs during iteration do not affect it. Thus, the calculation amounts to multiplying the squared differences between the observed and implied z for each group by N-3 for that group, and summing over groups.

This procedure, while used for convenience in the example of Chapter 4 (Table 4-17), is not strictly proper there, because some of the groups--in particular, those from the adoption study--are not independent. Many of the same fathers enter, for example, into the father-adopted-child and father-natural-child correlations. There is some evidence to suggest that under such circumstances the model χ^2s will be somewhat underestimated, although the parameter estimates are little affected (Rao et al., 1977; McGue, Wette & Rao, 1984). In the present case, a rather clumsy LISREL approach gave solutions to the models in lines 3 and 6 of Table 4-17 having χ^2s of 8.84 and 2.68, compared to the 8.47 and 2.60 in the table; the parameter estimates were .76 and -.04 in both cases for the first, and .69, .02, -.18, and .13, compared to .68, .02, -.17, and .14, for the second. These results are certainly in good enough agreement for most practical purposes.

The following modifications to IPSOL will allow it to carry out these calculations: Add a z-transform function $\ln((1+r)/(1-r))$, add a vector of Ns to the input and to the common statement, and suitably modify the function evaluation in FUNCT. For computational economy, one can transform the observed correlations to zs and the Ns to (N - 3)s once at the start when the data are read in to the executive program. Also, it is a good idea to provide a test for out-of-range rs prior to the z transformation in FUNCT; otherwise, if a trial r should happen to equal or exceed 1.0, it will abruptly shut down the calculations.

These can be implemented by making the following changes in the IPSOL program as given:

In both IPSOL and FUNCT, add ,XN(60) to COMMON statement, and add the following line after DIMENSION:

$$Z(R) = .5*ALOG((1.+R)/(1.-R))$$

In IPSOL, add after statement numbered 15:

```
        READ 16,(XN(I),I=1,NOV)
16      FORMAT (20F4.0)
        PRINT 17,(XN(I),I=1,NOV)
17      FORMAT('    NS: ',10F6.0)
        DO 25 I=1,NOV
        XN(I)=XN(I)-3.
        IF(XN(I).LT.0)XN(I)=0
25      OV(I)=Z(OV(I))
```

In FUNCT, replace statement numbered 20 with:

```
        IF(CV(I).GE.1.)CV(I)=.9999
        IF(CV(I).LE.-1.)CV(I)=-.9999
20      FX=FX+(Z(CV(I))-OV(I))**2*XN(I)
```

Add the following line of comment to IPSOL instructions for input, preceding the present item (4), which becomes (5):

(4) NS, NOV OF THEM, INTEGERS, IN 4-DIGIT FIELDS, 20 PER LINE.

And change other comments as appropriate.

Appendix C: Derivation of Matrix Version of Path Equations

In this appendix we show how the McArdle-McDonald matrix equation described in Chapter 2 can be derived from the structural-equation translation of a path diagram.

Figure C.1 repeats the path diagram used in the example, with the structural equations given to the right of the figure.

$$C = cB + aA + e$$

$$D = aA + d$$

Fig. C.1 Path model for example.

Now we write out these same equations so that each of them has on its right-hand side all the variables in the path diagram. This means putting in a lot of zero coefficients but gets the equations into a convenient form to express as matrices. For completeness, structural equations have been added for A and B, although these are not very exciting because neither has any incoming causal arrows from other variables in the diagram. In each equation, the first four terms indicate causal arrows from other variables (hence, the variable itself always gets a zero coefficient). The last term in each expression is the residual. Source variables such as A and B have by definition all their causes external to the path diagram, so they are treated as "all residual."

$$A = 0A + 0B + 0C + 0D + A$$
$$B = 0A + 0B + 0C + 0D + B$$
$$C = aA + cB + 0C + 0D + e$$
$$D = aA + 0B + 0C + 0D + d$$

Next we write this in matrix form.

$$
\begin{matrix}
A \\ B \\ C \\ D
\end{matrix}
\quad = \quad
\begin{matrix}
0 & 0 & 0 & 0 \\
0 & 0 & 0 & 0 \\
a & c & 0 & 0 \\
a & 0 & 0 & 0
\end{matrix}
\quad \times \quad
\begin{matrix}
A \\ B \\ C \\ D
\end{matrix}
\quad + \quad
\begin{matrix}
A \\ B \\ e \\ d
\end{matrix}
$$

(You might want to check to assure yourself that the matrix formulation is indeed the equivalent of the equations.)

Now let's call these matrices, from left to right, **v**, **A**, **v** (again), and **u**. The matrix equation can then be written:

$$v = Av + u.$$

By simple matrix algebra, we solve for **v**:

$$v - Av = u$$
$$(I - A)v = u$$
$$v = (I - A)^{-1}u.$$

If we assume the variables all to be in deviation-score form, the matrix of covariances among all the variables may be obtained as **vv´** /n, or

$$(I - A)^{-1}uu´(I - A)^{-1´}/n.$$

Let us call **uu´** /n --which is itself a covariance matrix--**S**. Then:

$$vv´/n = (I - A)^{-1} S (I - A)^{-1´}.$$

Pre- and postmultiplication by **F** and **F´** selects the observed variables **C**:

$$C = F (I - A)^{-1} S (I - A)^{-1´} F´,$$

which is the McArdle-McDonald equation.

Obtaining $(I - A)^{-1}$

McArdle and McDonald point out that the matrix $(I - A)^{-1}$ can be obtained for unlooped path diagrams as:

$$I + A + AA + AAA + \ldots,$$

where the series is carried out until the product terms become zero. If there are no compound paths in the diagram that contain more than one consecutive straight arrow in the same direction, this will occur after the term **A**; with a maximum of two consecutive straight arrows, it will be after **AA**; and so on.

The example of Fig. C.1 contains only single straight arrows in its paths. Thus, **AA** (as you should verify) is a null matrix. Therefore,

$$(I - A)^{-1} = I + A = \begin{matrix} 1 & 0 & 0 & 0 \\ 0 & 1 & 0 & 0 \\ a & c & 1 & 0 \\ a & 0 & 0 & 1 \end{matrix}$$

as used for the Chapter 2 example.

In Chapter 1, "direct" and "indirect" causal effects were discussed. Note that matrix **A** represents direct effects, and **AA**, **AAA**, etc. indirect effects.

Appendix D: Alpha and Canonical Factor Extraction--A Worked Example

In Chapter 5, the Alpha and Canonical rescalings were briefly described. As noted there, Alpha factor analysis rescales variables to equal communalities of 1.0, whereas Canonical factor analysis rescales variables to equal uniquenesses of 1.0.

Formally, the Alpha method rescales variables by $H^{-1}R_rH^{-1}$, where H^{-1} is a diagonal matrix of the reciprocals of the square roots of the commmunalities, and the Canonical method rescales by $U^{-1}R_rU^{-1}$, where U^{-1} contains the reciprocals of the square roots of the uniquenesses. (Recall that one obtains the inverse of a diagonal matrix by taking reciprocals of its elements.) The Alpha rescaling results in a matrix in which differences along the diagonal are eliminated, whereas the Canonical rescaling results in a matrix in which they are enhanced.

Table D-1 illustrates the process with the same reduced correlation matrix used for the centroid and principal factor solutions in Chapter 5; it is shown in the center of the top row. To the left is a column vector of the reciprocals of the square roots of the communalities (e.g., $1/\sqrt{.16} = 2.5$). These are used in the diagonal matrix H^{-1} which pre- and postmultiplies R_r to yield the matrix shown on the left in the second row. Note that this has rescaled all the diagonal elements to 1.0, and the other elements proportionately (zeroes, of course, stay zero).

To the right is the Canonical factor solution. At the top are the u^{-1} (e.g., $1-.16 = .84$; $1/\sqrt{.84} = 1.091$). In the second row is the rescaled R_r matrix. Note that the differences are now exaggerated: The high values tend to be scaled up much more than the low values--.16 becomes .19, whereas .91 becomes 10.11. This is because the uniqueness for the first variable is already large (.84) and only needs to be increased a little to equal 1.0, whereas the small uniqueness in the second case (.09) must be increased many times.

In the third row of the table are the factor patterns, obtained via VL from the eigenvalue-eigenvector solutions of the matrices above them, as with principal factors. Finally, the factors are returned to their original metric (the standardized variables of the correlation matrix) by the rescalings HP and UP, respectively.

Table D-1 Alpha and Canonical factor solutions (correlation matrix of Table 5-1, exact communalities)

h^{-1}		R_r				u^{-1}
2.500	.16	.20	.24	.00	.00	1.091
1.162	.20	.74	.58	.56	.21	1.961
1.348	.24	.58	.55	.41	.21	1.491
1.048	.00	.56	.41	.91	.51	3.333
1.667	.00	.21	.21	.51	.36	1.250

$H^{-1}R_rH^{-1}$					$U^{-1}R_rU^{-1}$				
1.000	.581	.809	.000	.000	.190	.428	.390	.000	.000
.581	1.000	.909	.682	.407	.428	2.846	1.696	3.661	.515
.809	.909	1.000	.580	.472	.390	1.696	1.222	2.037	.391
.000	.682	.580	1.000	.891	.000	3.661	2.037	10.111	2.125
.000	.407	.472	.891	1.000	.000	.515	.391	2.125	.562

Alpha factors			Canonical factors		
I	II	III	I	II	III
.586	.770	.253	.071	.383	.198
.918	.174	-.357	1.344	.992	-.236
.948	.315	.044	.783	.720	.301
.808	-.577	-.115	3.130	-.560	-.038
.694	-.638	.333	.634	-.270	.295

Rescaled Alpha factors			Rescaled Canonical factors		
I	II	III	I	II	III
.23	.31	.10	.06	.35	.18
.79	.15	-.31	.69	.51	-.12
.70	.23	.03	.53	.48	.20
.77	-.55	-.11	.94	-.17	-.01
.42	-.38	.20	.51	-.22	.24

Appendix E: Examples of Input for Factor Extraction by SPSS, BMDP, and SAS

These are examples of inputs to the factor analysis programs of three popular statistical packages. Each will carry out the extraction of three principal factors from the correlation matrix of Table 5-1, using prespecified communalities.

Table E-1 SPSS FACTOR

```
TITLE 'CHAPTER 5 EXAMPLE'
MATRIX DATA    VARIABLES=D E F G H /CONTENTS=CORR
BEGIN DATA
   1.00
    .20    1.00
    .24     .58    1.00
    .00     .56     .41    1.00
    .00     .21     .21     .51    1.00
END DATA
LIST
FACTOR   MATRIX=IN (COR=*)
   /DIAGONAL=.16 .74 .55 .91 .36
   /CRITERIA=FACTORS (3)
   /EXTRACTION=PAF
   /ROTATION=NOROTATE
```

Table E-2 BMDP4M

```
/PROBLEM   TITLE='CHAPTER 5 EXAMPLE'.
/INPUT     VAR=5.
           FORMAT='(5F5.2)'.
           TYPE=CORR.
/FACTOR    METH=PFA.
           NUMB=3.
           CONST=.001.
           COMM=.16,.74,.55,.91,.36.
           ITER=1.
/ROTATE    METH=NONE.
/PRINT     NO SHADE.
/END.
  1.00
   .20 1.00
   .24   .58 1.00
   .00   .56   .41 1.00
   .00   .21   .21   .51 1.00
```

Table E-3 SAS PROC FACTOR

```
DATA EXAMP(TYPE=CORR);
_TYPE_ ='CORR';
INPUT _NAME_ $ D E F G H;
CARDS;
D 1.0 . . . .
E .20 1.0 . . .
F .24 .58 1.0 . .
G .00 .56 .41 1.0 .
H .00 .21 .21 .51 1.0
  ;
PROC FACTOR   METHOD=PRIN NFACT=3;
   PRIORS .16 .74 .55 .91 .36;
   TITLE 'CHAPTER 5 EXAMPLE';
RUN;
```

Appendix F: Data Matrix for Thurstone's Box Problem

Table F-1 contains the raw data for the Thurstone box example in Chapter 6.

Table F-1 Data matrix for 40 boxes on 10 variables (after Kaiser & Horst, 1975, all scores x 10)

Box	V1	V2	V3	V4	V5	V6	V7	V8	V9	V10
1	89	50	27	56	34	21	11	8	3	23
2	94	45	38	54	81	34	11	6	4	98
3	69	102	7	103	42	32	11	11	0	99
4	122	96	41	78	61	66	11	11	9	145
5	88	91	92	90	96	82	11	12	11	286
6	182	16	1	96	37	20	14	7	-1	154
7	167	47	30	70	77	36	14	7	7	201
8	169	110	3	118	45	29	14	11	1	60
9	185	87	40	137	77	48	14	10	8	231
10	158	89	104	118	116	94	14	11	11	401
11	137	158	2	149	47	39	14	14	-1	180
12	160	144	41	134	77	85	14	14	8	293
13	164	140	93	143	117	117	15	15	11	492
14	265	36	16	100	43	17	16	7	0	157
15	253	41	37	99	101	26	15	6	7	186
16	229	107	38	143	122	56	17	11	7	351
17	252	74	92	150	138	104	17	11	12	486
18	256	158	4	194	48	43	16	14	0	210
19	249	160	33	226	87	73	17	14	7	432
20	253	165	85	196	151	132	16	13	11	604
21	97	29	18	52	27	28	11	7	0	48
22	91	39	45	57	65	33	11	7	7	124
23	81	80	10	101	28	16	10	12	-1	77
24	83	75	39	83	62	63	12	10	9	148
25	88	108	95	91	96	97	12	12	11	315
26	159	29	7	88	41	16	13	7	1	50
27	166	57	42	86	94	45	14	6	7	223
28	157	90	6	117	47	28	14	10	0	95
29	122	85	35	112	74	63	14	12	7	265
30	171	80	101	114	130	93	14	11	12	393

Table F-1 (continued)

Box	V1	V2	V3	V4	V5	V6	V7	V8	V9	V10
31	174	163	18	173	39	54	15	14	-1	200
32	158	148	49	158	80	88	14	14	7	383
33	165	142	86	146	101	114	14	14	12	445
34	246	46	13	113	52	4	15	7	-1	107
35	263	38	58	87	110	37	16	6	9	207
36	215	85	41	149	101	65	16	10	6	311
37	231	87	83	144	144	82	17	12	13	483
38	235	176	21	185	48	35	16	14	-2	168
39	252	159	43	199	90	78	16	14	7	418
40	248	157	83	199	139	124	16	14	13	554

Note: The boxes are ordered in the table by increasing X dimension; boxes 21 to 40 represent a repetition of boxes 1 to 20, with different errors.

Appendix G: Table of Chi-Square

df	P= .99	.90	.70	.50	.30	.10	.05	.01
1	.00	.02	.15	.46	1.07	2.71	3.84	6.64
2	.02	.21	.71	1.39	2.41	4.60	5.99	9.21
3	.12	.58	1.42	2.37	3.66	6.25	7.82	11.34
4	.30	1.06	2.20	3.36	4.88	7.78	9.49	13.28
5	.55	1.61	3.00	4.35	6.06	9.24	11.07	15.09
6	.87	2.20	3.83	5.35	7.23	10.64	12.59	16.81
7	1.24	2.83	4.67	6.35	8.38	12.02	14.07	18.48
8	1.65	3.49	5.53	7.34	9.52	13.36	15.51	20.09
9	2.09	4.17	6.39	8.34	10.66	14.68	16.92	21.67
10	2.56	4.86	7.27	9.34	11.78	15.99	18.31	23.21
11	3.05	5.58	8.15	10.34	12.90	17.28	19.68	24.72
12	3.57	6.30	9.03	11.34	14.01	18.55	21.03	26.22
13	4.11	7.04	9.93	12.34	15.12	19.81	22.36	27.69
14	4.66	7.79	10.82	13.34	16.22	21.06	23.68	29.14
15	5.23	8.55	11.72	14.34	17.32	22.31	25.00	30.58
16	5.81	9.31	12.62	15.34	18.42	23.54	26.30	32.00
17	6.41	10.08	13.53	16.34	19.51	24.77	27.59	33.41
18	7.02	10.86	14.44	17.34	20.60	25.99	28.87	34.80
19	7.63	11.65	15.35	18.34	21.69	27.20	30.14	36.19
20	8.26	12.44	16.27	19.34	22.78	28.41	31.41	37.57
21	8.90	13.24	17.18	20.34	23.86	29.62	32.67	38.93
22	9.54	14.04	18.10	21.34	24.94	30.81	33.92	40.29
23	10.20	14.85	19.02	22.34	26.02	32.01	35.17	41.64
24	10.86	15.66	19.94	23.34	27.10	33.20	36.42	42.98
25	11.52	16.47	20.87	24.34	28.17	34.38	37.65	44.31
26	12.20	17.29	21.79	25.34	29.25	35.56	38.88	45.64
27	12.88	18.11	22.72	26.34	30.32	36.74	40.11	46.96
28	13.56	18.94	23.65	27.34	31.39	37.92	41.34	48.28
29	14.26	19.77	24.58	28.34	32.46	39.09	42.56	49.59
30	14.95	20.60	25.51	29.34	33.53	40.26	43.77	50.89
z	-2.33	-1.28	-.52	.00	.52	1.28	1.64	2.33

Note: Table entries are values of χ^2 exceeded P proportion of the time, for given df. Abridged from Table III, in R. A. Fisher (1958), *Statistical methods for research workers* (13th ed.), New York: Hafner. Used by permission. For df greater than 30, the quantity $[2\chi^2]^{1/2} - [2df-1]^{1/2}$ may be evaluated as a normal deviate (bottom row).

Appendix H: Noncentral Chi-Square for Estimating Power

df	.50	.60	Power .70	.80	.90	.99
1	3.84	4.90	6.17	7.85	10.51	18.37
2	4.96	6.22	7.71	9.64	12.66	21.40
3	5.76	7.16	8.79	10.91	14.17	23.52
4	6.42	7.93	9.69	11.94	15.41	25.25
5	6.99	8.59	10.46	12.83	16.47	26.73
6	7.51	9.19	11.15	13.63	17.42	28.05
7	7.97	9.74	11.77	14.35	18.29	29.25
8	8.41	10.24	12.35	15.03	19.09	30.36
9	8.82	10.71	12.90	15.66	19.84	31.40
10	9.20	11.16	13.41	16.25	20.54	32.37
20	12.27	14.72	17.50	20.97	26.14	40.11
30	14.61	17.44	20.62	24.56	30.39	45.95
40	16.57	19.70	23.22	27.55	33.93	50.82
50	18.31	21.71	25.52	30.20	37.07	55.13
60	19.88	23.53	27.60	32.59	39.89	58.99
70	21.32	25.20	29.51	34.78	42.48	62.54
80	22.66	26.75	31.29	36.83	44.89	65.84
90	23.92	29.10	32.95	38.74	47.15	68.93
100	25.12	29.58	34.53	40.55	49.29	71.85

Note: Entries are noncentral χ^2s required for indicated power (top) for given df (side), at .05 significance level. Abridged from Haynum, Govindarajulu, & Leone (1973), Tables of the cumulative non-central chi-square distribution. In *Selected tables in mathematical statistics* (Vol. 1, pp. 1-42), Providence, RI: American Mathematical Society. Used by permission of the American Mathematical Society.

Answers to Exercises

Chapter 1

1. & 2. Various legitimate diagrams are possible, depending on assumptions made--for example, those shown in Fig. I.1.

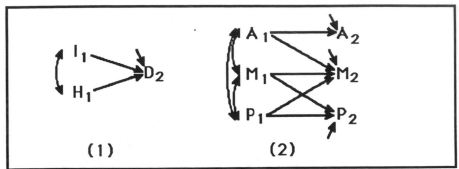

Fig. I.1 Problems 1 & 2--possible answers.

3. Source variables: A, B, W, X, Y, Z. Downstream variables: C, D, E, F, G.

4. That it is completely determined by A and B.

5. $r_{AF} = ae + bf + hcf$; $r_{DG} = cdg + bhdg$; $r_{CE} = ahd$; $r_{EF} = dcf + dhbf + dhae$.

6. $s^2{}_C = a^2 + i^2$; $s^2{}_D = b^2 + c^2 + 2bhc$; $s^2{}_F = e^2 + f^2 + 2eabf + 2eahcf + j^2$.

7. No. There are $(4 \times 3)/2 = 6$ observed correlations, and 8 unknowns (excluding residuals)--a, b, c, d, e, f, g, h.

8. $c_{CD} = a^* s^2{}_A b^* + a^* c_{AB} c^*$
    $c_{FG} = e^* a^* c_{AB} d^* g^* + f^* b^* c_{AB} d^* g^* + f^* c^* s^2{}_B d^* g^*$
    $c_{AG} = c_{AB} d^* g^*$
    $s^2{}_G = g^{*2} s^2{}_E + l^{*2} s^2{}_Z$ [or] $g^{*2} k^{*2} s^2{}_Y + g^{*2} d^{*2} s^2{}_B + l^{*2} s^2{}_Z$
    $s^2{}_D = b^{*2} s^2{}_A + c^{*2} s^2{}_B + 2b^* c^* c_{AB}$

9. $D = bA + cB$; $E = dB + kY$; $F = eC + fD + jX$.

10.

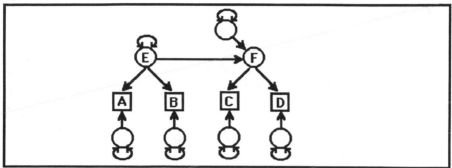

Fig I.2 RAM path diagram, problem 10

11. $r_{BC} = c + ba = .70$; $r_{CD} = a^2 + cba = .48$; $r_{BD} = ba = .30$.
   $a = .6$; $b = .5$; $c = .4$ [or] $a = -.6$; $b = -.5$; $c = .4$.
   $d = \sqrt{(1 - .36)} = .8$; $e = \sqrt{(1 - .36 - .16 - .24)} = .49$.

12. $ab \times bc/ac = b^2 = .42 \times .14/.12 = .49$; $b = .7$.
   $a = .6$; $c = .2$; [or] $b = -.7$; $a = -.6$; $c = -.2$.

13. Centroid factor loadings: .604, .673, .805, .503. Communality estimates--
   .36, .44, .63, .25; column sums--1.56, 1.74, 2.08, 1.30; $\Sigma\Sigma = 6.68$; $\Sigma = 2.5846$.

Chapter 2

Note: In this and the next two chapters, suggestions are sometimes given regarding problem setups in LISREL and EQS. If you are using CALIS, inputs will be similar to those for EQS. If you are using EzPATH or AMOS, inputs should follow directly from your path diagram.

1. Equations: CV(1)=X(1)*X(2)   Input: PROBLEM 1 CHAPTER 2
                CV(2)=X(1)*X(3)   3   3   2
                CV(3)=X(2)*X(3)   .30   .40   .35
                                               .5 .5 .5
                                               .1 .1 .1

Solutions: $a = .585$, $b = .512$, $c = .684$ (or all negative). Reproduced correlations, to three places, equal to originals (e.g., $.585 \times .512 = .300$). Residual paths: $x = .859$, $y = .811$, $z = .729$ (e.g., $\sqrt{[1-.512^2]} = .859$).

2. For example:

Fig. I.3 A difficult terrain for IPSOL.

3. **A**

	A	B	C	D
A	0	0	0	0
B	a	0	0	0
C	0	b	0	0
D	0	c	0	0

S

	A	B	C	D
A	1	0	0	0
B	0	y^2	0	0
C	0	0	x^2	0
D	0	0	0	z^2

F

	A	B	C	D
A	1	0	0	0
C	0	0	1	0
D	0	0	0	1

4. **PH, GA, PS, BE** = 1 x 1; **LX** = 3 x 1; **LY** = 2 x 1; **TD** = 3 x 3; **TE** = 2 x 2.

5.

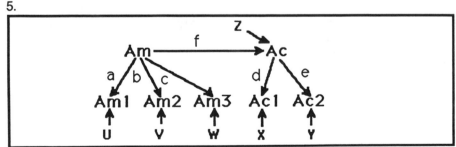

Fig. I.4 Path model for Problem 5.

For LISREL, there will be 1 K (Am), 1 E (Ac), 3 Xs (Am 1 to 3), and 2 Ys (Ac1 and 2). The matrix does not need to be reordered. One way to solve the model is to let all matrices take on their default values, then set *a* and *d* to 1.0, and free *b* and *c* in **LX** and *e* in **LY**. Ask for SS in the output. For EQS, solved the same way, there will be six EQUations, five for V1 to V5 (Am1 to Ac2) and one for F2 (Ac). The first two would be V1 = F1 + E1 and V2 = *F1 + E2. There will be seven VARiances (F1, E1 to E5, and D2). There will be asterisks corresponding to *b, c, e, f, u* to *z*, and the variance of Am. Results: Standardized paths: $a = .920$, $b = .761$, $c = .652$, $d = .879$, $e = .683$, $f = .356$. Residual variances: U= .153, V = .420, W = .575, X = .228, Y = .534, Z = .873. $\chi^2 = 5.80$, 4 df, p > .20. The model is consistent with the data. It implies that a little more than one-third (.356) of ambition translates into achievement, when both are expressed in standard-score units.

6. Model 1 ($\chi^2 = 16.21$, 7 df) is a significantly poor fit to the data, and a significantly worse fit than any of the other three (χ^2_{diff} 8.09, 2 df; 13.71, 3 df; 16.13, 6 df). None of the others can be rejected (p > .05 for each), but the third fits significantly better than the second (χ^2_{diff} 5.62, 1 df).

7.

Model	χ^2	Unknowns	df	nfi	pfi	AIC
null	25.00	0	10			25.00
1.	16.21	3	7	.352	.246	22.21
2.	8.12	5	5	.675	.338	18.12
3.	2.50	6	4	.900	.360	14.50
4.	.08	9	1	.997	.100	18.08

Model 4 in absolute terms is a very close fit (nfi = .997), but involves many parameters. Model 3 is the most parsimonious fit, by either pfi or AIC.

8.

Fig. I.5 Path diagram for problem 8.

LISREL matrices: **LX** 1   **PH** e   **TD** (diag.) f g h i
                                   b
                                   c
                                   d

In EQS, there will be 4 EQUations, for V1 through V4 (= W through Z); there will be VARiances for F1 (= e) and E1 to E4 (= *f* to *i*).
Results: Unstandardized: $a^* = 1.000$, $b^* = 1.120$, $c^* = 1.351$, $d^* = .829$, $e^* = .364$.
           Standardized: $a = .604$, $b = .676$, $c = .815$, $d = .500$, $e = 1.000$.
           Residual variances: $f = .636$, $g = .543$, $h = .335$, $i = .749$.
Standardized solution is very similar to centroid solution in Chapter 1.

9. $a = 1.0 \times \sqrt{.364} / 1 = .603$, $b = 1.120 \times \sqrt{.364} / 1 = .676$, etc.

Chapter 3

1. One way of setting up LISREL matrices:
LX 1.0   **PH** a   **TD** (diag)   b   b   b   [parallel]
     1.0   **TD** (diag)   b   c   d   [tau-equivalent]
     1.0
In EQS, there will be 3 EQUations and 4 VARiances, and a CONstraint
statement of the form (E1,E1)=(E2,E2)=(E3,E3) for parallel tests.
Goodness of fit (maximum likelihood solution):

     parallel: $\chi^2 = 10.35$, 4 df, p < .05

     tau-equivalent: $\chi^2 = 5.96$, 2 df, p > .05
Reject hypothesis that tests are parallel; hypothesis of tau-equivalence cannot
be rejected (but with this small sample, this does not mean that it fits very well).

2. First 3 equations, corresponding to r_{12}, r_{13}, and r_{14}:
     CV(1) = X(1)*X(2)
     CV(2) = X(1)*X(3)
     CV(3) = X(1)*X(10)*X(4)
(unknowns are in the same order as in Fig. 3.4).
IPSOL solution: .73, .64, .58, .74, .66, .67, .78, .71, .61, .63, -.41, -.25; in good
agreement with Table 3-4 solution (maximum discrepancy ≈ .03).

3. Within trait across method: .71, .53, .43, .48, .42, .22, .46, .24, .31;
median = .43.
     Within method across trait: .37, -.24, -.14, .37, -.15, -.19, .23, -.05, -.12;
median absolute value = .19.
     Across method and trait: .35, -.18, -.15, .39, -.27, -.31, .31, -.22, -.10, .17,
-.04, -.13, .36, -.15, -.25, .09, -.04, -.11; median absolute value=.175.
Suggests reasonable convergent and discriminant validity of traits, and not a
great deal of influence of measurement method.

4. One way of setting up LISREL matrices (both trait and method factors):
LX   a   0   0   j   0   0   **TD** (diag): 9 free values
      0   b   0   k   0   0
      0   0   c   l   0   0   obs. values: 9 x 10/2 = 45
      d   0   0   0   m   0   unknowns = 30; df = 15
      0   e   0   0   n   0
      0   0   f   0   o   0
      g   0   0   0   0   p
      0   h   0   0   0   q
      0   0   i   0   0   r

PH 1

   s 1

   t u 1

   0 0 0 1

   0 0 0 0 1

   0 0 0 0 0 1

For EQS there will be 9 EQUations corresponding to the rows of **LX** plus **TD**; 6 fixed variances (diagonal of **PH**) and 9 free variances (**TD**); and 3 COVariances corresponding to those in **PH**.

Goodness of fit (maximum likelihood solution):

    both kinds of factors $\chi^2 = 14.15$, 15 df, p > .50

    trait only: $\chi^2 = 21.94$, 24 df, p > .50

    method only: $\chi^2 = 232.77$, 27 df, p < .001

Trait factors, with or without method factors, fit well. Method factors alone do not yield an acceptable fit. Method factors do not add significantly to the fit of trait factors ($\chi^2_{diff} = 7.79$, 9 df, p > .50).

5.

	χ^2	Unknowns	df	nfi	pfi	AIC
null	290.68	9	36			308.7
method	232.77	18	27	.20	.15	268.8
trait	21.94	21	24	.92	.62	63.9
both	14.15	30	15	.95	.40	74.2

The model with both trait and method factors gives the best absolute fit (nfi = .95), but the one with trait factors only gives a good absolute fit (nfi = .92) and is the most parsimonious by both pfi and AIC.

6. One way of setting up LISREL matrices:

LX 1 1 1   **PH** a   **TD** (diag): g g g g

      1 1 -1   b c

      1 -1 1   d e f   [second run: same, except c=a]

      1 -1 -1

In EQS, 4 EQUations; 3 VARiances of Fs and 3 COVariances; 4 Es constrained equal, plus 2 Fs in second run.

Trait and acquiescence variances differ: $\chi^2 = 2.61$, 3 df, p > .40; trait and acquiescence variances the same: $\chi^2 = 156.66$, 4 df, p < .001; $\chi^2_{diff} = 154.05$, 1 df, p < .001; reject the hypothesis that trait and acquiescence variances are equal.

Answers

7.	CZ	r_{XZ}	r_{XY}	$r_{XY \cdot Z}$
	.7	.504	.5184	.3544
	.9	.648	.5184	.1698
	1.0	.72	.5184	.0
	.5	.36	.5184	.4467
	.0	.00	.5184	.5184

Only as CZ approaches 1.0 does $r_{XY \cdot Z}$ become small. With values of .5 or less it is only slightly reduced.

8 & 9.

Chapter 4

1. Line 2 solution: $\chi^2 = 18.89$, 28 df. Without z for occupational aspiration: $\chi^2 = 30.62$, 29 df, $\chi^2_{diff} = 11.73$, 1 df, $p < .001$. Without z for educational aspiration: $\chi^2 = 19.32$, 29 df; $\chi^2_{diff} = .43$, 1 df, $p > .50$. Residual correlation of the friends' educational aspirations is not statistically significant, but that for occupational aspirations is.

2. Show that inclusion of curved arrows between the residuals from RPA and REA or ROA, and FPA and FEA or FOA, leads to a significant decrease in χ^2. A problem would be presented by the fact that LISREL does not admit covariances between independent and dependent variables. It would be necessary to reformulate the model (e.g., by putting it all on the Y side) in order to test it using LISREL.

3. One way of setting up LISREL matrices:

```
LX  a e 0 0 0    PH: Identity    TD(diag): i j k l i j k l
    b 0 f 0 0
    c 0 0 g 0
    d 0 0 0 h
    a e 0 0 0    χ² = 72.14, 24 df, p < .001;
    b 0 f 0 0    reject such a model.
    c 0 0 g 0
    d 0 0 0 h
```

In EQS, 8 EQUations for V1 to V8 corresponding to LX plus TD (examples: V1 = *F1 + *F2 + E1; V2 = *F1 + *F3 + E2); 5 F VARiances set to 1 and 8 E variances solved; CONstraints as indicated in LISREL matrices.

4. Allow all 8 parameters in the first column of **LX** in problem 3 to be different. $\chi^2 = 65.53$, 20 df. $\chi^2_{diff} = 6.61$, 4 df, $p > .10$. This model does not fit significantly better.

5. With different structural and measurement models (text), $\chi^2 = 24.56$, with 32 df. Requiring the measurement model to be the same (**LY** and **TE** invariant across groups in LISREL, comparable CONstraints in EQS) yields $\chi^2 = 119.33$ with 56 df; $\chi^2_{diff} = 94.77$, with 24 df, p < .001. The same measurement model does not fit in both groups.

6. Four groups, differing only in the fixed genetic covariance. One way of setting up LISREL matrices for the hypothesis of parallel tests is (e.g., for DZ twins):

LX			**PH**				**TD**					
a	0		1				b					
a	0		.5	1			c	b				
a	0						c	c	b			
0	a						d	e	e	b		
0	a						e	d	e	c	b	
0	a						e	e	d	c	c	b

In each group, EQS will have 6 EQUations for V1 to V6; VARiances of F1 and F2 set to 1 with appropriate COVariance; CONstraints among variances and covariances of Es and regression weights of Fs, as required (see **TD** and **LX**). Solution: The χ^2 is 91.59 with 79 df, p > .15, and $\chi^2_{diff} = 16.76$, 10 df, p > .05. Thus, one would not reject the hypothesis that the three scales are parallel tests of numerical ability. (Under this model, the genetic paths *a* are .665, the residual variances *b* are .561, and the residual covariances are *c* = .209 across tests within persons, *d* = .244 for the same test across persons, and *e* = .150 across both tests and persons.)

Chapter 5

1. Eigenvalues: 1.6912,   .9458,   .7866,   .5764

Eigenvectors:

-.601	.109	.282	-.740
-.476	.256	-.834	.107
.277	.951	.128	-.037
-.579	.133	.456	.663

Principal Factors:

-.781	.106	.250	-.562
-.620	.249	-.740	.081
.361	.925	.114	-.028
-.753	.129	.404	.503

R_1

.61			
.48	.38		
-.28	-.22	.13	
.59	.47	-.27	.57

R_2

.62			
.51	.45		
-.18	.01	.99	
.60	.50	-.15	.58

R_3

.68			
.33	.99		
-.16	-.08	1.00	
.70	.20	-.11	.75

$R_4 = R$

1. (cont.) Successive matrices do improve in fit, but much of this improvement, after R_1, is in fitting the diagonal elements.

2. R_r

.49	.28	-.14	.42
.28	.16	-.08	.24
-.14	-.08	.04	-.12
.42	.24	-.12	.36

Eigenvalues: 1.0500, .0000, .0000, .0000

v_1		p_1	
	.683		.700
	.390		.400
	-.195		-.200
	.586		.600

PP' reconstructs R_r exactly.

3. Column sums: 1.26   .88   .48   1.20
   Factor loadings: .645   .450 -.246   .614

4. SMCs: .962, .800, .962, .791, .842

5. Eigenvalues: 2.867, 1.798, .217, .098, .019.   Two factors by either criterion.

6. C_r

11388427				
62	3			
4140969	335	1481764		
174064	143	72785	10455	
438118	9858	948323	571210	34152979

P from R_r

.625	.764
.707	-.550
.711	.679
.882	-.161
.741	-.579

P from C_r (rescaled)

.043	.980
.937	-.026
.152	.980
.859	.409
.918	-.020

The two solutions are quite different, due to the markedly different scales on which the solution was carried out.

7. First factor loadings: .977, .137, .984, .530, .132. $\chi^2 = 243.74$, 10 df, $p < .001$. Reject hypothesis of one common factor.

8.

Chapter 6

1.
P			F			S		
	.79	.06		1.00	.57		.82	.51
	.89	-.06		.57	1.00		.85	.45
	.07	.68					.45	.72
	-.08	.61					.26	.56

2.

Fig. I.6 Path diagrams for unrotated (a) and rotated (b) factors.

3. Path diagram h^2s: .62, .79, .46, .37.
   h^2s from P_0 rows: .68, .73, .52, .32.

The two are similar but not identical. The h^2s from the path diagram may be either larger or smaller because some of the small omitted paths are positive and some negative, resulting in covariance contributions of both signs.

4.
$P_{varimax}$			$P_{oblimin}$			P_{orthob}		
	.78	.28		.79	.07		.78	.07
	.83	.19		.88	-.04		.88	-.05
	.28	.67		.10	.66		.06	.68
	.11	.55		-.05	.59		-.09	.61

$F_{varimax}$			$F_{oblimin}$			F_{orthob}		
	1.00	.00		1.00	.52		1.00	.56
	.00	1.00		.52	1.00		.56	1.00

Either oblique **P** is similar to the Problem 1 solution. The orthogonal **P** has similar high loadings, but its low loadings are not as close to zero.

5.

6. $\mathbf{P}_{promax}$

			$\mathbf{F}$		
.77	.09		1.00	.53	
.86	-.02		.53	1.00	
.07	.68				
-.08	.60		Quite similar to other oblique solutions.		

7.

$\mathbf{P}_{-1}$			$\mathbf{P}_0$			$\mathbf{P}_{+.5}$		
.06	.09	.50	.01	.01	.58	-.28	-.18	.98
.05	.04	.46	.01	-.00	.50	-.24	-.26	.95
.08	.63	.38	.01	.65	.33	-.52	1.04	.33
.72	.05	.07	.74	.02	.01	1.32	-.34	-.34
.06	.74	.04	.02	.81	-.06	-.40	1.53	-.48
.72	.02	.04	.75	-.02	-.01	1.37	-.40	-.37

$\mathbf{F}$			$\mathbf{F}$			$\mathbf{F}$		
1.00	.26	.33	1.00	.41	.49	1.00	.89	.91
	1.00	.50		1.00	.65		1.00	.94
		1.00			1.00			1.00

With increasing w, the factors become more highly correlated. Quartimin, $w = 0$, gives the cleanest solution in this case--the small loadings are quite close to zero and split between positive and negative; $w = -1.0$ gives a passable but probably slightly too orthogonal a solution--the low loadings are larger than for the quartimin solution, and all are positive. The solution for $w = +.5$ has clearly gone much too oblique--the factor intercorrelations are approaching unity, the low loadings have become substantial and negative, and the high loadings are implausibly high, yielding an essentially uninterpretable solution.

8. Add a row .17 .55 to **S** and a row -.14 .62 to **P**.

9.

Chapter 7

1. A path model for part (a) is shown in Fig. I.7. In LISREL, it is convenient to set up the model entirely on the Y side; this permits the variations of parts (a) through (d) without major reformulation of the model. The matrices will be **LY** (the fixed 1.0 paths, and a and b), **PS=DI** (e and d), **BE=FU** (c), and **TE** (f, g, h, i), for part (a). Changes in **BE** will produce parts (b) and (c); no **BE**, and **PS** default, will yield part (d). In EQS, there will be 5 EQUations, for V1 through V4

Fig. I.7 Path diagram for problem 1, part (a)

and F2 (HH1 through WH2 and WH), and 6 VARiances (Es for *f* through *i*, D2 for *d*, and F1 for *e*), for part (a), and equivalent changes for the other models. Result: All fits identical (χ^2 = 1.78, 1 df, p > .10), but path values and residual variances change in the structural model.

2. The implied matrix will consist of .36s within and .18s across factors. χ^2 = 5.08, 9 df, yields a power of < .50 from the table. The N required for 80% power is about (15.66/5.08) x 50 = 154.

3. In LISREL 7 use the special matrices **KA** (fixed and free, respectively, in the two groups) and **TX** (free and invariant). In EQS include the special variable V999 in each equation, analyze moments, and impose comparable constraints.
    A single-factor model with factor pattern the same for both sexes, but latent variable mean and variance and residual variances allowed to differ, fits the data quite adequately: χ^2 = 9.25, 10 df, p > .50 (by LISREL with maximum likelihood criterion). Allowing the factor patterns to differ between men and women does not significantly improve the fit: χ^2 = 4.61, 7 df; χ^2_{diff} = 4.64, 3 df, p ≈ .20. (If in the first condition the residuals are also required to be equal, the fit is still satisfactory: χ^2 = 15.71, 14 df, p > .30.)

4. (a) $C_{S1D2} = aV_{M1}d + eV_{M2}h + iV_{F1}l + mV_{F2}p$
$+ aC_{M1M2}h + eC_{M2M1}d + aC_{M1F1}l + iC_{F1M1}d$
$+ aC_{M1F2}p + mC_{F2M1}d + eC_{M2F1}l + iC_{F1M2}h$
$+ eC_{M2F2}p + mC_{F2M2}h + iC_{F1F2}p + mC_{F2F1}l$

(b) $C_{S1D2} = $ .15 + .10 + .08 + .04 + .15 + .036 + .02 + .024 + .02 + .003
$+ .004 + .02 + .024 + .015 + .080 + .01 = .776$
$C_{S1D1} = $ .779

4. (c)

	A	B	C	D	C_M	C_F	C_{MF}
	.5 .2	.5 .3	.4 .1	.3 .2	1.0 .6	1.0 .5	.2 .1
	.2 .4	.3 .5	.1 .2	.2 .4	.6 1.0	.5 1.0	.1 .3

C_{SD} = .779 .776 C_{S1D1} and C_{S1D2} agree with top
       .579 .651   row of C_{SD}.

5. $V_A = V_X + V_S$ $C_{AC,AD} = hV_{XZ} + hV_{ZS}$
   $C_{B,AC} = 0$ $V_Y = c^2V_X + d^2V_Z + 2cdi + eV_{XZ} + V_W$

6. **P**   .13   .98
        -.91 -.09
        -.16 -.98
        .82   .04
        .86   .39

Large coefficients on the first factor correspond to equations that give relatively large weights to X, and on the second, to equations that give relatively large weights to X^2.

7. P_{12} .56
            .74
            .88

8. $P_{02} = P_{01}P_{12}$.   The coefficients are .52, .45, .78, .44, .56, and .40.

9.   **P** h^2 h^2_{PF}
         .52 .01 .01 .28   .35   .34
         .45 .01 -.00 .24   .26   .25
         .78 .01 .44 .16   .83   .83
         .44 .61 .01 .00   .57   .58
         .56 .02 .55 -.03   .62   .61
         .40 .62 -.01 -.00   .54   .55

The two sets of communalities agree within rounding error.

10. **P**   .778 Al   Eigenvalues: 3.12, .67, .15, .06
         -.999 Ben   (factor solution--principal factors
         .943 Carl   with iteration for communalities,
         -.643 Zach   starting from SMCs)

The data are fairly well described by a single factor, on which Carl and Al are alike and opposite to Ben and Zach.

11. For example, one might obtain a measure of motor skill for a sample of persons under a number of different conditions, and intercorrelate and factor the conditions to study the major dimensions of their influence on motor skill.

12. Conceivably, but it is perhaps better described as a three-mode analysis carried out in two groups (college and noncollege). The three modes are persons, occasions ('72, '74, '76), and attitudes (toward busing, criminals, jobs).

13.

References

Akaike, H. (1987). Factor analysis and AIC. *Psychometrika, 52*, 317-332.

Anderson, J. C., & Gerbing, D. W. (1982). Some methods for respecifying measurement models to obtain unidimensional construct measurement. *Journal of Marketing Research, 19*, 453-460.

Anderson, J. C., & Gerbing, D. W. (1984). The effect of sampling error on convergence, improper solutions, and goodness-of-fit indices for maximum likelihood confirmatory factor analysis. *Psychometrika, 49*, 155-173.

Anderson, J. C., & Gerbing, D. W. (1988). Structural equation modeling in practice: A review and recommended two-step approach. *Psychological Bulletin, 103*, 411-423.

Anderson, J. C., Gerbing, D. W., & Hunter, J. E. (1987). On the assessment of unidimensional measurement: Internal and external consistency, and overall consistency criteria. *Journal of Marketing Research, 24*, 432-437.

Arbuckle, J. L. (1989). AMOS: Analysis of moment structures. *American Statistician, 43*, 66.

Asher, H. B. (1983). *Causal modeling* (2nd ed.). Beverly Hills, CA: Sage Publications.

Babakus, E., Ferguson, C. E., Jr., & Jöreskog, K. G. (1987). The sensitivity of confirmatory maximum likelihood factor analysis to violations of measurement scale and distributional assumptions. *Journal of Marketing Research, 24*, 222-228.

Bagozzi, R. P., & Van Loo, M. F. (1988). An investigation of the relationship between work and family size decisions over time. *Multivariate Behavioral Research, 23*, 3-34.

Bagozzi, R. P., & Yi, Y. (1989). On the use of structural equation models in experimental designs. *Journal of Marketing Research, 26*, 271-284.

Bagozzi, R. P., & Yi, Y. (1990). Assessing method variance in multitrait-multimethod matrices: The case of self-reported affect and perceptions at work. *Journal of Applied Psychology, 75*, 547-560.

Baker, R. L., Mednick, B., & Brock, W. (1984). An application of causal modeling techniques to prospective longitudinal data bases. In S. A. Mednick, M. Harway, & K. M. Finello (Eds.), *Handbook of longitudinal research: Vol. I. Birth and childhood cohorts* (pp.106-132). New York: Praeger.

Bartholomew, D. J. (1987). *Latent variable models and factor analysis*. New York: Oxford University Press.

Baumrind, D. (1983). Specious causal attributions in the social sciences: The reformulated stepping-stone theory of heroin use as exemplar. *Journal of Personality and Social Psychology, 45*, 1289-1298.

References

Bentler, P. M. (1980). Multivariate analysis with latent variables: Causal modeling. *Annual Review of Psychology, 31*, 419-456.

Bentler, P.M. (1983). Some contributions to efficient statistics in structural models. *Psychometrika, 48*, 493-517.

Bentler, P. M. (1986). Structural modeling and *Psychometrika:* An historical perspective on growth and achievements. *Psychometrika, 51*, 35-51.

Bentler, P. M. (1989). *EQS structural equations program manual.* Los Angeles: BMDP Statistical Software.

Bentler, P. M. (1990). Comparative fit indexes in structural models. *Psychological Bulletin, 107*, 238-246.

Bentler, P. M., & Bonett, D. G. (1980). Significance tests and goodness of fit in the analysis of covariance structures. *Psychological Bulletin, 88*, 588-606.

Bentler, P. M., & Chou, C.-P. (1990). Model search with TETRAD II and EQS. *Sociological Methods & Research, 19*, 67-79.

Bentler, P. M., & Huba, G. J. (1979). Simple minitheories of love. *Journal of Personality and Social Psychology, 37*, 124-130.

Bentler, P. M., & Lee, S.-Y. (1979). A statistical development of three-mode factor analysis. *British Journal of Mathematical and Statistical Psychology, 32*, 87-104.

Bentler, P. M., & McClain, J. (1976). A multitrait-multimethod analysis of reflection-impulsivity. *Child Development, 47*, 218-226.

Bentler, P. M., & Weeks, D. G. (1980). Linear structural equations with latent variables. *Psychometrika, 45*, 289-308.

Bentler, P. M., & Weeks, D. G. (1985). Some comments on structural equation models. *British Journal of Mathematical and Statistical Psychology, 38*, 120-121.

Bentler, P. M., & Woodward, J. A. (1978). A Head Start reevaluation: Positive effects are not yet demonstrable. *Evaluation Quarterly, 2*, 493-510.

Biddle, B. J., & Marlin, M. M. (1987). Causality, confirmation, credulity, and structural equation modeling. *Child Development, 58*, 4-17.

Bielby, W. T. (1986). Arbitrary metrics in multiple-indicator models of latent variables. *Sociological Methods & Research, 15*, 3-23.

Bock, R. D., Dicken, C., & Van Pelt, J. (1969). Methodological implications of content-acquiescence correlation in the MMPI. *Psychological Bulletin, 71*, 127-139.

Bohrnstedt, G. W., & Felson, R. B. (1983). Explaining the relations among children's actual and perceived performances and self-esteem: A comparison of several causal models. *Journal of Personality and Social Psychology, 45*, 43-56.

Bollen, K. A. (1989a). A new incremental fit index for general structural equation models. *Sociological Methods & Research, 17*, 303-316.

Bollen, K. A. (1989b). *Structural equations with latent variables.* New York: Wiley.

References

Bollen, K. A. (1990). Overall fit in covariance structure models: Two types of sample size effects. *Psychological Bulletin, 107*, 256-259.

Bollen, K. A., & Jöreskog, K. G. (1985). Uniqueness does not imply identification. *Sociological Methods & Research, 14*, 155-163.

Bollen, K. A., & Liang, J. (1988). Some properties of Hoelter's CN. *Sociological Methods & Research, 16*, 492-503.

Bone, P. F., Sharma, S., & Shimp, T. A. (1989). A bootstrap procedure for evaluating goodness-of-fit indices of structural equation and confirmatory factor models. *Journal of Marketing Research, 26*, 105-111.

Boomsma, A. (1982). The robustness of LISREL against small sample sizes in factor analysis models. In K. G. Jöreskog & H. Wold (Eds.), *Systems under indirect observation* (Part I, pp.149-174). Amsterdam: North-Holland.

Boomsma, A. (1985). Nonconvergence, improper solutions, and starting values in LISREL maximum likelihood estimation. *Psychometrika, 50*, 229-242.

Boomsma, D. I., Martin, N. G., & Neale, M. C. (Eds.). (1989). Genetic analysis of twin and family data: Structural modeling using LISREL. *Behavior Genetics, 19*, 3-161.

Bozdogan, H. (1987). Model selection and Akaike's Information Criterion (AIC): The general theory and its analytical extensions. *Psychometrika, 52*, 345-370.

Bracht, G. H., & Hopkins, K. D. (1972). Stability of educational achievement. In G. H. Bracht, K. D. Hopkins, & J. C. Stanley (Eds.) *Perspectives in educational and psychological measurement* (pp. 254-258). Englewood Cliffs, NJ: Prentice-Hall.

Bramble, W. J., & Wiley, D. E. (1974). Estimating content-acquiescence correlation by covariance structure analysis. *Multivariate Behavioral Research, 9*, 179-190.

Brecht, M.-L., Bentler, P. M., & Tanaka, J. S. (1986). A case study in evaluating statistical computer programs: Comparison of three programs for specifying and testing structural equation models. *Journal of Educational Technology Systems, 14*, 217-227.

Breckler, S. J. (1990). Applications of covariance structure modeling in psychology: Cause for concern? *Psychological Bulletin, 107*, 260-273.

Brenner, S.-O., & Bartell, R. (1984). The teacher stress process: A cross-cultural analysis. *Journal of Occupational Behaviour, 5*, 183-195.

Brown, R. L. (1986). A comparison of the LISREL and EQS programs for obtaining parameter estimates in confirmatory factor analysis studies. *Behavior Research Methods, Instruments, & Computers, 18*, 382-388.

Browne, M. W. (1984). Asymptotically distribution-free methods for the analysis of covariance structures. *British Journal of Mathematical and Statistical Psychology, 37*, 62-83.

Browne, M. W. (1987). Robustness of statistical inference in factor analysis and related models. *Psychometrika, 74*, 375-384.

References

Burt, C. (1917). *The distributions and relations of educational abilities.* London: London County Council.

Burt, R. S. (1981). A note on interpretational confounding of unobserved variables in structural equation models. In P. V. Marsden (Ed.), *Linear models in social research* (pp. 299-318). Beverly Hills, CA: Sage

Busemeyer, J. R., & Jones, L. E. (1983). Analysis of multiplicative combination rules when the causal variables are measured with error. *Psychological Bulletin, 93*, 549-562.

Byrne, B. M. (1989). *A primer of LISREL.* New York: Springer-Verlag.

Campbell, D. T., & Fiske, D. W. (1959). Convergent and discriminant validation by the multitrait-multimethod matrix. *Psychological Bulletin, 56*, 81-105.

Cattell, R. B. (1952). The three basic factor-analytic research designs--Their interrelations and derivatives. *Psychological Bulletin, 49*, 499-520.

Cattell, R. B. (1966a). The data box: Its ordering of total resources in terms of possible relational systems. In R. B. Cattell (Ed.), *Handbook of multivariate experimental psychology* (pp. 67-128). Chicago: Rand McNally.

Cattell, R. B. (1966b). The scree test for the number of factors. *Multivariate Behavioral Research, 1*, 245-276.

Cattell, R. B. (1978). *The scientific use of factor analysis.* New York: Plenum.

Cattell, R. B., & Cross, K. P. (1952). Comparison of ergic and self-sentiment structures found in dynamic traits by R- and P-techniques. *Journal of Personality, 21*, 250-271.

Cattell, R. B., & Jaspers, J. (1967). A general plasmode (No. 30-10-5-2) for factor analytic exercises and research. *Multivariate Behavioral Research Monographs, 67-3*, 1-211.

Cattell, R. B., & Muerle, J. L. (1960). The "maxplane" program for factor rotation to oblique simple structure. *Educational and Psychological Measurement, 20*, 569-590.

Cattell, R. B., & Sullivan, W. (1962). The scientific nature of factors: A demonstration by cups of coffee. *Behavioral Science, 7*, 184-193.

Chatterjee, S. (1984). Variance estimation in factor analysis: An application of the bootstrap. *British Journal of Mathematical and Statistical Psychology, 37*, 252-262.

Cliff, N. (1983). Some cautions concerning the application of causal modeling methods. *Multivariate Behavioral Research, 18*, 115-126.

Coan, R. W. (1959). A comparison of oblique and orthogonal factor solutions. *Journal of Experimental Education, 27*, 151-166.

Cohen, J. (1977). *Statistical power analysis for the behavioral sciences* (rev. ed.). New York: Academic Press.

Cohen, P., Cohen, J., Teresi, J., Marchi, M., & Velez, C. N. (1990). Problems in the measurement of latent variables in structural equations causal models. *Applied Psychological Measurement, 14*, 183-196.

Connell, J. P., & Tanaka, J. S. (Eds.). (1987). Special section on structural equation modeling. *Child Development, 58*, 1-175.

References

Cote, J. A., & Buckley, M. R. (1987). Estimating trait, method, and error variance: Generalizing across 70 construct validation studies. *Journal of Marketing Research, 24,* 315-318.

Cronbach, L. J. (1984). A research worker's treasure chest. *Multivariate Behavioral Research, 19,* 223-240.

Cudeck, R. (1988). Multiplicative models and MTMM matrices. *Journal of Educational Statistics, 13,* 131-147.

Cudeck, R. (1989). Analysis of correlation matrices using covariance structure models. *Psychological Bulletin, 105,* 317-327.

Cudeck, R., & Browne, M. W. (1983). Cross-validation of covariance structures. *Multivariate Behavioral Research, 18,* 147-167

Cudeck, R., & Henly, S. J. (1991). Model selection in covariance structures analysis and the "problem" of sample size: A clarification. *Psychological Bulletin, 109,* 512-519.

Cuttance, P., & Ecob, R. (Eds.). (1987). *Structural modeling by example.* Cambridge, England: Cambridge University Press.

Davidon, W. C. (1975). Optimally conditioned optimization algorithms without line searches. *Mathematical Programming, 9,* 1-30.

DeFries, J. C., Johnson, R. C., Kuse, A. R., McClearn, G. E., Polovina, J., Vandenberg, S. G., & Wilson, J. R. (1979). Familial resemblance for specific cognitive abilities. *Behavior Genetics, 9,* 23-43.

de Leeuw, J., Keller, W. J., & Wansbeek, T. (Eds.). (1983). Interfaces between econometrics and psychometrics. *Journal of Econometrics, 22,* 1-243.

Dijkstra, T. (1983). Some comments on maximum likelihood and partial least squares methods. *Journal of Econometrics, 22,* 67-90.

Dixon, W. J. (Ed.). (1988). *BMDP statistical software manual.* Berkeley: University of California Press.

Donaldson, G. (1983). Confirmatory factor analysis models of information processing stages: An alternative to difference scores. *Psychological Bulletin, 94,* 143-151.

Duncan, O. D. (1966). Path analysis: Sociological examples. *American Journal of Sociology, 72,* 1-16.

Duncan, O. D. (1975). *Introduction to structural equation models.* New York: Academic Press.

Duncan, O. D., Haller, A. O., & Portes, A. (1968). Peer influences on aspirations: A reinterpretation. *American Journal of Sociology, 74,* 119-137.

Dwyer, J. H. (1983). *Statistical models for the social and behavioral sciences.* New York: Oxford University Press.

Endler, N. S., Hunt, J. M., & Rosenstein, A. J. (1962). An S-R inventory of anxiousness. *Psychological Monographs, 76* (17, Whole No. 536).

Etezadi-Amoli, J., & McDonald, R. P. (1983). A second generation nonlinear factor analysis. *Psychometrika, 48,* 315-342.

References

Everitt, B. S. (1984). *An introduction to latent variable models*. London: Chapman and Hall.

Fornell, C., & Bookstein, F. L. (1982). Two structural equation models: LISREL and PLS applied to consumer exit-voice theory. *Journal of Marketing Research, 19*, 440-452.

Fox, J. (1980). Effect analysis in structural equation models: Extensions and simplified methods of computation. *Sociological Methods & Research, 9*, 3-28.

Fox, J. (1985). Effect analysis in structural equation models: II. Calculation of specific indirect effects. *Sociological Methods & Research, 14*, 81-95.

Fraser, C., & McDonald, R. P. (1988). COSAN: Covariance structure analysis. *Multivariate Behavioral Research, 23*, 263-265.

Fredricks, A. J., & Dossett, D. L. (1983). Attitude-behavior relations: A comparison of the Fishbein-Ajzen and the Bentler-Speckart models. *Journal of Personality and Social Psychology, 45*, 501-512.

Freedman, D. A. (1987a). As others see us: A case study in path analysis. *Journal of Educational Statistics, 12*, 101-128.

Freedman, D. A. (1987b). A rejoinder on models, metaphors, and fables. *Journal of Educational Statistics, 12*, 206-223.

Gerbing, D. W., & Anderson, J. C. (1985). The effects of sampling error and model characteristics on parameter estimation for maximum likelihood confirmatory factor analysis. *Multivariate Behavioral Research, 20*, 255-271.

Glymour, C., Scheines, R., Spirtes, P., & Kelly, K. (1988). TETRAD: Discovering causal structure. *Multivariate Behavioral Research, 23*, 279-280.

Goldberger, A. S. (1971). Econometrics and psychometrics. *Psychometrika, 36*, 83-107.

Gorsuch, R. L. (1983). *Factor analysis* (2nd ed.). Hillsdale, NJ: Lawrence Erlbaum Associates.

Guttman, L. (1954). A new approach to factor analysis: The radex. In P. F. Lazarsfeld (Ed.), *Mathematical thinking in the social sciences* (pp. 258-348). Glencoe, IL: The Free Press.

Haller, A. O., & Butterworth, C. E. (1960). Peer influences on levels of occupational and educational aspiration. *Social Forces, 38*, 289-295.

Hambleton, R. K., & van der Linden, W. J. (Eds.). (1982). Advances in item response theory and applications. *Applied Psychological Measurement, 6*, 373-492.

Harlow, L. L., & Newcomb, M. D. (1990). Towards a general hierarchical model of meaning and satisfaction in life. *Multivariate Behavioral Research, 25*, 387-405.

Harman, H. H. (1976). *Modern factor analysis* (3rd ed., rev.). Chicago: University of Chicago Press.

Harris, C. W. (1962). Some Rao-Guttman relationships. *Psychometrika, 27,* 247-263.

Harris, C. W., & Kaiser, H. F. (1964). Oblique factor analytic solutions by orthogonal transformations. *Psychometrika, 29,* 347-362.

Hayduk, L. A. (1987). *Structural equation modeling with LISREL: Essentials and advances.* Baltimore: Johns Hopkins Press.

Heise, D. R. (1975). *Causal analysis.* New York: Wiley.

Hendrickson, A. E., & White, P. O. (1964). Promax: A quick method for rotation to oblique simple structure. *British Journal of Mathematical and Statistical Psychology, 17,* 65-70.

Hinman, S., & Bolton, B. (1979). *Factor analytic studies 1971-1975.* Troy, NY: Whitston Publishing.

Holahan, C. J., & Moos, R. H. (1991). Life stressors, personal and social resources, and depression: A 4-year structural model. *Journal of Abnormal Psychology, 100,* 31-38.

Homer, P. M., & Kahle, L. R. (1988). A structural equation test of the value-attitude-behavior hierarchy. *Journal of Personality and Social Psychology, 54,* 638-646.

Huba, G. J., & Bentler, P. M. (1982). On the usefulness of latent variable causal modeling in testing theories of naturally occurring events (including adolescent drug use): A rejoinder to Martin. *Journal of Personality and Social Psychology, 43,* 604-611.

Huba, G. J., & Harlow, L. L. (1983). Comparison of maximum likelihood, generalized least squares, ordinary least squares, and asymptotically distribution free parameter estimates in drug abuse latent variable causal models. *Journal of Drug Education, 13,* 387-404.

Huba, G. J., & Harlow, L. L. (1987). Robust structural equation models: Implications for developmental psychology. *Child Development, 58,* 147-166.

Hunter, J. E., Gerbing, D. W., & Boster, F. J. (1982). Machiavellian beliefs and personality: Construct invalidity of the Machiavellianism dimension. *Journal of Personality and Social Psychology, 43,* 1293-1305.

Hurley, J. R., & Cattell, R. B. (1962). The Procrustes program: Producing direct rotation to test a hypothesized factor structure. *Behavioral Science, 7,* 258-262.

IMSL (1987). *IMSL user's manual, math/library* (Version 1.0). Houston: IMSL.

James, L. R., Mulaik, S. A., & Brett, J. M. (1982). *Causal analysis: Assumptions, models, and data.* Beverly Hills: Sage Publications.

James, L. R., & Singh, B. K. (1978). An introduction to the logic, assumptions, and basic analytic procedures of two-stage least squares. *Psychological Bulletin, 85,* 1104-1122.

Jennrich, R. I., & Sampson, P. F. (1966). Rotation for simple loadings. *Psychometrika, 31,* 313-323.

References

Jöreskog, K. G., & Lawley, D. N. (1968). New methods in maximum likelihood factor analysis. *British Journal of Mathematical and Statistical Psychology, 21*, 85-96.

Jöreskog, K. G., & Sörbom, D. (1979). *Advances in factor analysis and structural equation models.* Cambridge, MA: Abt Books.

Jöreskog, K. G., & Sörbom, D. (1989). *LISREL 7: A guide to the program and applications* (2nd ed.). Chicago: SPSS Inc.

Jöreskog, K. G., & Sörbom, D. (1990). Model search with TETRAD II and LISREL. *Sociological Methods & Research, 19*, 93-106.

Judd, C. M., & Milburn, M. A. (1980). The structure of attitude systems in the general public: Comparisons of a structural equation model. *American Sociological Review, 45*, 627-643.

Kaiser, H. F. (1958). The varimax criterion for analytic rotation in factor analysis. *Psychometrika, 23*, 187-200.

Kaiser, H. F. (1990). On initial approximations for communalities. *Psychological Reports, 67*, 1216.

Kaiser, H. F., & Caffrey, J. (1965). Alpha factor analysis. *Psychometrika, 30*, 1-14.

Kaiser, H. F., & Horst, P. (1975). A score matrix for Thurstone's box problem. *Multivariate Behavioral Research, 10*, 17-25.

Kaiser, H. F., & Madow, W. G. (1974, March). *The KD method for the transformation problem in exploratory factor analysis.* Paper presented at the meeting of the Psychometric Society, Palo Alto, CA.

Kaplan, D. (1990). Evaluating and modifying covariance structure models: A review and recommendation. *Multivariate Behavioral Research, 25*, 137-155.

Kenny, D. A. (1979). *Correlation and causality.* New York: Wiley.

Kenny, D. A., & Judd, C. M. (1984). Estimating the nonlinear and interactive effects of latent variables. *Psychological Bulletin, 96*, 201-210.

Kiiveri, H., & Speed, T. P. (1982). Structural analysis of multivariate data: A review. In S. Leinhardt (Ed.), *Sociological methodology 1982* (pp. 209-289). San Francisco: Jossey-Bass.

Kim, J.-O., & Ferree, G. D., Jr. (1981). Standardization in causal analysis. *Sociological Methods & Research, 10*, 187-210.

Kroonenberg, P. M. (1983). Annotated bibliography of three-mode factor analysis. *British Journal of Mathematical and Statistical Psychology, 36*, 81-113.

Kroonenberg, P. M., Lammers, C. J., & Stoop, I. (1985). Three-mode principal components analysis of multivariate longitudinal organizational data. *Sociological Methods & Research, 14*, 99-136.

Kühnel, S. M. (1988). Testing MANOVA designs with LISREL. *Sociological Methods & Research, 16*, 504-523.

Kumar, A., & Dillon, W. R. (1987a). The interaction of measurement and structure in simultaneous equation models with unobservable variables. *Journal of Marketing Research, 24*, 98-105.

References

Kumar, A., & Dillon, W. R. (1987b). Some further remarks on measurement-structure interaction and the unidimensionality of constructs. *Journal of Marketing Research, 24*, 438-444.

Kuusinen, J., & Leskinen, E. (1988). Latent structure analysis of longitudinal data on relations between intellectual abilities and school achievement. *Multivariate Behavioral Research, 23*, 103-118.

La Du, T. J., & Tanaka, J. S. (1989). Influence of sample size, estimation method, and model specification on goodness-of-fit assessments in structural equation models. *Journal of Applied Psychology, 74*, 625-635.

Lance, C. E. (1991). Evaluation of a structural model relating job satisfaction, organizational commitment, and precursors to voluntary turnover. *Multivariate Behavioral Research, 26*, 137-162.

Lance, C. E., Cornwell, J. M., & Mulaik, S. A. (1988). Limited information parameter estimates for latent or mixed manifest and latent variable models. *Multivariate Behavioral Research, 23*, 171-187.

Land, K. C., & Felson, M. (1978) Sensitivity analysis of arbitrarily identified simultaneous-equation models. *Sociological Methods & Research, 6*, 283-307.

Langeheine, R., & Rost, J. (1988). *Latent trait and latent class models.* New York: Plenum.

LaRocco, J. M. (1983). Job attitudes, intentions, and turnover: An analysis of effects using latent variables. *Human Relations, 36*, 813-825.

Lawley, D. N., & Maxwell, A. E. (1971). *Factor analysis as a statistical method* (2nd ed.). London: Butterworths.

Lazarsfeld, P. F. (1950). The logical and mathematical foundation of latent structure analysis. In S. A. Stouffer, L. Guttman, E. A. Suchman, P. F. Lazarsfeld, S. A. Star, & J. A. Clausen, *Measurement and prediction* (pp. 362-412). Princeton, NJ: Princeton University Press.

Lazarsfeld, P. F., & Henry, N. W. (1968). *Latent structure analysis.* New York: Houghton Mifflin.

Lee, S., & Hershberger, S. (1990). A simple rule for generating equivalent models in covariance structure modeling. *Multivariate Behavioral Research, 25*, 313-334.

Lee, S.-Y. (1985). Analysis of covariance and correlation structures. *Computational Statistics and Data Analysis, 2*, 279-295.

Lee, S.-Y. (1986). Estimation for structural equation models with missing data. *Psychometrika, 51*, 93-99.

Lee, S.-Y., & Jennrich, R. I. (1984). The analysis of structural equation models by means of derivative free nonlinear least squares. *Psychometrika, 49*, 521-528.

Lehmann, D. R., & Gupta, S. (1989). PACM: A two-stage procedure for analyzing structural models. *Applied Psychological Measurement, 13*, 301-321.

References

Li, C.-C. (1975). *Path analysis: A primer.* Pacific Grove, CA: Boxwood Press.

Lindsay, P., & Knox, W. E. (1984). Continuity and change in work values among young adults: A longitudinal study. *American Journal of Sociology, 89,* 918-931.

Lingoes, J. C., & Guttman, L. (1967). Nonmetric factor analysis: A rank reducing alternative to linear factor analysis. *Multivariate Behavioral Research, 2,* 485-505.

Loehlin, J. C. (1985). Fitting heredity-environment models jointly to twin and adoption data from the California Psychological Inventory. *Behavior Genetics, 15,* 199-221.

Loehlin, J. C. (in press). *Genes and environment in personality development.* Newbury Park, CA: Sage Publications.

Loehlin, J. C., & Vandenberg, S. G. (1968). Genetic and environmental components in the covariation of cognitive abilities: An additive model. In S. G. Vandenberg (Ed.), *Progress in human behavior genetics* (pp. 261-278). Baltimore: Johns Hopkins Press.

Loehlin, J. C., Willerman, L., & Horn, J. M. (1985). Personality resemblances in adoptive families when the children are late-adolescent or adult. *Journal of Personality and Social Psychology, 48,* 376-392.

Lohmöller, J.-B. (1988). The PLS program system: Latent variables path analysis with partial least squares estimation. *Multivariate Behavioral Research, 23,* 125-127.

Long, J. S. (1983a). *Confirmatory factor analysis: A preface to LISREL.* Beverly Hills, CA: Sage Publications.

Long, J. S. (1983b). *Covariance structure models: An introduction to LISREL.* Beverly Hills, CA: Sage Publications.

MacCallum, R. (1983). A comparison of factor analysis programs in SPSS, BMDP, and SAS. *Psychometrika, 48,* 223-231.

MacCallum, R. (1986). Specification searches in covariance structure modeling. *Psychological Bulletin, 100,* 107-120.

Maiti, S. S., & Mukherjee, B. N. (1990). A note on the distributional properties of the Jöreskog-Sörbom fit indices . *Psychometrika, 55,* 721-726.

Marsden, P. V. (Ed.). (1981). *Linear models in social research.* Beverly Hills, CA: Sage Publications.

Marsh, H. W., Balla, J. R., & McDonald, R. P. (1988). Goodness-of-fit indexes in confirmatory factor analysis: The effect of sample size. *Psychological Bulletin, 103,* 391-410.

Marsh, H. W., & Hocevar, D. (1983). Confirmatory factor analysis of multitrait-multimethod matrices. *Journal of Educational Measurement, 20,* 231-248.

Marsh, H. W., & Hocevar, D. (1985). Application of confirmatory factor analysis to the study of self-concept: First- and higher order factor models and their invariance across groups. *Psychological Bulletin, 97,* 562-582.

References

Marsh, H. W., & Hocevar, D. (1988). A new, more powerful approach to multitrait-multimethod analyses: Application of second-order confirmatory factor analysis. *Journal of Applied Psychology, 73*, 107-117.

Martin, J. A. (1982). Application of structural modeling with latent variables to adolescent drug use: A reply to Huba, Wingard and Bentler. *Journal of Personality and Social Psychology, 43*, 598-603.

Maruyama, G., & McGarvey, B. (1980). Evaluating causal models: An application of maximum-likelihood analysis of structural equations. *Psychological Bulletin, 87*, 502-512.

Mason, W. M., House, J. S., & Martin, S. S. (1985). On the dimensions of political alienation in America. In N. Tuma (Ed.), *Sociological methodology 1985* (pp. 111-151). San Francisco: Jossey-Bass.

Maxwell, A. E. (1977). *Multivariate analysis in behavioural research.* New York: Wiley.

McArdle, J. J. (1980). Causal modeling applied to psychonomic systems simulation. *Behavior Research Methods and Instrumentation, 12*, 193-209.

McArdle, J. J. (1986). Latent variable growth within behavior genetic models. *Behavior Genetics, 16*, 163-200.

McArdle, J. J. (1988). Dynamic but structural equation modeling of repeated measures data. In J. R. Nesselroade & R. B. Cattell (Eds.), *Handbook of multivariate experimental psychology* (2nd ed.; pp. 561-614). New York: Plenum.

McArdle, J. J., & Boker, S. M. (1990). *RAMpath: Path diagram software.* Denver: Data Transforms Inc.

McArdle, J. J., & Epstein, D. (1987). Latent growth curves within developmental structural equation models. *Child Development, 58*, 110-133.

McArdle, J. J., & McDonald, R. P. (1984). Some algebraic properties of the Reticular Action Model for moment structures. *British Journal of Mathematical and Statistical Psychology, 37*, 234-251.

McDonald, R. P. (1962). A general approach to nonlinear factor analysis. *Psychometrika, 27*, 397-415.

McDonald, R. P. (1967). Nonlinear factor analysis. *Psychometric Monographs, No. 15.*

McDonald, R. P. (1978). A simple comprehensive model for the analysis of covariance structures. *British Journal of Mathematical and Statistical Psychology, 31*, 59-72.

McDonald, R. P. (1985). *Factor analysis and related methods.* Hillsdale, NJ: Lawrence Erlbaum Associates.

McDonald, R. P. (1989). An index of goodness-of-fit based on noncentrality. *Journal of Classification, 6*, 97-103.

McDonald, R. P., & Marsh, H. W. (1990). Choosing a multivariate model: Noncentrality and goodness of fit. *Psychological Bulletin, 107*, 247-255.

References

McDonald, R. P., & Mulaik, S. A. (1979). Determinacy of common factors: A nontechnical review. *Psychological Bulletin, 86*, 297-306.

McGue, M., Wette, R., & Rao, D. C. (1984). Evaluation of path analysis through computer simulation: Effect of incorrectly assuming independent distribution of familial correlations. *Genetic Epidemiology, 1*, 255-269.

McIntosh, A. R., & Gonzalez-Lima, F. (1991). Structural modeling of functional neural pathways mapped with 2-deoxyglucose: Effects of acoustic startle habituation on the auditory system. *Brain Research, 547*, 295-302.

McIver, J. P., Carmines, E. G., & Zeller, R. A. (1980). Appendix: Multiple indicators. In R. A. Zeller & E. G. Carmines, *Measurement in the social sciences* (pp. 162-185). Cambridge, England: Cambridge University Press.

McNemar, Q. (1969). *Psychological statistics* (4th ed.). New York: Wiley.

Morrison, D. F. (1976). *Multivariate statistical methods* (2nd ed.). New York: McGraw-Hill.

Mulaik, S. A. (1972). *The foundations of factor analysis.* New York: McGraw-Hill.

Mulaik, S. A. (1986). Factor analysis and *Psychometrika*: Major developments. *Psychometrika, 51*, 23-33.

Mulaik, S. A. (1987). Toward a conception of causality applicable to experimentation and causal modeling. *Child Development, 58*, 18-32.

Mulaik, S. A., James, L. R., Van Alstine, J., Bennett, N., Lind, S., & Stilwell, C. D. (1989). Evaluation of goodness-of-fit indices for structural equation models. *Psychological Bulletin, 105*, 430-445.

Muthén, B. (1984). A general structural equation model with dichotomous, ordered categorical, and continuous latent variable indicators. *Psychometrika, 49*, 115-132.

Muthén, B. O. (1989). Latent variable modeling in heterogeneous populations. *Psychometrika, 54*, 557-585.

Muthén, B., & Jöreskog, K. G. (1983). Selectivity problems in quasi-experimental studies. *Evaluation Review, 7*, 139-174.

Muthén, B., & Kaplan, D. (1985). A comparison of some methodologies for the factor analysis of non-normal Likert variables. *British Journal of Mathematical and Statistical Psychology, 38*, 171-189.

Muthén, B., Kaplan, D., & Hollis, M. (1987). On structural equation modeling with data that are not missing completely at random. *Psychometrika, 52*, 431-462.

Muthén, B., & Speckart, G. (1985). Latent variable probit ANCOVA: Treatment effects in the California Civil Addict Programme. *British Journal of Mathematical and Statistical Psychology, 38*, 161-170.

Neale, M. C., & Fulker, D. W. (1984). A bivariate analysis of fear data on twins and their parents. *Acta Geneticae Medicae et Gemellologiae, 33*, 273-286.

Neuhaus, J. O., & Wrigley, C. (1954). The quartimax method: An analytic approach to orthogonal simple structure. *British Journal of Statistical Psychology, 7*, 81-91.

Newcomb, M. D., & Bentler, P. M. (1983). Dimensions of subjective female orgasmic responsiveness. *Journal of Personality and Social Psychology, 44*, 862-873.

Newton, R. R., Kameoka, V. A., Hoelter, J. W., & Tanaka-Matsumi, J. (1984). Maximum-likelihood estimation of factor structures of anxiety measures: A multiple group comparison. *Educational and Psychological Measurement, 44*, 179-193.

Overall, J. E., & Klett, C. J. (1972). *Applied multivariate analysis.* New York: McGraw-Hill.

Pearson, K., & Filon, L. N. G. (1898). Mathematical contributions to the theory of evolution. *Philosophical Transactions of the Royal Society (London), Series A, 191*, 229-311.

Rahe, R. H., Hervig, L., & Rosenman, R. H. (1978). Heritability of Type A behavior. *Psychosomatic Medicine, 40*, 478-486.

Rao, C. R. (1955). Estimation and tests of significance in factor analysis. *Psychometrika, 20*, 93-111.

Rao, D. C., Morton, N. E., Elston, R. C., & Yee, S. (1977). Causal analysis of academic performance. *Behavior Genetics, 7*, 147-159.

Rice, T., Fulker, D. W., & DeFries, J. C. (1986). Multivariate path analysis of specific cognitive abilities in the Colorado Adoption Project. *Behavior Genetics, 16*, 107-125.

Rindskopf, D. (1984a). Stuctural equation models: Empirical identification, Heywood cases, and related problems. *Sociological Methods & Research, 13*, 109-119.

Rindskopf, D. (1984b). Using phantom and imaginary latent variables to parameterize constraints in linear structural models. *Psychometrika, 49*, 37-47.

Rindskopf, D., & Everson, H. (1984). A comparison of models for detecting discrimination: An example from medical school admissions. *Applied Psychological Measurement, 8*, 89-106.

Rindskopf, D., & Rose, T. (1988). Some theory and applications of confirmatory second-order factor analysis. *Multivariate Behavioral Research, 23*, 51-67.

Rozeboom, W. W. (1978). Estimation of cross-validated multiple correlation: A clarification. *Psychological Bulletin, 85*, 1348-1351.

Ryan, B. F., Joiner, B. L., & Ryan, T. A., Jr. (1985). *Minitab handbook* (2nd ed.). Boston: Duxbury Press.

Saris, W. E., de Pijper, M., & Mulder, J. (1978). Optimal procedures for estimating factor scores. *Sociological Methods & Research, 7*, 85-106.

Saris, W. E., & Stronkhorst, L. H. (1984). *Causal modelling in nonexperimental research.* Amsterdam: Sociometric Research Foundation.

References

SAS Institute (1990a). *SAS/IML software: Usage and reference* (Version 6, 1st ed.). Cary, NC: SAS Institute.

SAS Institute (1990b). *SAS/STAT user's guide* (Version 6, 4th ed.). Cary, NC: SAS Institute.

Satorra, A. (1989). Alternative test criteria in covariance structure analysis: A unified approach. *Psychometrika, 54,* 131-151.

Satorra, A., & Saris, W. E. (1985). Power of the likelihood ratio test in covariance structure analysis. *Psychometrika, 50,* 83-90.

Schmid, J., & Leiman, J. M. (1957). The development of hierarchical factor solutions. *Psychometrika, 22,* 53-61.

Schmitt, N. (1982). The use of analysis of covariance structures to assess beta and gamma change. *Multivariate Behavioral Research, 17,* 343-358.

Schmitt, N., & Stults, D. M. (1986). Methodology review: Analysis of multitrait-multimethod matrices. *Applied Psychological Measurement, 10,* 1-22.

Schoenberg, R., & Richtand, C. (1984). Application of the EM method: A study of maximum likelihood estimation of multiple indicator and factor analysis models. *Sociological Methods & Research, 13,* 127-150.

Sharma, S., Durvasula, S., & Dillon, W. R. (1989). Some results on the behavior of alternate covariance structure estimation procedures in the presence of non-normal data. *Journal of Marketing Research, 26,* 214-221.

Silvia, E. S. M., & MacCallum, R. C. (1988). Some factors affecting the success of specification searches in covariance structure modeling. *Multivariate Behavioral Research, 23,* 297-326.

Skaalvik, E. M., & Hagtvet, K. A. (1990). Academic achievement and self-concept: An analysis of causal predominance in a developmental perspective. *Journal of Personality and Social Psychology, 58,* 292-307.

Snyder, C. W., Jr. (1988). Multimode factor analysis. In J. R. Nesselroade & R. B. Cattell (Eds.), *Handbook of multivariate experimental psychology* (2nd ed.; pp. 289-316). New York: Plenum.

Sörbom, D. (1974). A general method for studying differences in factor means and factor structure between groups. *British Journal of Mathematical and Statistical Psychology, 27,* 229-239.

Spearman, C. (1904). "General intelligence," objectively determined and measured. *American Journal of Psychology, 15,* 201-292.

Spirtes, P., Scheines, R., & Glymour, C. (1990a). Simulation studies of the reliability of computer-aided model specification using the TETRAD II, EQS, and LISREL programs. *Sociological Methods & Research, 19,* 3-66.

Spirtes, P., Scheines, R., & Glymour, C. (1990b). Reply to comments. *Sociological Methods & Research, 19,* 107-121.

SPSS Inc. (1990). *SPSS reference guide.* Chicago: SPSS Inc.

Steiger, J. H. (1980). Tests for comparing elements of a correlation matrix. *Psychological Bulletin, 87,* 245-251.

References

Steiger, J. H. (1988). Aspects of person-machine communication in structural modeling of correlations and covariances. *Multivariate Behavioral Research, 23*, 281-290.

Steiger, J. H. (1989). *EzPATH: Causal modeling.* Evanston, IL: SYSTAT Inc.

Stelzl, I. (1986). Changing a causal hypothesis without changing the fit: Some rules for generating equivalent path models. *Multivariate Behavioral Research, 21*, 309-331.

Tanaka, J. S. (1987). "How big is big enough?": Sample size and goodness of fit in structural equation models with latent variables. *Child Development, 58*, 134-146.

Tanaka, J. S., & Huba, G. J. (1985). A fit index for covariance structure models under arbitrary GLS estimation. *British Journal of Mathematical and Statistical Psychology, 38*, 197-201.

Tanaka, J. S., & Huba, G. J. (1987). Assessing the stability of depression in college students. *Multivariate Behavioral Research, 22*, 5-19.

Tanaka, J. S., & Huba, G. J. (1989). A general coefficient of determination for covariance structure models under arbitrary GLS estimation. *British Journal of Mathematical and Statistical Psychology, 42*, 233-239.

ten Berge, J. M. F., & Knol, D. L. (1985). Scale construction on the basis of components analysis: A comparison of three strategies. *Multivariate Behavioral Research, 20*, 45-55.

Tesser, A., & Paulhus, D. L. (1976). Toward a causal model of love. *Journal of Personality and Social Psychology, 34*, 1095-1105.

Thurstone, L. L. (1947). *Multiple-factor analysis.* Chicago, University of Chicago Press.

Tucker, L. R. (1964). The extension of factor analysis to three-dimensional matrices. In N. Frederiksen & H. Gulliksen (Eds.), *Contributions to mathematical psychology* (pp. 109-127). New York: Holt, Rinehart & Winston.

Tukey, J. W. (1954). Causation, regression and path analysis. In O. Kempthorne, T. A. Bancroft, J. W. Gowen, & J. L. Lush (Eds.), *Statistics and mathematics in biology* (pp. 35-66). Ames, IA: Iowa State College Press.

Undheim, J. O., & Gustafsson, J.-E. (1987). The hierarchical organization of cognitive abilities: Restoring general intelligence through the use of linear structural relations (LISREL). *Multivariate Behavioral Research, 22*, 149-171.

Vandenberg, S. G. (1962). The Hereditary Abilities Study: Hereditary components in a psychological test battery. *American Journal of Human Genetics, 14*, 220-237.

Verhees, J., & Wansbeek, T. J. (1990). A multimode direct product model for covariance structure analysis. *British Journal of Mathematical and Statistical Psychology, 43*, 231-240.

References

Vogler, G. P. (1985a). *Multivariate path analysis of cognitive abilities in reading-disabled and control nuclear families and twins.* Unpublished doctoral dissertation, University of Colorado, Boulder, CO.

Vogler, G. P. (1985b). Multivariate path analysis of familial resemblance. *Genetic Epidemiology, 2,* 35-53.

Vogler, G. P., & DeFries, J. C. (1985). Bivariate path analysis of familial resemblance for reading ability and symbol processing speed. *Behavior Genetics, 15,* 111-121.

Walters, R. G., & MacKenzie, S. B. (1988). A structural equations analysis of the impact of price promotions on store performance. *Journal of Marketing Research, 25,* 51-63.

Wellhofer, E. S. (1984). To "educate their volition to dance in their chains": Enfranchisement and realignment in Britain, 1885-1950. *Comparative Political Studies, 17,* 3-33, 351-372.

Werts, C. E., & Linn, R. L. (1970). Path analysis: Psychological examples. *Psychological Bulletin, 74,* 193-212.

Werts, C. E., Linn, R. L., & Jöreskog, K. G. (1977). A simplex model for analyzing academic growth. *Educational and Psychological Measurement, 37,* 745-756.

Widaman, K. F. (1985). Hierarchically nested covariance structure models for multitrait-multimethod data. *Applied Psychological Measurement, 9,* 1-26.

Williams, R., & Thomson, E. (1986). Normalization issues in latent variable modeling. *Sociological Methods & Research, 15,* 24-43.

Windle, M., Barnes, G. M., & Welte, J. (1989). Causal models of adolescent substance use: An examination of gender differences using distribution-free estimators. *Journal of Personality and Social Psychology, 56,* 132-142.

Wold, H. (1982). Soft modeling: The basic design and some extensions. In K. G. Jöreskog & H. Wold (Eds.), *Systems under indirect observation* (Part II, pp. 1-54). Amsterdam: North-Holland.

Wothke, W., & Browne, M. W. (1990). The direct product model for the MTMM matrix parameterized as a second order factor analysis model. *Psychometrika, 55,* 255-262.

Wright, S. (1920). The relative importance of heredity and environment in determining the piebald pattern of guinea-pigs. *Proceedings of the National Academy of Sciences, 6,* 320-332.

Wright, S. (1960). Path coefficients and path regressions: Alternative or complementary concepts? *Biometrics, 16,* 189-202.

Index